WARRIOR TALK

WARRIOR TALK
A Study of War, Peace and Politics

Sally Watson

Peter Lang
Oxford · Bern · Berlin · Bruxelles · New York · Wien

Bibliographic information published by Die Deutsche Nationalbibliothek
Die Deutsche Nationalbibliothek lists this publication in the Deutsche
Nationalbibliografie; detailed bibliographic data is available on the Internet at http://dnb.d-nb.de.

A catalogue record for this book is available from the British Library.

Library of Congress Cataloging-in-Publication Data
Names: Watson, Sally Elaine, 1951- author.
Title: Warrior talk : a study of war, peace and politics / Sally Elaine Watson.
Description: New York : Peter Lang, 2021. | Includes bibliographical references and index.
Identifiers: LCCN 2020057941 (print) | LCCN 2020057942 (ebook) | ISBN 9781789977509 (paperback) | ISBN 9781789977660 (ebook) | ISBN 9781789977677 (epub) | ISBN 9781789977684 (mobi)
Subjects: LCSH: Communication in politics. | Discourse analysis--Political aspects. | Political violence. | Sinn Fein. | Peace movements--Northern Ireland--Case studies.
Classification: LCC JA85 .W38 2021 (print) | LCC JA85 (ebook) | DDC 320.01/4--dc23
LC record available at https://lccn.loc.gov/2020057941
LC ebook record available at https://lccn.loc.gov/2020057942

Cover image: Vector illustration, symbol of competition, corporate conflict, tug-of-war, working mechanism. Conflict resolution.

ISBN   978-1-78997-750-9 (print)   •   ISBN   978-1-78997-766-0 (ePDF)
ISBN   978-1-78997-767-7 (ePub)   •   ISBN   978-1-78997-768-4 (mobi)

© Peter Lang Group AG 2021

Published by Peter Lang Ltd, International Academic Publishers,
52 St Giles, Oxford, OX1 3LU, United Kingdom
oxford@peterlang.com, www.peterlang.com

Sally Watson has asserted her right under the Copyright, Designs and Patents Act, 1988, to be identified as Author of this Work.

All rights reserved.
All parts of this publication are protected by copyright.
Any utilisation outside the strict limits of the copyright law, without the permission of the publisher, is forbidden and liable to prosecution.

This applies in particular to reproductions, translations, microfilming, and storage and processing in electronic retrieval systems.

This publication has been peer reviewed.

For my parents and Tony

Table of contents

Abbreviations, key political actors and terms		ix
Preface		xvii
Acknowledgements		xix
Chapter 1	An introduction to warrior talk	1
Chapter 2	Decoding political discourses	15
Chapter 3	The Republican code	39
Chapter 4	The political journey of Sinn Féin	69
Chapter 5	'War is a waste if we don't win the peace'	101
Chapter 6	'A greyhound trained to race'	133
Chapter 7	Transformational discourses and warrior talk	173
Chapter 8	Warrior talk and peace	213
Internet sources		235
Newspapers		237
Journals		239
Bibliography		241
Index		245

Abbreviations, key political actors and terms

Abbreviations

ANC: African National Congress and the main political force opposing Apartheid in South Africa.
CAC: Continuity Army Council.
CIRA: Continuity IRA, formed in 1986 and shares an ideology with Republican Sinn Féin.
CLMC: Combined Loyalist Military Command grouping of loyalist paramilitaries including UVF, UFF, UDA and Red Hand Commandos.
DSD: Downing Street Declaration.
DUP: Democratic Unionist Party, formed by Ian Paisley.
INLA: Irish National Liberation Army formed 1974 known as the military wing of the Irish republican socialist party and involved in republican hunger strikes in 1981.
IRB: Irish Republican Brotherhood, predecessors of the IRA.
New IRA: A merger of RAAD, Real IRA and republicans operating independently.
NICRA: Northern Ireland Civil Rights Association.
NIWC: Northern Ireland Women's coalition.
OIRA: Official Irish Republican Army, a republican paramilitary organization reluctant to get involved in the violence in Northern Ireland in 1969. Their politics was far left and focussed on uniting the six counties with the thirty-two counties into a republic with a federal structure of government.
ONH: Óglaigh na hÉireann is a term used OIRA, PIRA and now various republican groups. It means 'Soldiers of Ireland'.
PIRA: Provisional Irish Republican Army founded in 1969 and disbanded 2005.
PSF: Provisional Sinn Féin.

PSNI: Police Service of Northern Ireland.
RAAD: Republican Action Against Drugs.
Real IRA: republican armed group formed in 1997
Real UFF: Real Ulster Freedom Fighters founded in 2007 by ex UDA and UFF members.
Red Hand Commandos a loyalist paramilitary group whose aim is to keep Northern Ireland as part of the United Kingdom. They are historic enemies of the IRA but disarmed in 2009.
RNU: Republican Network for Unity formed 2007.
RSF: Republican Sinn Féin formed in 1986 in protest at the political strategies of Provisional Sinn Féin, which were deemed to be counter to Irish republican principles.
RUC: Royal Ulster Constabulary and replaced by PSNI in 2001.
SDLP: Social Democratic Labour Party.
UDA: Ulster Defence Association, an Ulster Loyalist defence organization, formed in 1971 and key participant of the 'Troubles' in Northern Ireland, ended armed campaign, 2007.
UDR: Ulster Defence Regiment. An infantry regiment of the British Army, 1970–1992.
UFF: Ulster Freedom Fighters, a paramilitary group formed by more militant members of the UDA.
UUP: Ulster Unionist Party, dominant unionist party that governed Northern Ireland from 1921 to 1972. Unlike Sinn Féin, unionist MP's taken their seats in the Westminster parliament in London.
UVF: Ulster Volunteer Force, a loyalist paramilitary organization formed in 1966 and active throughout the 'Troubles'.

Key political actors

Adams, Gerry: President of Sinn Féin, 1983–2018.
Ahern, Bertie: Irish Prime Minister, 1997–2008.
Blair, Tony: British Prime Minister during the peace talks and Good Friday Agreement, 1998.
Brooke, Peter: Secretary State for Northern Ireland, 1989–1992.
Brownie: a pseudonym by Gerry Adams for his writings in the 1970s.
Clinton, Bill: US president during the Good Friday Agreement.
Costello, Seamus: formed the republican group IRSP, 1974.
Goulding, Cathal: Chief of Staff, OIRA, 1962–1972.
Hartley, Tom: Sinn Féin politician responsible for the 'Language of Invitation' appearing in the political discourses of the 1990s.
Hume, John: Leader of SDLP, 1979–1998, won the Nobel Peace prize, 1998, jointly shared with David Trimble, UUP for their efforts in the Northern Ireland peace prize.
MacStiofáin, Seán: Chief of Staff, PIRA, 1969–1972.
Major, John: British Prime Minister and signatory of the Downing Street Declaration 1993.
Martin Micheal: current leader of Fianna Fáil.
McDonald, Mary Lou: President of Sinn Féin (2018–present day) and currently leaders of opposition in the Irish parliament in Dublin (27 June 2020).
McGuinness, Martin: Deputy First Minister of Northern Ireland, 2007–2017, chief republican negotiator during the peace talks, senior leader in Sinn Féin and previously IRA volunteer.
Mitchell George: US senator and chair of the peace negotiations in Northern Ireland.
Morrison, Danny: author of the 'Armalite and Ballot' statement and ex republican prisoner.
Mowlam, Mo: Secretary of State for Northern Ireland, 1997–1999, and a key player in the Good Friday Agreement.
Ó Brádaigh, Ruarirí: President of RSF and former President of Sinn Féin.
Ó Conaill, Dáithí: Member of the Army Council, PIRA, Vice President of RSF and Chief of Staff, CIRA, 1986–1991.

O'Neill, Michelle: Northern leader of Sinn Féin, 2017, and appointed deputy First Minister of Northern Ireland, 2020.

Paisley, Ian: leader of the Democratic Unionist Party, First Minister of Northern Ireland, 2007–2008. His relationship with Martin McGuinness was famously described as the 'Chuckle Brothers'.

Pearse, Padráig: One of the leaders of the Easter Rising 1916 who was executed He read the Proclamation on 24 April 1916 and this is commemorated annually by Irish republicans, in the Republic of Ireland and Northern Ireland.

Reynolds, Albert: Taoiseach of the Republic of Ireland and signatory to the Downing Street Declaration, 1993.

Thatcher, Margaret: British Prime Minister during republican hunger strikes, 1980/1981, also known as the 'Iron Lady'.

Trimble, David: First Minister of Northern Ireland, 1998–2002 and leader of the UUP, 1995–2005.

Terms

Abstention policy: traditional republican principle of abstaining from taking seats in the British Parliament, London and the Irish Parliament, Dublin.

Active Abstentionism: the empowerment of grass roots was a political concept promoted by Gerry Adams in the 1970s.

Ard Chomhairle: republican leadership or 'high council'.

Ard Fheis: Annual convention for the republican movement.

Blanket Protest: A protest about the removal of special category status for republican prisoners which allowed them to wear their own clothes instead of prison uniforms. The blanket became a symbol of protest from 1976 until 1980/1981 when republicans, in prison, started their hunger strikes.

Bodenstown Cemetery: Burial place of Wolfe Tone, the 'Father' of Irish republicanism.

Ceasefire: A temporary lull or truce in a conflict to enable talks between opponents or to build trust.

Cessation: The process of bringing hostilities to an end.

Colonization of discourse: The appropriation of language and terms from another source into existing discourses.

Cumann: Sinn Féin local organizations.

Dáil: Irish Parliament comprised of twenty-six counties.

Discourse: a network of language and terms which *constructs* a particular version of events and which *positions* subjects in relation to those events.

Discourse Analysis: a process by which the strategies of *constructing* meaning are made visible and an important source of understanding both context and content of political discourses.

Downing Street Declaration, 1993: A joint declaration between John Major, and Albert Reynolds which introduced the principle of consent which meant that the people of the island of Ireland had an exclusive right to solve the issues between North and South by mutual consent.

Easter Rising, 1916: the mobilization of Irish nationalists to free Ireland from British rule.

Éire: Irish term for Ireland.

éirígí: radical republican group formed in 2006 and means 'arise'.

Fianna Fáil: Twenty-six county national party committed to Irish unity but more conservative and more to the centre of Irish politics. The name means 'Soldiers of Destiny' and in 2019, they formed a partnership with SDLP in Northern Ireland.

Fine Gael: A centre right political party operating in the Irish Republic. The name means 'Family of Ireland' and was founded in 1933.

First Dáil Éireann: formed by Sinn Féin in 1918 after they gained seats in the Westminster parliament, abstained according to republican principles and formed their own parliament on 21 January 2019.

Good Friday Agreement, 1998: An agreement reached by the British and Irish governments on how Northern Ireland should be governed. Strand one established the Northern Ireland Assembly and a power – sharing Northern Ireland Executive. Strand two created institutions to promote the formation of common policies across the North and South. Strand three established bodies and institutions to promote greater co-operation between British and Irish governments.

Green Book: IRA training manual, 1977 and the extract below is an insight into historic relationship between Irish republicans and the British state:

- A war of attrition against enemy personnel which is aimed at causing as many casualties and deaths as possible so as to create a demand from their people at home for their withdrawal
- A bombing campaign aimed at making the enemy's financial interests in our country unprofitable while at the same time curbing the long-term investment in our country
- To make the Six Counties as at present and for the past several years ungovernable except by colonial military rule
- To sustain war and gain support for its ends by National and International propaganda and publicity campaigns
- By defending the war of liberation by punishing criminals, collaborators and informers

H Blocks: part of the prison at Long Kesh and the site of the 1981 republican hunger strikes.

Her Majesty's Prison, Long Kesh: a large prison also known as the 'Maze'.

Abbreviations, key political actors and terms xv

Loyalists: individuals and groups, in Northern Ireland, loyal to the British monarchy with some groups engaged in paramilitary violence.

Radical republicanism: a generic term used for republicans who challenge Sinn Féin's political strategies because they have abandoned republican principles and accepted the continued influence of the British government in Northern Ireland affairs.

Republican movement: a modern version of the Irish republican tradition which draws on eighteenth century French republicanism and the influence of Wolfe Tone, United Irishmen, Irish republicanism.

Saoirse: Republican Sinn Féin newspaper.

Saoradh: republican political group formed in 2016. The name means 'freedom'.

SDLP: Social Democratic and Labour Party, a nationalist political party in Northern Ireland.

Sinn Féin: also refereed to as Provisional Sinn Féin to differentiate this group from Republican Sinn Féin.

Stormont: Parliament Buildings in the Stormont Estate area of Belfast and the seat of the Northern Ireland Assembly. The Northern Ireland Executive is located at Stormont Castle.

Taoiseach: Irish Prime Minister.

Ulster: are four traditional provinces in the North of Ireland comprised of nine counties? Six counties became Northern Ireland and three counties became part of the Republic of Ireland.

Unionist: an individual or group who believes in preserving the United Kingdom of Great Britain and Northern Ireland.

Warrior talk: language, terms and metaphors associated with war and violence used in political discourses or appropriated into everyday settings to influence people and situations.

Preface

In 1998, I was awarded a Masters in Peace Studies by the Richardson Institute, at Lancaster University, the oldest peace and conflict research centre in the UK. I researched the Oslo Accords (1990/1991) and was fascinated by the work of Norwegian facilitators in brokering a peace settlement in the Middle East. I was intrigued by the behaviours of German and British soldiers on Christmas Day 1914 (the Christmas Day Truce) and decided to study this phenomenon in greater detail. During the year of study, my interests in the dynamics of global war and peace grew until a chance remark stopped me in my tracks. One of my fellow students from Sri Lanka asked me about the conflict in Northern Ireland. In that moment, I suddenly realized the magnitude of events in a part of the world, 188 nautical miles from Lancaster. A moment in time that changed my thinking, my career path and me.

My Masters dissertation was focussed on the Good Friday Agreement and a study of the unionist, nationalist and republican discourses generated during 1997–1998. In 2002, I published a PhD on Sinn Fein political transformation from 1969 to 2002 and developed a discourse model to support further research into republican discourses. Between 2003 and 2019, the research work continued and the content of each book chapter is supported by extracts from the material collated during those years. The focus on republican discourses was a deliberate choice to ensure a sound basis for the analysis of warrior talk. The timeline of republican discourses allowed me to concentrate on observable patterns and themes and look more closely at both the surface rhetoric and deeper meaning.

The warrior talk of all parties to conflict is a critical component of a sustainable peace process and the source of material for facilitators and mediators in conflict resolution. My commentary on warrior talk in other settings is based on a long career in conflict resolution in the private and public sectors and more recently with not for profit organizations.

My writing intention was to create a book about warrior talk that was easy to read, with a balance of theory and practice, and the opportunity for the reader to apply their learning in a practical way. This aspiration resulted in chapters designed to integrate theory and practice combined with opportunities for practical application and further reading. Readers may have different learning preferences and interests and therefore each chapter presents a range of options on how the material can be studied.

The book has been written for a varied audience of readers. Some of you may be interested in Northern Ireland or Irish republican history and its impact on current Northern Ireland politics.

For readers intrigued by discourse analysis, there is chapter on research methodology with practical tools and exercises for you to test out. For those readers primarily interested in peace studies and conflict resolution, the case study acts as a practical context for your learning and deeper understanding of the cycles of violence and retaliation that can emerge in a lengthy conflict.

Finally, there is a commentary, at the close of the book, on the forms of warrior talk in our everyday lives and while this is short, I hope it will leave you thoughtful about how language impacts your thinking and actions, and how warrior talk impacts your communities and the wider world.

Dr Sally E Watson
Lancaster, UK

Acknowledgements

I would like to personally thank my family, friends and colleagues for the support given to me during the writing of this book, the team at Kentmere Book Services, Tony Mason and the staff at Peter Lang.

A special thank you to my nephew Greg, a timely conversation in a coffee shop showed me how important it was to make this book a practical read.

Chapter 1

An introduction to warrior talk

Introduction

> We are always writing the history of war, even when we are writing the history of peace.[1]

The focus of this book is the enduring nature of warrior talk, its role in political discourses and impact on human relationships. Warrior talk is a fundamental part of our human existence and exists in many forms of communication between individuals, groups and nations. On a global level, it is perplexing that so few modern conflicts have been resolved and sadly many continue to display a disturbing level of direct physical violence.[2] There is very rarely a neat symmetrical outcome that is sustainable despite the rhetoric of peace talks and the high-profile events where peace agreements are signed. This study of warrior talk will help to illuminate why some conflicts remain in perpetual cycles of violence and retaliation. The roots and causes of conflict are communicated through stories, metaphors and symbolic language: this process serves to trap conflicting parties in past grievances. A peace process represents an imagined future and is therefore unknown whereas the past is well known, albeit often contested.

The language of war may have a role to play in obstructing the progress of peace negotiations, but the language of peace is equally problematic because it brings with it an expectation that there will need to be a compromise in positions and interests. In practice, a peace process can be challenging to initiate and sustain, and it frequently moves through phases of 'process fatigue'.[3] A major stumbling block to sustainable peace is the trust that is needed between all the stakeholders, and this includes the conflicting parties, politicians, grassroots communities, armed groups, negotiators and facilitators.[4] In this context, warrior talk can be a potent communication tool with a positive influence that can be used to force an endgame within a peace negotiation, but there is always the risk of destroying trust.

The language of war has a key role in human conflict whether on a global level or in the day-to-day experiences of human life because it sustains a narrative that one party or position will eventually dominate the outcome. Warrior talk contains stories of good and evil deeds; its narratives need heroes, villains and scapegoats to support the storyline. The outcomes are frequently a polarized interpretation of complexity, a situation which reduces social and political discourses to an alternative 'battleground' with exchanges as fearsome as the rallying cries of an advancing army.

The purpose of this book is to raise awareness of the potency of warrior talk and the forms it takes in human experiences, whether in crises, conflicts or war. The research approach draws on a case study of the Northern Ireland peace process and examines a timeline of Irish republican discourses, 1969–2019, to investigate the role of warrior talk through a period of violent conflict, a lengthy peace process and the political consequences of a peace agreement. A generic definition of warrior talk will be applied throughout this book to encompass the forms which have emerged in the research study:

> Language, terms and metaphors associated with war and violence used in political discourses or appropriated into everyday settings to influence people and situations.[5]

Research context

The history and legacy of the *Troubles*[6] in Northern Ireland have been extensively documented but not necessarily well understood. This book focusses on the multiple discourses produced by republicans to demonstrate that Irish republicanism is a more complex political phenomenon than has historically been acknowledged. For example, the development of Sinn Féin from a political wing to a mainstream political party is frequently presented as a linear process of transition from war to peace, from notoriety to community champions. The reality is more convoluted than that, and this can be observed in the co-existence of the language of war and the language of peace within republican political discourses.

Republican discourses and the language of warrior talk have traditionally been used to provide legitimacy, consistency and continuity for the republican cause. However, the political development of Sinn Féin since the 1970s has resulted in a major expansion of discourses, many of which were colonized from sources outside the republican movement. Warrior talk was clearly a key communication tool used by republicans in Northern Ireland and full of heroic stories of courage and personal sacrifice. Warrior talk became a visible thread running through Sinn Féin political discourses, and this has become arguably the greatest challenge to Sinn Féin's political credibility.[7] Sinn Féin appear to have achieved significant political success but at a cost to unity within the republican movement. The rise of new republican groups, the voices of republican prisoners and republican academics are all now bracketed within the label of 'dissidents', and this indicates the emergence of new forms of warrior talk.

The peace process

The Good Friday Agreement (1998) marked a pivotal moment for republicans in Northern Ireland. It heralded a peace process and brought a serious challenge to the physical force tradition of Irish republicanism. The negotiations were facilitated with international support, brokered by key international figures, and engaged a full spectrum of political stakeholders including Irish republicans. In 1998 the presence of Sinn Féin at the negotiating table made history and accelerated their political rise over the following twenty years. On the surface, the peace process was a successful story of intervention by governments and international third parties, and its culmination was marked by an event that would be lodged in the history of conflict resolution.[8] Within the republican movement, the negotiations for peace presented a seismic challenge to traditional republican views on the British state, and the outcomes presented a philosophical dilemma for Sinn Féin. The Good Friday Agreement provided all parties with a structured process towards peace in Northern Ireland, but it did not promise an early removal of British influence. This meant the British government remained a legal entity in Northern Ireland.

The Good Friday Agreement altered the terrain for all political groups in Northern Ireland, but it is possibly Sinn Féin who gained the most. They accelerated their political transformation and have achieved political power in Northern Ireland – but they also have the most to lose. Their credibility as serving elected officials in two governments, Northern Ireland and the Irish Republic, could be seriously damaged with a return to violence. In that sense, the war for Sinn Féin is over, but the conditions for more violence in Northern Ireland continue to exist.

How the research was done

> Your job is to pick out what is our warrior talk and what is relevant.[9]

During the research that underpins this book the origins of republican warrior talk were examined to establish how their discourses have presented the republican cause. In the first period of research, the discourse findings were analysed to build a rich picture of republican warrior talk. A practical discourse model was created to track the relationship between core and colonized discourses across a time period between 1969 and 1998. During this period warrior talk appeared in several guises despite a significant development in Sinn Féin's political strategies, and these findings were published in 2002. In a second phase of research, which focussed on republican discourses from 1999 to 2019, warrior talk continued to feature in Sinn Féin political discourses despite their rhetoric of peace, transition and transformation. Through this period of significant political change within the republican movement, warrior talk remained a key communication tool.

At the time of writing strands of militaristic language remain in the Sinn Féin repertoire of discourses, appearing as set pieces at republican gatherings and commemorations. On the surface it seems paradoxical that a political party positioning itself within a peace process should continue to use the language of battle. However, the discourse findings reveal clear patterns in the ways that warrior talk was used and the role it continues to play in republican politics. The outcomes from the two phases of discourse research (1969–1998 and 1999–2019) will be presented as a narrative which spans five decades and which provides a comparative analysis of warrior talk in the context of war, peace and politics.

Peace is not just the absence of war[10]

The differentiation between the terms 'peace' and 'war' will be an important framework in this exploration of republican warrior talk and specifically the analysis of colonized Sinn Féin discourses after the Good Friday Agreement. The language of war and the language of peace were evident throughout the timeline of republican discourses, 1969–2019, and this co-existence of apparently oppositional messages was a good source of research material.

A war is generally defined as a state of armed conflict between groups. The term 'war' instantly polarizes opponents into 'good' or 'evil' and influences external perceptions of the situation. The polarizing effect of the language of war with terms such as 'the enemy' heightens emotional reactions. The term 'conflict' does not necessarily mean that the situation is violent. The terms 'conflict' and 'war' have been used interchangeably in Northern Ireland, by different political stakeholders, to account for violence involving the British state and sectarian violence between communities. The precision of these terms will be important to the exploration of republican warrior talk.

Galtung's[11] definition of peace will be used to differentiate between 'negative peace', which means stopping the violence, and 'positive peace', which addresses the root causes of the conflict through structural and attitudinal changes. A sustainable positive peace is therefore more than a peace treaty but a collective will between all parties to change and operate differently. Violence does not necessarily manifest as armed conflict or war. This means that violence is not simply a physical act but a complex chemistry of diverse human needs, interests and behaviours which can result in a range of acts, including some that may be non-physical. For example:

- Direct violence: killing, maiming, rape
- Structural violence: repressive regimes, injustice, disenfranchisement, exploitation
- Cultural violence: religious beliefs and language to deny or debase the values or identity of another or justify structural violence
- Behavioural violence: domestic abuse, coercion and bullying

The range of approaches to resolving conflict may appear complex, but this is a reflection of the multiplicity of settings which involve direct or indirect violence. The field of conflict resolution has developed through concepts from organizational behaviour, psychology, sociology and political science, and by good practice developed by those working in the field. The following framework will be referred to in later chapters on peace, transitional and transformational discourses:

- Conflict prevention, where actions are taken to prevent escalation into violence
- Conflict settlement, a negotiating process to end violent behaviour and reach a peace agreement
- Conflict resolution, which involves addressing the root causes of the conflict and seeking new and lasting relationships with opposing groups
- Conflict transformation, which addresses the wider social and political context of the conflict and brings positive social and political change

How to get the best from each chapter

The approach taken by this book is one of collaboration between the writer and the reader. This is not a conventional textbook, and it will not repeat what has already been written about Northern Ireland in other than brief terms and to illustrate the conditions in which political discourses were generated.

The book chapters are written to provide a structured process flow through the discourse material and build a comprehensive picture of the political journey of republicans in Northern Ireland from the 1970s to the present day. Each chapter has a purpose and a role in presenting a timeline of discourse material. Early chapters introduce the reader to discourse analysis and present a political context for the research process. The origins of republican core discourses are explored and form a basis for understanding the political development of Sinn Féin into mainstream politicians. In later chapters the development of Sinn Féin's peace, transitional and transformational discourses are studied with specific reference to the Good Friday Agreement and its impact on the republican movement. The role of warrior talk as a component of republican core discourses will be compared with the forms of warrior talk used in Sinn Féin's colonized discourses. The paradox of the continued presence of Sinn Féin warrior talk during what is essentially a time of peace will be used to highlight the current challenges facing the republican movement in Northern Ireland.

Format of chapters

Each chapter will contain extracts from discourse findings along with a commentary about the different themes. Key findings will be supplemented with some suggested reading from a range of authors that includes academics, journalists, republican activists and republican veterans. Each chapter will close with a practical study task and references to support further secondary research. The practical study tasks are tailored to the chapter content and designed to help the reader conduct their own research and make their own analysis of republican discourses.

Throughout each chapter, Provisional Sinn Féin will be termed 'Sinn Féin' to distinguish the organization from other republican groups. The Provisional Irish Republican Army will be termed 'the IRA' to distinguish them from other armed republican groups. Republican opposition to provisional republicanism is termed 'radical republicanism' throughout this book and further explanations of different republican grouping can be found in the glossary and in Chapter 6.

Reading and study resources

The book is focussed on political discourses and the role of warrior talk in the context of the Northern Ireland peace process. It would, therefore, be presumptuous of the author to give an expert view on Northern Ireland politics, and this is the rationale for including an additional resources section in each chapter. The reader will be able to draw on further ideas on a range of topics depending on their specific needs and interests, for example, the Northern Ireland peace process, Irish republicanism, political discourse analysis, or theory and practice in peace studies.

Each chapter is designed to bring a balance between theory and practice to the study of warrior talk in recognition that some readers may be part of an academic programme and others will be engaged in their own research. For some readers, the material of the book will intrigue them and draw them to further study. Each chapter offers a customized approach to learning with three resources:

- Suggested reading section
- Practical study task
- Chapter references and endnotes

The suggested reading sections focus on the specific themes of each chapter and includes material that the author found useful in preparing this book. All discourses are political in nature and created in a specific context and for a specific purpose, and this is the reason for the inclusion of secondary material from a broad spectrum of writers and time periods. In discourse research, it is important to avoid the temptation to search for a concrete answer or to drop into a polarized position on the topic. The key is to stay focused on analysing presentation and rhetoric rather than questioning content and truthfulness.

The practical study tasks are an opportunity for the reader to consolidate their understanding of the chapter findings and test out their skills at

An introduction to warrior talk

political discourse analysis. The purpose of the study tasks is to integrate theory and practice and to encourage a critically reflective approach to the material on warrior talk. Each study task relates to the themes of the chapter. The tasks become progressively more challenging and will require some additional reading to get the most from the experience. The suggested reading section contains practical tips to guide the reader efficiently to what they need.

Practical study tasks include:

- *Chapter 1: Are we at war with Covid?*
- *Chapter 2: A personal case study*
- *Chapter 3: Easter commemoration*
- *Chapter 4: How to recognize core and colonized discourses.*
- *Chapter 5: Maskey lays Somme wreath*
- *Chapter 6: New IRA Easter speech*
- *Chapter 7: Writing assignments and personal development task*

References and endnotes provide additional information and explanations on specific points in the chapter. This may include additional contextual detail that helps the reader to understand why and how discourses were created or specific historical detail that is important to a critical analysis of the material. Finally, a glossary can be found at the front of the book and a bibliography follows Chapter 8.

Book structure

Glossary, abbreviations, key political actors and terms

Chapter 1: An introduction to warrior talk

This chapter is an overview of the rationale and purpose for the book with an introduction to the research process and the specific focus on warrior talk. It is a guide to the book structure, flow of chapters and additional resources to make the learning experience both meaningful and practical.

Chapter 2: Decoding political discourses

This chapter presents the research methodology, theoretical research perspectives and an introduction to discourse analysis. A conceptual framework of core and colonized discourses is outlined with illustrations from republican discourses. This framework is used throughout the book to analyse the relationship between political discourses and warrior talk.

Chapter 3: The republican code

This is an important contextual chapter that sets out a brief history of Irish republicanism and establishes the origins of warrior talk. The development of republican core discourses is used to understand the historical legacy behind republican politics in Northern Ireland and the emergence of the provisional republican movement.

Chapter 4: The political journey of Sinn Féin

The political transformation of the provisional movement is studied through their discourses and responses to changing political opportunities and the potential threats to the republican goal. The dynamics between republican core discourses and the politics of the provisional movement is used to explore the role of warrior talk in Sinn Féin politics.

Chapter 5: War is a waste if we don't win the peace

This chapter examines the political development of Sinn Féin through their production of peace discourses and subsequent engagement with the Northern Ireland peace process. The role of warrior talk in the context of peace is used to illustrate the complexity and plurality of the republican movement and the internal tensions that emerged during the peace talks in 1997.

Chapter 6: A greyhound trained to race

The impact of decommissioning on the republican movement is used to examine the relationship between provisional and radical republicans.[12] The development of Sinn Féin transitional discourses is studied in the context of the emergence of new republican groups and their reasons for opposing the Good Friday Agreement. The emergence of new war-like discourses, for example, 'Dissidents', is explored to understand further the political dynamic between provisional republicans and the wider republican movement.

Chapter 7: Transformational discourses and warrior talk

This chapter charts the rise of Sinn Féin transformational discourses following the Good Friday Agreement and explores their role in facilitating a political republican route to a united Ireland. The role of warrior talk is analysed in the context of Sinn Féin's transformational agenda for Northern Ireland. Current political challenges facing the republican movement are reviewed using both theoretical perspectives and good practice from peace building and transformational change.

Chapter 8: Warrior talk and peace

This final chapter summarizes discourse findings from all previous chapters and presents a commentary on the role of warrior talk and its various forms. The potential relevance of warrior talk for Sinn Féin in the future is analysed, along with the wider implications for the sustainability of the Northern Ireland peace process. Some observations will be made on the role of warrior talk in other conflict settings and the power of symbolic language to bring peace or fuel conflict.

Practical study task

Are we at war with Covid?

This first exercise is for you to consider the role of warrior talk in a context that is not a conflict or all-out war: this will help you become more aware of the prevalence of warrior talk in your life. Read the extract below and then use the questions which follow to reflect on the appropriation of warrior talk to a global medical crisis. The full article is referenced below.

Coronavirus and the language of war[13]

It is portrayed as a battle against a cruel enemy that must be defeated. At the 'front line', health care professionals put themselves at risk. In research laboratories, scientists endeavor to find a vaccine to repel the invading pathogen.

In China, Xi Jinping summoned the words and spirit of Mao Zedong as he declared a 'people's war'.

In France, Emmanuel Macron put the country on a 'war footing'. Donald Trump calls coronavirus a foreign threat and pronounces himself a wartime president.

There are a number of objections to the war analogy. It is offensive to suggest that those inflicted by the disease have been called to combat and their response is a test of character. When governments use war analogies to respond to national emergencies they invite disappointment e.g. wars on poverty, crime, drugs and cancer.

Reflective study questions

The following prompts are to guide you through an analysis of the political discourses used to respond to the global pandemic of Covid-19. The purpose of the exercise is to become more aware of your current views on warrior talk:

An introduction to warrior talk

- *What do you notice about the use of warrior talk from each leader?*
- *What has surprised you about their language?*
- *What forms of war-like metaphor are used in the extract above?*
- *What might be a positive impact of warrior talk in a crisis?*
- *What could be the implications of using warrior talk in a crisis?*
- *What is my own relationship with warrior talk?*

It is worth making some notes at the beginning of the book and keeping a journal of your insights and learning before you move onto another chapter. When you reach Chapter 8, return to your reflections from this exercise and notice if there are any changes in the way you perceive warrior talk and its role in shaping your perceptions of others.

Notes

1. Foucault, M. (2003). *Society Must Be Defended*, London: Penguin.
2. <https://www.cfr.org/global-conflict-tracker/?category=us> 12 November 2020. <https://www.cfr.org/programs/center-preventive-action> 2 December 2020.
3. Powell, J. (2014). *Talking to Terrorists: How to End Armed Conflicts*, London: Random House. Jonathan Powell uses a 'bicycle theory' to describe how to keep a peace process moving, p. 205.
4. A differentiation is made in this book between negotiators (who frequently represent the interests of one party in a conflict) and facilitators (who generally have a third-party role that is focussed on the process rather than the substantive content of the negotiation).
5. This definition has been developed by the author based on findings from discourse research and will be applied in each chapter.
6. The 'Troubles' is a term used to describe the conflict in Northern Ireland, 1968–1998. From a discourse perspective, this term reflects the complexity of the political issues in Northern Ireland and the different perceptions of the key stakeholders involved. The 'Troubles' describes both a political/nationalist conflict and a long history of ethnic and sectarian violence. In the 1970s the level of violence could be described as a low-level war.
7. Maillot, A. (2005). *New Sinn Féin: Irish Republicanism in the Twenty-First Century*, Oxford: Routledge.
8. Mitchell, G. (1999). *Making Peace: The Inside Story of the Making of the Good Friday Agreement*, London: Heinemann.

9. Watson, S. E. (2002). *Sinn Féin Politics and Republican Ideology: A Study of Republican Discourse and Political Transition*, Lancaster University, p. 3. This statement was by way of a challenge from Eoin Ó Broin, a Sinn Féin republican activist in Belfast, 1999 and currently an elected MP for the Dublin Mid West constituency.
10. Galtung, J. (1996). *Peace by Peaceful Means: Peace and Conflict, Development and Civilization*, London: Sage.
11. *Ibid.*
12. The distinction between these terms is discussed in the glossary. This distinction will be explored throughout this book.
13. Freedman, L. (2020). Coronavirus and the Language of War, *New Statesman*, 11 April 2020.

Chapter 2

Decoding political discourses

Introduction

> Changes in republicanism are rarely conducted in public.[1]

Political discourses have many roles and it is essential that a robust study looks beyond the surface level for the deeper meaning of the symbolic language being used. In the previous chapter, an international case study of a peace process was introduced as a source of learning about the discourses of war and peace and specifically the part played by warrior talk. In this study of republican discourses during the period 1969–2019, the Good Friday Agreement (1998) represents an event that saw a major expansion of Sinn Féin's peace discourses using language such as *reconciliation*, *forgiveness*, *cultural change* and *transformation*.

Despite the proliferation of peace discourses, warrior talk has remained in Sinn Féin's repertoire of political speeches and it still occurs in the present day. The role of warrior talk has evolved over time and is disseminated in different ways and a variety of contexts. Warrior talk can be a powerful catalyst in a conflict situation because it presents the situation through clearly defined positions and encourages stakeholders to take sides psychologically and, at times, physically. The outcome is an increased polarization of views and a decreased appreciation of the complexity and history of the conflict.

The rhetoric of war and the rhetoric of peace draw us into creating rigid mental models and norms, which then shape our behaviours and allegiances. We rally around emblems and flags and find ourselves fiercely defending our views and – worse – we defend our assumptions. It could be argued that warrior talk is a crude linguistic tool to agitate, inspire, compete and even go to war. However, in some settings, especially negotiations, warrior talk can be used more peaceably, as a deliberate tactic to force an opponent to back down.

Chapter purpose

This chapter presents a rationale for discourse analysis as a research approach in the study of republican warrior talk. A conceptual framework is introduced, including an outline of the philosophical influences that have shaped the research design. In preparation for the next four chapters, a practical model of core and colonized discourses is discussed and illustrated with text from republican discourses. This model will be used throughout the book and provides a practical structure to examine republican discourses.

The political context in which republican discourses were created is presented along with some recommended reading to allow the reader to study political events in more detail and according to their specific interests. It is important to recognize that the various commentaries about and analyses of the Troubles also constitute forms of discourse, each written for a purpose and within a specific political context. The chapter will equip you with practical tools and theoretical insights to expand your knowledge and research skills, and at the same time, develop a discerning, critical approach to political discourse.

Chapter structure

Research methodology: Theoretical perspectives

Interpretative research
Positive research
Universal and particular
Structure and agency
Identity and power

Discourse analysis
Research methodology: Practical considerations
　A conceptual framework for discourse analysis
　Core and colonized discourses
Core discourses (1969–2019)
　Historical discourses
　Justification discourses
Colonized discourses (1969–2019)
　Peace Discourses
　Transitional Discourses
　Transformational Discourses (1998–2019)
Chapter summary
Suggested reading (chapter specific)
Practical study task: A personal case study

Research methodology: Theoretical perspectives

This section presents a short summary on the theoretical perspectives behind the choice of research methodology. It is not a detailed study of relevant philosophy but an introduction to the key concepts that have shaped the field of discourse analysis. The recommended reading contains a selection of both specific and general reading material for the reader to follow up on their specific interests. Chapter 2 is a preparatory chapter will provide concepts and practical tools for use in later chapters.

This form of study requires close, patient reading of the text, to appreciate how individuals and groups, engaged in peace building communicate their identity and values. The struggle between conflicting parties is frequently a struggle over the meaning and interpretation of a shared history. In a conflict situation, language is frequently used to legitimize war as an option to resolve social, economic, religious or political differences between groups, organizations and nations. The justification for conflict may be sustained by symbolic language such as stories, myths and metaphors. Political discourses are a complex choreography of signals to create and sustain the legitimacy and continuity of political ideologies. Closer examination of discourse production reveals anomalies, paradoxes and places where the continuity of the message has been radically challenged or changed.

The story of Northern Ireland and the influence of republicanism has been predominantly told in terms of a stark duality between war and peace. The research methodology outlined in this chapter has been designed to look beyond the discursive certainties and ambiguities of republican discourse over time. While changes in republicanism are rarely conducted in public, their discourses provide a powerful insight into the relationship between their core philosophy, political ideologies and political strategies. The question of why and how republicans continue to use warrior talk will be explored through rigorous discourse analysis and attention to the political context in which republican discourses are created, developed or abandoned.

The following section will outline the key concepts that informed the research design and provide a summary of the key challenges that face a researcher of political discourse.

Interpretative research

The main focus of an interpretative research approach is the subjective responses of human beings. The researcher acknowledges that humans rarely respond objectively to their experiences. An interpretative approach is based on the assumption that our reality is not a concrete fixture but a construction of the mind. Individuals see the same situation in different ways but may choose to communicate with one another in an effort to understand those differences and develop a shared meaning.

Politics is a socially constructed phenomenon between humans that is observable through symbolic language and discourses. Human beings are social actors with the capacity to create, interpret and modify discourses. Language becomes more than a vehicle for communication but a process where people can understand, organize and express their political positions. The surface level of discourse or rhetoric is therefore an access code to understand the deeper underlying political dynamics and power relationships.

If human beings are social actors and symbol users, then the collective medium of language, even with misunderstandings and mixed messages, provides rich material to study. The discourse patterns and anomalies that emerge over time can be mapped against the political context in which the discourses were generated. A rigorous approach is key, as it enables countering of challenges about the reliability and credibility of a subjective approach.

Positivist research

A fundamentally different approach to that taken in interpretative research is known as positivism. This assumes that political organizations are closed systems where reality is more concrete and human behaviour more predictable. The principle of cause and effect shapes the research design and it is likely to be quantitative and to emphasize the search for clarity. In this research paradigm the priority is to achieve an outcome that is a rational and objective with a concrete answer. The research priority is to find the 'right' answer and prove it is reliable and predictable. Historically, the positivist approach was the research philosophy of the physical sciences: these fields dominated academic research and over time legitimized a positivist perspective as superior.

In the field of peace and conflict resolution, critics of a positivist approach argue that an objective reality of the social world is not the central issue.[2] It is the way the social world is interpreted by the human actors that is important. In the specific context of the Northern Ireland peace process, it was clear that the scale of plurality and complexity in republican discourses challenged the conventional polarized interpretations of republican politics. This meant that a research study of warrior talk required a methodology that would bring greater understanding of multiple and, at times, conflicting discourses.

Universal and particular

Human beings are born with organizing principles in their minds to make sense of their experiences.

A simple example is how we might categorize an experience as 'good' or 'bad'. Over time, we develop a repertoire of categories derived from previous experiences, and through interactions with others we are able to envisage new categories. These organizing principles can be *universal* or *particular* depending on our reaction to changing circumstances. This process is observable in both the content and context of discourse formation.

The categories may be time-bound especially if the context changes and requires a new response. The universal nature of Irish republicanism can be seen in their core principles, which are often perceived as a sacred message about Irish freedom that has passed through several generations. Outsiders to the republican movement may not possess the necessary 'category' to fully understand this or the desire to look beyond the absolute nature of the categories. This can be illustrated in their historical position on the British state:

> We are on firm ideological ground and our analysis of the political situation has proved correct. We look to the future – a future without a British military presence. We will never be reconciled with British rule in Ireland nor will we accept any dilution of the national demand. The sovereignty and unity of the Irish Republic are inalienable and non-judicable.[3]

In direct contrast to this absolutist view is the concept of the particular nature of the human mind which can be observed in the new terms and categories created to manage with the unknown or unexpected. The peace discourses created by Sinn Féin during the Northern Ireland peace process are a good example of the particular nature of republicanism. The peace process brought a fundamental change in the relationship between republicans and the British state and this required new discourses to articulate the new particular categories. The text below represents a clear contrast between the universal, philosophical position, shown above, and a particular, ideological position taken by Sinn Féin and revealed in their 1990s peace discourses:

> The British government's departure must be preceded by a sustained period of peace and this will arise out of negotiations … such negotiations will involve different shades of Irish nationalism and Irish Unionism engaging with the British government.[4]

Both universal and particular aspects of republicanism were important to the research underpinning this book because they helped to explain some of the complexity of multiple discourses evolving over time. The role of warrior talk took on many forms and reflected both *universal* and *particular* aspects of republicanism.

Structure and agency

Another philosophical consideration underpinning the research design was the need to understand how a structural explanation of human nature might impact the production of discourse. An example of a structural perspective can be seen in speeches made by the Sinn Féin leadership in 1997, when republicans were prevented from joining peace talks. The Mitchell Principles outlined a series of requirements for the negotiations and one of them was a cessation of violence.[5] Republicans argued that other parties to the talks were still armed and active:

> What excuse can there be in this new situation for refusing to recognize the rights of a sizeable section of the electorate here and for them to be represented at the talks.[6]

This text represents the republican response to an external structure which appears, in the above statement as preconditions imposed on Sinn Féin to allow them to join peace talks. The discourse cited above uses the notion of a 'political mandate' to communicate a political moral high ground for the republican cause. 'Agency' is a term used to describe the notion of human 'free will', which can be applied to individuals, groups or organizations. The collective agency of a group of human beings within a political or social structure is termed 'empowerment'. A good example is the electoral success for Sinn Féin as a result of hunger strikes in 1981. Republicans mobilized political support from their grass roots and communities and challenged the status quo of social and political inequality:

> We believe the age-old struggle for Irish self-determination has been immeasurably advanced by this hunger strike and therefore we claim a massive political victory.[7]

The concepts of *structure* and *agency* impact research into discourse formation because they bring a vital source of information about the context in which the discourses are being produced. The relationship between structure and agency is key to understanding the power dynamics operating between different stakeholders within a social or political system. Neither philosophical position fully addresses the fact that not all human beings in a social or political system are equally powerful. A focus on structure versus agency without a deeper understanding of the power dynamics runs the risk of polarizing the interpretation of republican politics. To counter this, the work of Paul Dixon and his 'strategic relational' approach was incorporated into the research design of this book.[8]

For research purposes, language operates as the medium for an exchange of human understanding and their relationships with both structural power and an expression of free will. The role of myths, metaphors and stories embedded within discourses indicates that language is more than a messaging system and the words that people use are key to understanding how the discourses of war, peace and politics interact.

Identity and power

Both structural and agency perspectives fall short of a deeper understanding of how power relations are signalled in political discourses. By the 1990s, academics and thinkers were searching for new concepts to explain the complexity of discourses and challenge the bipolar explanations of structure and agency, as these were deemed to be too narrow. An era of post-structuralism emerged and offered a more integrated view of human actors, power and their organizations:

> The weak always have some capabilities of turning resources back onto the strong.[9]

The formation of groups is heavily influenced by discourses that polarize through the creation of the 'Other'. Linguistic tactics such as *scapegoating*, *victimizing*, *disapproving* and *trivializing* all conceal relations of power between different groups and different individuals. The current republican

'Other' refers to republicans and a variety of groups who oppose the political strategies of the current Sinn Féin leadership with discourses which bracket a diverse body of republicans under a category termed 'dissident'.

Power can also be described as a form of discipline arising from within the social system or organization rather than a process of domination from outside the system.[10] Republican power is communicated through their core discourses as both a historical response to British colonial power (structural perspective) and as a justification for armed struggle in Northern Ireland (agency perspective). Another reading of power is the link with identity. Power relationships are observable in discourses by the way in which they shape and sustain different identities. The power dynamic between humans may be more complex than a surface reading of the discourse.[11] Authority is therefore an exercise of power over those who are subjected to it but it is vital to understand that those subjected to power may have decided not to resist as a tactical response. This outcome immediately challenges the duality of the structure/agency perspective on power. This makes an analysis of power within republican discourses more complex than it first appears and this requires a research method that can accommodate plurality and subjectivity.

Discourse analysis

Discourses are consciously and unconsciously produced by people and groups to influence key internal and external stakeholders. To a researcher, discourses provide an early warning device that may reveal, signal or even mask a changing situation. Discourses contain empty signifiers, which operate as containers to transmit political messages.[12] Empty signifiers may appear to have a clear message and a good example is *united Ireland* which sustains the illusion of a political closure. Another example of an empty signifier is the term '*inequality*' which represents a powerful universal message which can influence individuals and groups to initiate change. Empty signifiers are an effective way of making shifts in political strategy and at the same time appear committed to a historical political ideology.

The production and communication of discourses is an effective way for leaders to reassure both internal and external stakeholders and boost confidence in the leadership strategies. In practice, this manifests as multiple discourses which contain both transparent and hidden messages. The contradictions inherent in multiple discourses are a source of learning because they bring insights into the power relationships between stakeholders. This can be illustrated by the emergence of Sinn Féin peace discourses in the 1990s, which grew in complexity as they communicated the republican position on peace to different audiences. New discourses emerged to signal a transition from armed struggle to a political route towards a united Ireland, but the armed struggle discourses and warrior talk remained in use.

The role of language within discourses is key because it provides signals of political change. The signals may be subtle, but they are likely to represent social and power relations within a group or organization. Warrior talk is a form of language that is clear and binary in that a warrior needs an enemy to exist but when the war is over the identity of the warrior is challenged. In a peace process, roles and boundaries are shaken as key parties search for new meaning and new identities. New forms of language are needed to explain the anomalies and complexity of making peace. The irony is that warrior talk delivers a clear message and represents a level of consistency and continuity. The language of peace is full of empty signifiers which are open to multiple interpretations and which can be endlessly debated. The co-existence of war and peace discourses is a possibility, but it requires a research methodology that can accommodate competing narratives and analytical framework that supports the political reality of modern societies.

Of particular importance is Foucault's work on *archaeological* and *genealogical* perspectives on discourse.[13] An archaeological interpretation considers the political context in which the discourse was created. A genealogical perspective takes into account the use of discourse to account for events in the past. This is a useful conceptual model when reading and conducting literature reviews. All discourses, written or spoken are political acts situated in a specific time or context and therefore it is important to look beyond what the writer is saying and question why and how they are communicating. A traditional approach to literature is to compare opposing views; a good exercise in intellectual development but the process runs the risk of reducing complex issues into polarized arguments.

Research methodology: Practical considerations

The continued presence of warrior talk in republican discourse presented a clear focus for the research. The research design is grounded in the notion that language can function as an access code embedded in discourses, and close analysis of language can enable the researcher to study power relationships. Language is both an expression of intent and a mechanism for understanding why and how the discourse was generated. For practical purposes, the discourse and language sources examined in this book were drawn from speeches, conference reports, newspaper articles and reports of specific events such as annual conferences and republican commemorations.

A conceptual framework for discourse analysis

Two phases of research that underpin this book were conducted, firstly focused on the period 1969–2002, and secondly 2002–2019. This provided an opportunity to compare republican discourses before and after the Good Friday Agreement (1998). The first phase of research resulted in an analytical model of four major discourse themes: *historical, justification, peace* and *transitional* which will be applied throughout this book. In the second phase of research, the model was adapted to include a *transformational* theme, a new form of colonized discourse which became more obvious in Sinn Féin speeches after the Good Friday Agreement. While the final five-theme model is a practical research tool, it is important to recognize that these discourse themes are another set of labels and, as such, the social construction of the author. To avoid the trap of simplifying and polarizing republican discourses into manageable but unreliable concepts, the reader is invited to test out the practical study task at the close of each chapter and conduct their own analysis.

Core and colonized discourses

During the construction of the original discourse model, a differentiation was made between *core* and *colonized* discourses.[14] This proved an essential distinction and has been used to compare early republican discourse production with the later proliferation of Sinn Féin colonized discourses. The political context impacting the production of republican discourse continuously changed and the use of language shifted to respond to internal, local, national and global influences. Over time, the major changes in discourse formation emerged from Sinn Féin who systematically colonized new language to secure their influence in a wider arena of national and international politics. The core republican discourses remained constant and communicated the traditional republican principles.

The contrast between early core discourses and the later colonized discourses became stark over the time period of the study:

- Core discourses focus on republican identity and are used to maintain consistency and continuity for the republican goal of a united Ireland. These republican discourses generally relate to a historical legacy, signal a political response or provide a justification for radical actions. During violent events in Northern Ireland, core discourses were used to sustain the republican identity and limit the damage to Sinn Féin's reputation as a political party. Core discourses emerged as repeating patterns or fresh adaptations of previous historical discourses. A practical example is shown in this recurring theme in many Ard Fheis speeches:

    Guided by our patriot dead.[15]

- Colonized discourses include ideas and language from sources outside Irish republicanism. These forms of discourse emerged at different times in response to changing political opportunities and threats. For example, in the 1980s, colonized discourses included themes such as transition and change signifying a shift towards a Sinn Féin peace strategy. Colonized discourses can stay dormant for long periods and their re-emergence may shock both internal and external stakeholders when they appear in speeches and documents. Beneath the surface, new colonized discourses may signal changes in fundamental ideology or developments in practical strategy. Over time, colonized Sinn Féin discourses have appeared to edge the party politically further away from core republican philosophy and closer to constitutional politics. Notice how this statement from Gerry Adams used the language of change to strengthen the republican position in the peace process:

> Change must be managed and the anchor of change is dialogue.[16]

The interaction between core and colonized discourses provides key insights into the political role of warrior talk for republicans. The next section will illustrate the discourse model and illustrate with practical examples:

- Core discourses; *historical*; *political*; *justification* (1969–2019)
- Colonized discourses; *transitional*; *peace* (1969–2019)
- Later colonized discourses *transformational* (2003–2019)

Core discourses (1969–2019)

Historical discourses

In 1916, republicans articulated the Irish republican goal as a revolution against a colonial power. This communicated a clear republican rationale for armed struggle, which over time positioned the IRA as champions of justice, freedom and democracy. This historical context shaped republican politics across Ireland and had a major influence on a new generation of republican activists in the 1970s. Historical discourses were full of stories of heroic deeds and represented the enduring nature of republican values. This form of discourse provided a moral high ground to sustain the republican tradition, and, at the same time, keep the message relevant for the next generation. The ability to create and retain a republican moral high ground became a repeating pattern for over fifty years.

The sacrifice of previous republican generations was used to legitimize a military strategy and sustain the republican goal as a noble project. Historical discourses evolved over time to account for new heroes and to include civilians, for example innocent bystanders (Bloody Sunday, 1972 republican prisoners and hunger strikers, 1981/1982):

> The Irish Republic was proclaimed by the only way possible, by force of arms and only by force of arms can the Republic we seek be established.[17]

Justification discourses

Sinn Féin's justification discourses developed in two ways. The traditional republican principle of physical force was a moral justification, especially in response to the intervention by an arguably rogue British state. However, a growing civil rights movement in Northern Ireland was helping to politicize local communities and it was unsurprising that republican communities would turn to their 'Army' for protection against sectarian violence. A new form of justification discourse presented physical force as a defensive necessity:

> Our people's only means of support is the IRA. The only thing that will prevent wholesale slaughter is a strong IRA.[18]

Over time, justification discourses became a powerful source of the republican moral high ground and frequently expressed as warrior talk. This extract is one of many examples of a distinctive *'no choice'* justification for violence:

> Evidence confronts us of the determination of the British government to pursue its senseless policy of military oppression. The Irish Republican Army has no choice but to continue the campaign of armed resistance.[19]

Historical and justification discourses appear to have a complementary role and both provide an explicit explanation for republican actions.

Colonized discourses (1969–2019)

Colonized discourses have different characteristics from core discourses. Sinn Féin's colonized discourses use material from sources outside republicanism to a secure a political moral high ground externally. This material is adapted and used internally to present new political strategies to the republican movement. In this discourse model, they are subdivided into transitional and peace discourses.

Transitional discourses focus on change as a series of planned stages and the achievement of the republican goal is framed as a journey. They are different from justification discourses, which are used to account for a past event and apportion blame to another party. Transitional discourses tend to be colonized from external sources or are adaptions of earlier core discourses. The job of transitional discourse is to normalize unpredictable futures and outcomes. The transition to a united Ireland is presented as a dynamic and evolving process that might involve inclusive politics.

Peace discourses

The emergence of Sinn Féin peace discourses represented a major shift away from the traditional goal of Irish unity. Sustainable peace requires a cessation of military action combined with a structural reform of the political and social systems which caused the original conflict.[20] The statement below delivers a clue about the relationship between Sinn Féin and the wider republican community. In an interview given in 1995, Gerry Adams made an explicit statement that social reform in Northern Ireland was crucial to peace:

> It is not just a matter of Brits out. It is a matter of transforming Irish society.[21]

Sinn Fein became adept at colonizing discourses from other international conflicts and the addition of language such as forgiveness and reconciliation appeared pre-emptive when the British state was still in control in Northern Ireland. Peace discourses sought to communicate a new inclusive political message to all communities across Ireland. The leadership specifically promoted reconciliation across Northern Ireland as a politically acceptable precursor to Irish unity. This did not sit well with some, including those republicans and their families who had suffered from sectarian violence.

By the 1990s Sinn Féin peace discourses were discursively a long way from the traditional radical republican position:

> The depth of our republican vision is its capacity to lift us above our negative feelings. Our vision compels us to build a bridge into the hearts and minds of those whom we once described as our enemy.[22]

The moral high ground of peace discourses made it difficult for internal stakeholders to challenge the political direction of travel. For some republicans, the Sinn Féin peace strategy traded away the leverage of the armed struggle, criminalized IRA veterans and weakened the republican position in Irish politics.

Transitional discourses

In the 1970s there were few references to the concept of transition and little discursive evidence for a flexible political strategy to achieve the republican goal. Core republican discourses were primarily focused on the unification of Ireland after a forced withdrawal of the British government.

Transitional discourses started to develop more fully in the 1980s with language that described change as dynamic, chaotic but manageable. Phrases such as *taking stock*, *phases of struggle* and the *republican way* started to appear. This change signalled a realization amongst the Sinn Féin leadership that Irish unity was a long-term project. Neither the republican strategies of electoralism or military intervention were having quick results:

> There are no short cuts in the task of making revolution. Only by painstakingly perfecting, educating and structuring our organisation so it becomes relevant to our people.[23]

Transitional discourses reinforced the message that republicans could win their goal by using the electoral system and political power. Internally, the future was presented as a long road that delivered respite from armed struggle and included terms such as *phased demilitarization and release of political prisoners*. The power of transitional discourses is that they appear to offer a sturdy bridge between events of the past with political aspirations of the future. This allowed Sinn Féin to present armed struggle as a legitimate step towards political change and peaceful outcomes:

> The mass and popular uprising of the early seventies through intense armed conflict and prison struggles including the hunger strikes, electoralism and the Sinn Féin peace strategy.[24]

Transitional discourses appear to signal that old conventions and meanings were being challenged inside the discourse. The surface rhetoric claimed a moral high ground but beneath the surface were complex narratives and meanings.

Transformational discourses (1998–2019)

In the aftermath of the Good Friday Agreement (signed on 10 April 1998), Sinn Féin started to position themselves as custodians of peace. The language of *cordial union, primacy of community* and *reconciliation* appeared in their earlier peace discourses and they continued to use their transitional discourses to warn that Irish unity was a long journey. There was a distinctive turn in their discourse from transition to transformation, which gave them a multipurpose form of discourse, visionary and flexible if short on practical detail. Their strategy was, however, clear that the route to Irish unity was a societal transformation of Northern Ireland first followed by the ending of partition:

> That is why republicans have to be long-headed and strategic in our approach. We are the ones who want maximum change. Sinn Féin is the one party who wants to see a total transformation of the situation, so we have to be patient, resolute and magnanimous.[25]

Transformation was seen as both the transformation of Northern Ireland and the transformation of Irish society, which spelt out a major ambition for Sinn Féin to govern a united Ireland. The distinction between transitional and transformational discourses is subtle but important. Transition implies a series of planned stages to reach a destination and a metaphorical bridge which acts as a structure to travel across. Transformation implies that the destination will be totally different and the bridge is only a temporary structure and there is no going back. Indeed, a political or social transformation may be so dramatic there is little time to build a bridge or indeed question whether a bridge was the appropriate means to travel. The impact of transformational discourses is highly relevant to the study of conflict resolution and the processes of building a sustainable peace and will be explored in more detail in Chapter 7.

Chapter summary

An insightful examination of warrior talk requires a research methodology that goes beyond a literal interpretation of political discourses. It also requires a case study, which has substantial material to draw out patterns and themes in a range of discourses. The case study selected is a narrative of war, peace and politics and one that requires a research design to enable readers to look beyond surface rhetoric.

A philosophical framework to the research design has been introduced with a rationale for discourse analysis. In the suggested reading section, there is a selection of text for the reader to explore depending on your individual interests. Both theoretical and practical aspects of discourse research are outlined in this section. In this chapter, a practical discourse model has been introduced to guide the reader through the format of the next six chapters. The model is an easy to follow structure as each chapter examines an aspect of the republican journey in Northern Ireland, 1969–2019 to gather insights into the role played by warrior talk.

Suggested reading (chapter specific)

This chapter has outlined the limitations of a positivist approach to research and introduced the rationale for discourse analysis. Below is a brief summary of key thinkers and researchers who have contributed to the development of a more interpretative perspective on research. The reader will notice some of the sources are from the 1980s and 1990s, and this is a reflection of the scale and speed of change towards a more subjective interpretative approach to research. The legitimacy of discourse analysis grew in this time period and is now become embedded in social and political sciences. Many of the authors have continued to publish but the discourse of their early work brings an interesting insight into meeting the challenges from an established traditional paradigm. The bibliography at the end of the book will highlight further reading.

Research methodology: Theoretical perspectives

For those readers who are drawn to the theory of positivist and interpretive research paradigms and the case for qualitative research, *Sociological Paradigms and Organization Analysis* (1985) and *The Case for Qualitative Research* (1980)[26] provide more detail on post structural thinking and an appreciation of interpretative research approaches.

Prison Notebooks (1971)[27] is an important read because the author challenges an authoritarian conception of power and introduced the notion of collective will. The book also discusses the importance of symbolism and myths to the transformation of social relations.

The Phenomenology of the Mind (1931)[28] was an early challenge to a universal interpretation of social and political systems. This work opened up the way for an alternative explanation of human interactions and gives a philosophical basis for appreciating the plurality and diversity found in modern political discourses.

Consequences of Modernity (1990)[29] focuses on human agency and the transformative impact of collective power on social practices and systems that exercise control. His thinking on power will help the reader to develop a deeper understanding of the politics of hunger striking.

Two key books stand out for their integration of theory and practice in the research of political discourses. They bring a clear comprehensive analysis of the rise of postmodern thinking and the practical impact on research practices. *Situating Social Theory* (1999)[30] uses a timeline approach called the *Seven Traditions* (pp. 33–62) and *New Theories of Discourse* (1999)[31] gives a fuller explanation of terms such as structure/agency, universal/particular and power/authority.

Structural Anthropology (1963)[32] was an early work on myths as universal structures of the human mind, which promote collective understanding in groups and organizations. The topic of myths in the context of Irish republicanism will be covered in more detail in later chapters and the relevant literature sources will be outlined.

Research methodology: Practical considerations

The development of Discourse Analysis can be understood more fully by reading *Studies in Ethnomethodology* (1984)[33] and *Cognitive Sociology* (1974)[34] to gain an appreciation of the different strands such as linguistic analysis, ethnomethodology and conversation analysis.

For more detail on the term 'colonization' read *Language and Power* (1989)[35] and *New Labour, New Language* (2000)[36]. *Language, Power and Ideology* (1990)[37] is essential reading for all chapters of this book.

The Archaeology of Knowledge (1989)[38] A good text for more detail on archaeological and genealogical approaches to discourse production.

Talking Politics (1996)[39] brings a practical approach to demonstrate how discourse both constitutes social and political practice and is constituted by it. This means that discourses can be viewed as evolving, flexible processes that can change with external conditions or co-exist with other discourses.

Contingency, Irony and Solidarity (1989)[40] gives some good insights about language as a symbolic representation of reality. The author challenges the idea of knowing the 'truth' and this helps to understand the process of discourse analysis.

Course in General Linguistics (1981)[41] concludes that language is a medium for an exchange of consciousness between members of a human system. This work made a significant contribution to the development of a more linguistic approach to discourse analysis.

Language and Symbolic Power (1992)[42], *Hegemony and Socialist Strategy* (1985)[43] and *Discourse Theory and Political Analysis* (2000)[44] all impacted the research design for this book. These texts are representative of a new era of interpretative research and give practical understanding of how discourse analysis has gained credibility. They all highlight the importance of being curious about anomalies in political discourses. All these texts provide good explanations of the term 'empty signifiers'.

Practical study task: A personal case study

Preparation

Select a personal experience of a conflict, which you are familiar with or specifically interested in. This could be something in your personal or professional life or an issue in your team or community. It is important that the conflict situation is meaningful to you. If you are a student of politics, conflict resolution or related subject, then you may wish to select a conflict that is on your syllabus.

Analysis

Now use the following questions to explore the conflict in more detail:

- *What is the background to this conflict?*
- *What is the current context and challenge you face?*
- *How does history impact the situation?*
- *How does history impact your thoughts and feelings?*
- *What do you notice about your assumptions?*
- *How does it make you feel towards the different stakeholders?*
- *How is warrior talk used in this context?*

Keep notes of your observations and as you read a chapter, return to your notes and progressively develop your thinking on warrior talk.

Notes

1. Smyth, J. (2005). 'The Road to God Knows Where: Understanding Irish Republicanism', *Capital and Class*, 29, pp. 135–158.
2. Little, A. (2011). 'Debating Peace and Conflict in Northern Ireland: Towards a Narrative Approach', in Haywood, K., and O'Donnell, C. (eds), *Political Discourse and Conflict Resolution: Debating Peace in Northern Ireland*. London: Routledge, pp. 209–223.
3. Wolfe Tone Commemoration, 6 September 2000, Cathleen Knowles McQuirk, Vice President of Republican Sinn Féin, <http://free.freespeech.org/republicansf/boden00.htm> 2 December 2020.
4. Jim Gibney, Bodenstown Address, *An Phoblacht*, 25 June 1992.
5. Mitchell, G. (1999). *Making Peace*, London: Heinemann.
6. Adams, G. *The Irish People*, 2 August 1997, p. 8.
7. *An Phoblacht*, 10 October 1981.
8. Dixon, P. (2001). *Northern Ireland: The Politics of War and Peace*, Basingstoke: Palgrave, p. 27.
9. May, T. (1999). *Situating Social Theory*, Buckingham: Open University Press.
10. Foucault, M. (1972). *The Archaeology of Knowledge*, London: Tavistock.
    Foucault, M. (1986). Nietzshe, *Genealogy and History: The Foucault Reader*, London: Penguin.
11. Torfing, J. (1999). *New Theories of Discourse*, Oxford: Blackwell.

12. Laclau, E. (1990). *New Reflections on the Revolution of Our Time*. London: Verso.
13. Foucault, M. (1972). *The Archaeology of Knowledge*, London: Tavistock.
14. Fairclough, N. (2000). *New Labour: New Language*, London: Routledge.
15. IRA New Year speech, *Irish Republican News*, 2 January 2002, p. 1. Notice the date of this core discourse which illustrates the longevity of republican history.
16. Adams, G. (1998). *Belfast Telegraph*, 13 May 1998, p. 13.
17. *An Phoblacht*, April 1970, p. 1.
18. *An Phoblacht*, April 1971, p. 1.
19. IRA statement, *An Phoblacht*, 30 March, p. 1.
20. Galtung, J. (1990). 'Cultural Violence', *Journal of Peace Research*, 27, no. 3.
21. Adams, G. (1995). Interview with *Reality*, June 1995, p. 8.
22. Adams, G. *Belfast Telegraph*, 13 May 1998.
23. 80th Ard Fheis report, *An Phoblacht*, 4 November 1984.
24. Adams, G. (1998). *An Phoblacht*, 7 May 1998.
25. Adams, G. (2000). 'Crossing the Rubicon', article in the *Irish Republican News*, 18 May 2000.
26. Burrell, G., and Morgan, G. (1985). *Sociological Paradigms and Organizational Analysis*, Aldershot: Gower; Burrell, G., and Smircich, L. (1980). 'The Case for Qualitative Research', *Academy of Management Review*, 5, pp. 491–500.
27. Gramsci, A. (1971). *Selections from Prison Notebooks*, London: Laurence and Wishart.
28. Hegel, G. (1931). *The Phenomenology of the Mind*, London: George Allen and Unwin.
29. Giddens, A. (1990). *The Consequences of Modernity*, Cambridge: Polity.
30. May, T. (1999). *Situating Social Theory*, Buckingham: Open University Press.
31. Torfing, J. (1999). *New Theories of Discourse*, Oxford: Blackwell.
32. Levi-Strauss, C. (1963). *Structural Anthropology*, New York: Basic Books.
33. Garfinkel, H. (ed.) (1986). *Ethnomethodological Studies of Work*, London: Routledge and Kegan Paul.
34. Cicourel, A. (1975). *Cognitive Sociology*, London: Penguin.
35. Fairclough, N. (1989). *Language and Power*, London: Longman.
36. Fairclough, N. (2000). *New Labour, New Language*, London: Polity.
37. Wodak, R. (1990). *Language, Power and Ideology: Studies in Political Discourse*, Amsterdam: Benjamin.
38. Foucault, M. (1989). *The Archaeology of Knowledge*, London: Routledge.
39. Gamson, A. W. (1996). *Talking Politics*, New York: Cambridge University Press.
40. Rorty, R. (1989). *Contingency, Irony and Solidarity*, Cambridge: Cambridge University Press.
41. Saussure, F. (1981). *Course in General Linguistics*, Suffolk: Fontana.
42. Bourdieu, P. (1992). *Language and Symbolic Power*, Cambridge: Polity.
43. Laclau, E., and Mouffe, C. (1985). *Hegemony and Socialist Strategy: Towards a Radical Democratic Politics*, London: Verso.
44. Howarth, D., Norval, A. J., and Stavrakakis, Y. (eds) (2000). *Discourse Theory and Political Analysis: Identities, Hegemonies and Social Change*, Manchester: Manchester University Press.

Chapter 3

The Republican Code

Introduction

> The past emboldens the rebel in great matters.[1]

Irish republicanism has a long history of struggle with the British state that predates 1969 and the start of the conflict in Northern Ireland. The republican philosophical position has remained very clear and consistent with their demands for a united Ireland as well as an end to what they perceive as an illegal partition that was imposed by the British state in 1920. As the Northern Ireland peace process evolved, there were two key outcomes, the Good Friday Agreement (1998) and IRA decommissioning (2005), that signalled a major change in the traditional relationship between the republican movement and the British state. Fast forward to the current situation in Northern Ireland: the fact that it exists at all as a political entity indicates that a united Ireland has not been achieved. The peace process has brought greater political influence for republicans, but the British government is still in control.[2]

Two key principles have guided the republican movement in their ambitions for a united Ireland. The legitimacy of physical force to remove the British state from Ireland, and the concept of 'abstention', which is the refusal to recognize the British government as a legal entity within the island of Ireland. Both these principles represent deeply held convictions amongst republicans and are based on a long legacy of republican philosophy and ideology. This legacy is key to understanding the impact of the peace process on the republican movement and the continuing role of warrior talk in republican discourses.

While the philosophical basis for Irish republicanism is sacrosanct, republican ideologies have flexed to enable provisional republicans to engage in inclusive politics and electoral strategies. It is in the domain of republican ideology that the republican movement has experienced the greatest challenges to their internal unity. The peace process in Northern Ireland heightened external pressure on the republican leadership to abandon the physical force tradition and relax their position on the withdrawal of the British state.

The principle of republican abstention was debated in 1987 to enable Sinn Féin politicians to take up seats in the Stormont parliament. This was a shift in republican ideology presented as a political tactic and a practical route to Irish unity and was supported by all republicans because it challenged their core principles. The relationship between republican philosophy and ideology is key to understanding an internal dynamic that continues to exist within the republican movement. For some republicans, ideological shifts are pragmatic and represent a 'long game' with the British government that does not represent an abandonment of republican philosophy and principles. Others regard a change in republican principles as a betrayal of Irish republicanism and a noble cause:

> Republicanism is effectively decommissioned. Discursively it lives on but this is little more than lip service.[3]

Irish republicanism has a powerful legacy whether it is understood as a form of lip service or as a binding code, and the tension between these two positions continues to impact unity across the wider republican movement. Whether pragmatist or purist, republican political intentions have traditionally been communicated through a fiery mixture of political ideology and military intentions. Their warrior talk delivers a robust and consistent message:

> For mark this well, our enemies will never concede or surrender their Power, Position or Privileges to anything but armed men who are determined, committed and trained in every field of Revolution. Our strategy must be the perfect blending of politics and violence.[4]

This extract is a good example of justification discourse and illustrates a traditional republican perception of their relationship with their enemy, the British state. A second extract, cited below, illustrates a blend of historical and justification discourses. Here republican warrior talk is communicated in a poem used by Gerry Adams in 2016, eighteen years after the Good Friday Agreement.

The time span between the two extracts is over fifty years and this evidences the continuity and longevity of Irish republicanism:

> The men and women of that rising were right.
> It was Republic against Empire.
> Republicanism versus Imperialism.
> We know what side we are on.
> We stand by and for the Republic.[5]

Chapter purpose

This chapter maps the origins of Irish republicanism and the philosophical influences which have impacted republican politics in Northern Ireland. This is an introduction to a historical legacy that has influenced republican discourses rather than a detailed chronological account of Irish republicanism. There is a wealth of literature published on Northern Ireland available and a suggested reading section is at the close of this chapter.

The historical roots of Irish republicanism reveal the origins of both philosophical and practical dilemmas facing the republican movement today. Republican warrior talk is a legacy of that history and signifies a dilemma for the current republican leadership and their political aspirations in Northern Ireland. This chapter illustrates how warrior talk has evolved in this context over time and how it is used for different purposes and by different republican groups. The conceptual model of core and colonized discourses, introduced in the previous chapter, will continue to act as an analytical framework in this chapter.

Chapter structure

> Roots of republicanism
> Republicanism and physical force
> The legacy of the Easter Uprising, 1916
> The northern provisional movement (1970s)
> Republican hunger strikes (1980s)
> Republicanism and abstentionism
> Provisionals and republican unity
> Chapter summary
> Suggested reading (chapter specific)
> Practical study task: Easter commemoration

Roots of republicanism

> The hour of your emancipation is at length arrived.[6]

This exhortation to rebel against the British colonial system in Ireland in 1798 is attributed to Wolfe Tone as he prepared republicans for a military operation; ironically the rebellion failed but it left a lasting political legacy for republicans to cherish for generations. Tone advocated the co-operation of Catholics, Protestants and Dissenters, as Irishmen, to fight together against British interference.[7] His political position on an Irish republic was essentially inclusive and, in that sense, quite different from the exclusive republican politics which dominated Northern Ireland in the 1970s.

The origins of Irish republican roots and discourses can be traced back to ancient Greece, and two world-changing revolutions in France (1789) and America (1765).[8] From ancient philosophical roots and radical politics came the notion of a republic, identifying it as a viable form of government in the whole of Ireland. These roots became the cornerstone for Irish republicanism and a consistent moral high ground for republicans. An ancient Greek philosophy became a cornerstone for Irish republicanism and a lasting moral legitimacy for a democratic and just form of government.

Irish republican politics and their discourses were influenced by Cicero's notion of democracy.[9] Classical republicanism can be seen today in the republican language of *justice, freedom* and *democracy* and these words consistently permeate both their core and colonized discourses. Cicero believed that people were the foundation of a democracy. In his view, democracy was the property of the people and the safety and freedom of society should be enshrined in law. A manifestation of this can be seen in Northern Ireland when the republican leadership proposed People's Assemblies in the 1970s as an alternative power structure to the British state.[10] Northern republican views on democracy, at that time, illustrated a remarkable continuity of a political ideology. Cicero's influence can be seen consistently in the traditional republican perspective on the British state.

Republican discourses frequently use the writings of both Wolfe Tone, named the father of Irish republicanism, and Thomas Paine, who was a keen observer of the American War of Independence (1775–1783). Both men were heavily influenced by the French revolution (1789–1799), another key event which had a profound impact on modern history and triggered a decline in absolute monarchies. In France, workers rose up and rebelled against an unjust social and political system administered by a monarchy. In America, the rebellion was against an unjust colonial power, also a monarchy. Both revolutions were characterized by a willingness to use violence to achieve political freedom.

Both Wolfe Tone and Thomas Paine advocated the use of arms to secure a democratic political alternative and this could be seen in the Irish republican principle of physical force. For them, the American War of Independence against British rule provided historical evidence that a colonial power could be defeated through the force of arms. When Wolfe Tone established the Society for United Irishmen, he adopted the values of '*Liberty, Equality* and *Fraternity*' and colonized the discourse of the French revolution to rally people to the idea that inequality could be challenged by radical action. This theme also emerged in the American War of Independence and which created the political legitimacy for the people to rise up against an unjust state.

All these historical influences contributed to Irish republicanism and are present in their core discourses as a mechanism to transmit and sustain the continuity of their political legitimacy. From a republican perspective, this makes armed struggle a legitimate form of rebellion against injustice. The influence of Tone and Paine on Irish republicanism can be seen in language that positions the British state as an enemy of a republic. Republican warrior talk originates in a context where citizens took up arms and revolted against their unjust states. Citizens became warriors with a new identity of freedom fighters whose actions became heroic stories for another generation. Tone's vision of freedom was greater social, economic and religious equality across Ireland and his position on violence was a contributing factor to republican warrior talk:

> Swear with us the eternal war against the avarice and ambition of England to which your liberty, your property and your blood have been so long sacrificed.[11]

All republicans, irrespective of their political views and position on physical force, continue to commemorate Wolfe Tone and Thomas Paine at annual events.

Republicanism and physical force

> In its more extreme form it was thought not only right to die, but to kill for that version of Ireland.[12]

A key republican principle is the right to use physical force to achieve Irish unity. This position sanctions a military strategy as a legitimate response to injustice and sanctions violence as a moral choice. This rationale can be seen repeatedly in republican historical and justification discourses:

> I believe in the God-given right of the Irish nation to sovereign independence and the right of any Irish man or woman to assert this right in armed rebellion.[13]

In the late 1960s a civil rights movement had started to grow in Northern Ireland with supporters intent on bringing social justice for nationalist (mainly Catholic) communities and the political reform of a unionist-controlled government. In August 1969 an ongoing series of campaigns to gain civil rights for a minority Catholic nationalist population in Northern Ireland resulted in violent encounters with Protestant unionists and the Royal Ulster Constabulary (RUC).[14] The Irish Republican Army (IRA), traditionally the custodians of Catholic communities, was unprepared for the scale of street violence in Belfast and Derry. The provisional republican movement was originally a breakaway group of Northern republicans comprised of Provisional Sinn Féin (PSF) and the Provisional IRA (PIRA). Members of the IRA who stayed in the original formation were then termed the Official IRA (OIRA). The rise of the provisional movement is an important aspect in the timeline of Irish republicanism and will be discussed in more detail later in this chapter.

In 1969, the British Army were deployed to support the Royal Ulster Constabulary (RUC) to keep the peace and were initially given a positive reception from the communities under siege.[15] The relationship between nationalists and soldiers deteriorated as the promised neutrality of the British intervention started to be questioned by nationalists experiencing brutal responses from both RUC and the British Army. On Bloody Sunday, 30 January 1972, a civil rights march met with an armed response from the British military. The death of twenty-six unarmed civilians was a turning point for republicans. From their perspective, both OIRA and PIRA were now engaged in the protection of Catholic communities and at war with the British state.

Initially the primary republican goal was to achieve a declaration of intent by the British government to withdraw from Northern Ireland.[16] The shift to armed strategy was rapid and legitimized by the republican principle of physical force. Provisional republicans publicly argued that PIRA's escalation of retaliatory violence had a philosophical mandate that was deeply embedded in republican roots. However, Provisional Sinn Féin had political aspirations for Northern Ireland and was keen to promote civil rights, mobilize grass roots supporters and secure social justice for disenfranchised communities.[17]

The escalation of violence in Northern Ireland and especially the deployment of British troops reinforced the perception of the British state as enemy of the republic and the defender of a corrupt unionist government. The republican narrative was one of victimhood and that the IRA was forced to respond with physical force against, what they perceived to be an oppressive state security in Northern Ireland. This can be seen in the language of *self defence*, which became a recurring theme in republican justification discourses. The following extract is a clear indicator of the outrage felt by provisional republicans in the 1970s:

> A grim determination that never again would the forces of the British Crown run riot with impunity through any Irish city, town or village.[18]

In the 1970s the traditional republican principle of physical force was consistently used to legitimize both OIRA and PIRA activities in Northern Ireland. This brought a political complexity for northern republicans. Their discourses reveal two core strands of political aspirations: the historical demand for Irish unity and the pressing need for social justice for northern Catholics. Both aspirations were ambitious and complex, but the immediacy of escalating street violence bounced the IRA into an armed struggle. As the violence escalated, the provisional leadership turned to their historical roots to justify PIRA operations and positioned the British state as the enemy:

> Violence in Ireland is the result of British Imperialism; of the British connection and the British presence.[19]

The physical force tradition, and its main signifier – warrior talk – represented discourses that reflected only one facet of republican politics in the 1970s. Beneath the surface, the seeds of later discord within the provisional movement were being sown. The historical republican agenda was to create a democratic republic across the whole of Ireland and now some northern republicans could see the merits of a socialist agenda to create social, political and economic justice specifically in Northern Ireland. The primacy of republican philosophy and principles was in danger of being overtaken by the political opportunities for reform in Northern Ireland. For the next fifty years the internal debate within the republican movement continued to revolve around the 'means' and 'ends' of achieving Irish unity.

The legacy of the Easter Uprising, 1916

> A strange alchemy of Irish politics that transmuted sixteen executed men into martyrs.[20]

For republicans in 1916 the Easter Rising was seen as an attempt to change an unjust society that was administered by a rogue state. The British Army's armed response was followed by mass imprisonment, executions and backlash from nationalists and republicans. The Easter Rising brought physical force republicanism back into Irish politics, which for nearly fifty years had been dominated by constitutional nationalism. The warrior talk emerging from the Easter Rising became a potent rallying call for Irish freedom:

> It was one hundred years ago, on Easter Sunday 1916, in the centre of Dublin, when a small band of revolutionaries proclaimed an independent Irish republic. This group of poorly equipped Irish men and women took on the might of the largest empire the world has ever seen.[21]

> By executing the signatories and other leaders, the British government removed the revolutionary leadership and the most advanced and progressive thinkers.[22]

The American Revolution (1765–1783) against the British state had strengthened the justification for armed rebellion as the act of honest people against an unjust state. The Easter Rising delivered political gains and the chief beneficiary was Sinn Féin with a decisive General Election victory in Dublin in 1918.[23] Following this success, Sinn Féin established an Irish parliament in Dublin, the first Dáil Éirean in 1919.[24] In the aftermath of the executions, the British government came under international pressure to agree to Home Rule for Ireland but faced fierce opposition from a Protestant majority in the North. The result was a historic fudge manifested as the formal partition of Ireland in 1920, which established two parliaments, in Belfast and Dublin, both under British jurisdiction. Republicans have never accepted that partition or the continuing involvement of the British government was legal.

The impact of partition was brutal and it ruptured communities as both unionists and nationalists found themselves on the wrong side of the border. This division of Ireland was deemed to be undemocratic and illegal and, to this day, some republicans refer to the South as *the twenty-six counties* and the North as *the six counties*. In 1921, the South gained their independence and the Republic of Ireland (Éire) was created. Republicans have continued to push for the reunification of Ireland, using both political and military strategies.

In 1918, Sinn Féin electoral successes were boosted by a backlash at the decision by the British Government to execute the leaders of the Easter Rising for treason. This was a deliberate choice not to dignify the rebellion as an act of independence but to punish republicans for an act of treason. The executions created martyrs and their sacrifice became a powerful and emotive narrative for republicans. The Easter Rising remains a solemn annual commemoration.

The Easter Rising brought an awareness that armed rebellion could encourage renewed political support for a nationalist agenda. In the 1920s the electoral successes gained by Sinn Féin demonstrated an early engagement with constitutional politics when they won 124 out of 128 seats. The full impact of their political achievements was largely lost because Sinn Féin did not take up their seats in the Irish Dáil because of their principle of abstention. Republicans regarded the Irish Dáil as illegal government because it was administered by the British state and they set up their own Dáil.

The sacrificial nature of republican philosophy and ideology were further legitimized by stories of the Easter Rising, which added drama and richness to republican historical and justification discourses. This phenomenon can be seen in the core discourses of northern republicans throughout the 1970s and 1980s, which were greatly influenced by heroic deeds and courage. The following extract from Bobby Sands' diary illustrates a powerful moral timeline:

> I believe and stand by the God-given right of the Irish nation to sovereign independence and the right of any Irish man or woman to assert this right in armed rebellion. (1 March 1981.)[25]

Historically, republican ideology had been predominantly exclusive, offering universal principles about the relationship between the state and the people but focusing on the republican population. In the aftermath of the Easter Rising, however, Sinn Féin experienced the benefit of greater political collaboration across nationalist and republican communities. The republican values of *justice*, *freedom* and *democracy* had appeal for disadvantaged and disempowered groups, both Protestant and Catholic.

From 1916 onwards, republican historical and justification discourses were sustained by the story of the Easter Rising. The identity of Irish republicanism is a continuous unbroken chain, which has a clear consistent message to the present day. The emergence of the provisional movement in the North did not break that chain but the leadership of Provisional Sinn Féin brought existential challenges to the core republican principles of physical force and abstention that would have been inconceivable in 1916.

The northern provisional movement (1970s)

> The Good Friday Agreement now rests with a party that began its existence dedicated to the destruction of the government of Northern Ireland and the partition settlement that underlay it, but the same party has ended up utterly and absolutely reliant on them.[26]

The emergence of the provisional movement took place in the context of escalating violence in Northern Ireland and the perceived need to defend Roman Catholic communities against the actions of both a unionist government and the British state. This is the same movement that later engaged in a peace process, signed the Good Friday Agreement and decommissioned their army. The scale of political change initiated by the provisional leadership will be examined in more detail in Chapter 4.

August 1969 was a pivotal month in Northern Ireland. An explosive combination of civil rights activity, sectarian violence and overzealous policing by the Royal Ulster Constabulary tipped Northern Ireland into a period of time which became known as the *Troubles*. In the same month,

British troops were deployed to restore order and this effectively galvanized Northern republicans into an extensive civil rebellion. In the words of Seán MacStiofáin:

> A colonial power does not send in its army to hurry up social reforms.[27]

British troops were not trained in peacekeeping or community liaison and the escalation of sectarian violence between nationalists and unionists was met with a forceful response. It was Bloody Sunday, in 1972, that consolidated the perception of the British state as a colonial enemy. The civil rights movement in Northern Ireland had politicized republican and nationalist communities but the British Army conducted the policing of their civil rights marches. Bloody Sunday stands out in history because it resulted in civilian deaths and was a major traumatic event. In 1998 a judicial inquiry was established by the British government as part of the peace process; it finally produced a report in 2010.[28]

An armed response from the British government became the initial republican justification for the escalation of violence in Northern Ireland. The stated purpose of the British Army was to 'keep the peace' but in a very short time soldiers became embroiled in a conflict and, worse, they were not seen as neutral but as the instruments of state-sponsored violence inflicted on republican and nationalist communities. From the republican perspective, a unionist government supported by the British state continued to deny them their human rights:

> Those seeking an insight into the origins and development of the Provisional IRA need look no further than 1969 and subsequent state policy. British indifference created the organisation and British repression sustained it. Its volunteers did not carry some genetic code dating back to 1916 predisposing them toward physical violence.[29]

However, it noticeable that the provisionals adopted traditional historical discourses to provide a continuous link with 1916 and confer legitimacy on their new republican movement:

> Evidence confronts us of the determination of the British government to pursue its senseless policy of military oppression. The Irish Republican Army have no choice but to continue the campaign of armed resistance.[30]

The Republican code 51

Their surface rhetoric presented both military and political strategies, but in reality Sinn Féin activists were developing a political agenda based on socialist principles that made reforming Northern Ireland a priority over the traditional republican goal of a united Ireland. It is unsurprising that republican veterans would over time leave the provisional movement, shocked at the scale of departure from principles of Irish republicanism:

> The Provisional movement carefully manipulated and articulated the tradition of republican ideology into provisional discourse.[31]

> Today the ideals we fought for are never spoken of. Our beliefs are traded for the realities of the current process, a process that suits the interests of political parties and not the common people.[32]

The notion of physical force to eject a rogue state remained a key justification for the provisionals, but their new role of community protectors opened up the space for them to become politically active in Northern Ireland. The political development of Sinn Féin brought a spotlight to the unresolved tension between a universal message of republicanism and their pragmatic desire to influence northern politics. This meant that the republican principles of physical force and abstention would sooner or later be put the test.

Republican hunger strikes (1980s)

> It is not those who inflict the most but those who can suffer the most who will conquer.[33]

The words of Terence MacSwiney, who died on hunger strike in an English jail in 1920, became another powerful legacy adopted by provisional republicans. Hunger strikes were a political act of defiance against the perceived injustice inflicted by the British state and a means to draw attention to the plight of Catholic communities across Ireland. This personal sacrifice represented a different form of physical violence and enshrined martyrdom in republican culture for another 100 years. The discourse of personal sacrifice was reconstituted in the 1980s when the provisional movement resorted to hunger strikes in the North.

The language of the hunger strikers in the early 1980s indicates that they believed their actions to be an alternative front in a war with the British. Although engaged in a 'Long War' with the British state, the provisional leadership was discreetly drafting political strategies to steer the movement away from revolutionary violence.[34] Their political focus was on social and political reforms in the North and the hunger strikes gave them a route to move from a position of radical resistance to one of community politics:

> On a practical, and indeed at local level, it demonstrated the ability of the grass roots membership of the organisation to be an effective political force. The hunger strike campaign generally proved our ability to influence people in the community in which we lived.[35]

The election of Bobby Sands as an MP for the Westminster parliament in 1981 was a major watershed for northern republicans, even though the principle of abstention prevented him from taking his seat. The political support for Bobby Sands from nationalist and republican communities was an avalanche. His death, and the deaths of nine other young republicans, was a shocking event and reinforced the stories of martyrdom already embedded in republican historical discourses.[36] New stories of martyrdom and sacrifice portrayed the absorption of suffering rather than an infliction of violence on others. The original republican grievances against injustice in Northern Ireland were rational demands for economic, social and political justice. Republican hunger strikes evoked a strong emotional reaction from a wider body of people nationally and internationally. For republicans, the purpose of hunger striking was to communicate suffering as act of dignified rebellion and one that positions the enemy as a persecutor.

One of the key outcomes of the hunger strikes in the 1980s was an increasing politicization of nationalist communities in Northern Ireland and this increased republican political support. Sinn Féin learned the values of electoral power but there was a price, as this meant their political focus shifted closer to the nationalist community and constitutional politics.

They maintained their allegiance to the core republican goal of Irish unity but there was a distinctive shift to a broader pan-nationalist approach to their political strategy. Through their discourses, Sinn Féin were able to make political capital from the hunger strikes and stay faithful to the republican code:

> We believe that an age-old struggle for Irish self-determination has been immeasurably advanced by this hunger strike and therefore we claim a massive political victory.[37]

Sinn Féin's growing commitment to a political solution to ending partition during the 1980s was a qualitatively different message to their physical force republicanism in the previous decade. The hunger strikes started as a traditional republican response to the British state and were fundamentally about the status of republican volunteers in prison. With the international status of prisoner of war, their armed struggle was legitimized with a guarantee of special status in prison.[38] The identity of prisoner of war remains an important symbol for republicans because it recognizes the legitimacy of their struggle. In 1975 the special category status was dropped by the British government and overnight criminalized years of republican struggle. The republican response was to create a new battlefront in prison and that elevated their struggle to another form of sacrifice for the republican goal. The *blanket protest* was initiated and a different form of violent standoff confronted the British government.[39]

> The British government are responsible for the hunger strikes. The ending of special category status was a political tactic used to criminalize the Republican attack on British imperialism in Ireland.[40]
>
> Our comrades have lit with their lives an eternal beacon which will inspire this nation and people to rise up and crush oppression forever.[41]

In the years following the hunger strikes, a new transitional discourse started to emerge and this indicated that the Sinn Féin leadership were ready to challenge the traditional republican principle of abstention and take a more pragmatic stance to constitutional politics in Northern Ireland. The following extracts acknowledge the republican principle of physical force as a goal, but they also subtly challenge the principle of abstention. The discourses signal that Sinn Féin were anticipating a fundamental change in the traditional relationship between republicans and the British state:

> Those in favour of contesting elections that do so is a tactic – political gains must flow to the people associated with the armed struggle.[42]

> There is room for republicans to examine if the struggle for independence can be improved by an intervention in the electoral process in order to show clearly that people support radical republicanism. What should not be the basis for discussion is whether this intervention means the run-down of an armed struggle. It patently does not. We must fight on many fronts. The armed struggle has been historically shown to be important.[43]

The political terrain for republicans was about to change but their warrior talk of martyrdom and sacrifice remained. Despite the political leverage of the hunger strikes, the military rhetoric remained primary and the following statement was published during a period of inclusive talks with nationalist politicians. The warrior talk was directed at other republicans:

> Like other forms of struggle in Ireland, the armed struggle is about the political demands for national self-determination, and end to partition and the creation of a 32-county Irish Republic. Armed struggle is seen as a political option. Its use is considered in terms of achieving national political aims and the efficacy of other forms of struggle.[44]

Republicanism and abstentionism

> Sacred flame of abstention and the whole mantle of physical force republicanism.[45]

Abstentionism is a universal principle of Irish republicanism and represents a clear position that the partition of Ireland was illegal and therefore the Dublin government in the South and the Belfast government in the North are both deemed undemocratic and morally wrong. The reunification of Ireland does not imply bringing the two parts together as they currently exist but the creation of a new united republic. A major outcome of the 1980/81 hunger strikes was a change in republican policy around their core principle of abstention and forms a significant watershed in republican history. The death of ten hunger strikers added to the list of martyrs and further legitimized the republican cause, but it also freed Gerry Adams and Martin McGuinness to develop and communicate their electoral strategies in Northern Ireland:

> We must change our strategies but never let this change our aims.[46]

The republican principle of abstentionism is key to defining the republican relationship with the British state and positions them as the traditional enemy of Irish freedom. To this day, elected Sinn Féin MPs do not take their seats in the United Kingdom parliament. In the 1980s an amendment was proposed by the Sinn Féin leadership to allow their elected politicians to take up their seats in local government elections. This meant that republicans were being asked to change their ideology on abstention and it was not unanimously accepted. By 1987, Ruarírí Ó 'Brádaigh, a former provisional leader, had formed Republican Sinn Féin in protest at their proposal to change the republican position on abstentionism.

> All parties who broke from the Republican Movement and accepted partitionist institutions abandoned the 32 County Republic and ended up collaborating with English rule in Ireland.[47]

Provisional Sinn Féin argued that ideological shifts were simply political tactics to promote the republican goal of a united Ireland and therefore republican philosophy and principles have not been compromised. Opponents, such as Republican Sinn Féin, took the view that any change in republican principles was a betrayal of what it means to be a republican.

A vote was taken at a republican Ard Fheis in 1986 which Provisional Sinn Féin won. This was a very important political shift for northern republicans because it revived a long-standing philosophical debate about the *'means and ends'* to achieve a united Ireland. The amendment on abstention allowed Provisional Sinn Féin to engage in local elections in Northern Ireland and was a huge boost for their political aspirations and they grew in confidence. This change opened the door to a political route to Irish unity and perhaps more importantly, it enabled a focus on social and economic justice in Northern Ireland.

The formation of Republican Sinn Féin was an important event and the political discourses employed by Provisional Sinn Féin give an insight into way they worked to maintain unity in the republican movement. A fusion of political discourses with romantic rhetoric became a recurring feature of Sinn Féin speeches. Note, for instance, the use of the term 'unbeaten and unbroken':

> After seventeen years in the field, they have demonstrated time and time again that they are unbeaten and unbroken. Their tenacity in the face of a numerically stronger and better-equipped enemy has become a legend amongst the freedom-loving people of the world.[48]

In the extract above, Sinn Féin is addressing republicans and paying respect to republican volunteers – whether they were active volunteers, veterans or martyrs. This sample of discourse illustrates the careful way that Sinn Féin attempted to keep republicans on board, particularly when they were about to introduce a change in strategy. Their warrior talk was used rhetorically to sound out the readiness of the republican movement for new political tactics in Northern Ireland. The aspiration of a united Ireland was still promoted as a primary goal when in reality it was a secondary consideration to gaining power to shape the politics of Northern Ireland. The result was the creation of republican breakaway groups over the next twenty years: this is an important aspect of this study into warrior talk and will be explored in more detail in Chapter 6.

Provisionals and republican unity

> Republicans without republicanism are little different to constitutional nationalists.[49]

Republicans opposed to the political tactics of the provisional leadership are united in their allegiance to the core republican philosophy and see themselves as the living link that legitimizes Irish republicanism and which they sustain through words and actions. Both provisionals and their republican opponents use historical and justification discourses

The Republican code 57

to remind others of their republican lineage and the legacy of sacrifice. The rhetoric from both provisional and radical republican groups is similar because they share a history that includes 1916 (Easter Rising), 1969 (Civil Rights Movement), 1973 (Bloody Sunday) and 1981 (hunger strikes). Both groups believe themselves to be Irish republicans and the custodians of the sacred flame of republicanism. The tipping point for significant division within the movement was the Good Friday Agreement, when more republican groups and individuals formed in protest.

Despite their commitment to the peace process, the provisional leadership continues to stress their continuity with republican history using core discourses and warrior talk. Their journey towards constitutional politics taught them how to react through their discourses to external conditions and political opportunities. Their colonized discourses expanded and diversified as they navigated republicans into and through the Northern Ireland peace process. However, the traditions of Irish republicanism have not been extinguished as Marion Price illustrates in a speech:

> Fellow republicans, I call upon you to educate our youth and instill in them a sense of pride in, and understanding of, the sacrifices of countless generations of men and women in the pursuit of Irish freedom.
>
> Memories will come rushing back to many of you, of parents and grandparents, childhood friends, comrades-in-arms, the memories and camaraderie of the internment camps and the prisons.[50]

The language in these extracts is a fascinating glimpse into the perceptions of republicans who reject the pragmatic politics of the provisional movement and helps to understand the sense of betrayal felt by groups such as Republican Sinn Féin, that a historic compromise with unionists and the British government has effectively squandered a sacred inheritance.

Chapter summary

Warrior talk was an early linguistic device used by provisional republicans to justify military operations in Northern Ireland. Decades later, warrior talk remains in Sinn Féin discourses, and on a surface level this might appear a tactic to preserve unity across the spectrum of Irish republicanism. The forms of warrior talk have evolved in response to changes in context and Sinn Féin's political aspiration but the roots of republicanism and their historical legacy sustain a powerful cause. Warrior talk is a shorthand message to ensure the 'living link' to republican philosophy and the goal to unite Ireland is sustained.

In this chapter, the roots of Irish republicanism and impact of a powerful philosophical lineage on republican discourses were explored. A historical timeline of key events was introduced to demonstrate how republicans have used their discourse to legitimize their political and military strategies. It appears that warrior talk has served the purpose of maintaining the continuity of republican philosophy and principles. In 1969, republican philosophy, ideology and principles were perceived by republicans to be congruent. By 2019, republican ideology had shifted and republican principles had been parked.

From an ideological perspective, warrior talk presents an inconsistent message in the context of Sinn Féin's peace discourses. From a practical perspective, any return to an armed republican strategy would be deeply damaging to the political gains Sinn Féin have made and their future political ambitions. This leaves an interesting complexity for republican politics in Northern Ireland. Republican priorities of the past, current dilemmas and future visions are all circling around in their discourses.

The core discourses represent an alignment between philosophy, ideology and principles and as such provide a consistent and continuous message from one generation to the next. Colonized discourses signify changes in principles and ideology. Warrior talk is a key to understanding the current challenges facing Irish republicanism. The chapter also briefly outlined the emergence of provisional republicans who led the republican movement through a war, a peace process and are now elected politicians working in the government of Northern Ireland. The continued use of warrior talk may be a genuine outreach to other republicans or a collective denial that the provisional movement has entered mainstream politics and is no longer a radical political force. A bipolar explanation never quite delivers a comprehensive understanding of all the issues and discourse analysis allows us to consider that war and peace discourses could co-exist.

This next chapter will examine the emergence and development of Provisional Sinn Féin using a timeline of discourses from 1969 to 2019. The emergence of new forms of warrior talk in response to external events and political opportunities will address the question:

> How did the provisional movement of the 1970s develop into a constitutional political power?

Suggested reading (chapter specific)

This is not a traditional literature section but a short list of recommendations for further reading based on the content of Chapter 3. All discourses are political in nature and created in a specific context and for a specific purpose. This is where Foucault's work brings a helpful reminder to pay attention to the background detail and dates when discourses are formed or colonized. The same concept applies to literature sources. The political context at the time of the publication and the purpose of the writing will reveal the writer's interpretation of republicanism. A journalist's perspective may be different to a republican, veteran, academic or indeed any outsider to the republican movement.

In discourse analysis, it is important to read from a number of perspectives to understand the personal and political agendas of internal and external stakeholders. This will bring richness to your interpretation. The recommended reading is drawn from a full spectrum of perspectives including academics, journalists and republicans.

Some recommendations are *archaeological* accounts, which were written close to key events and in some cases the writers were active participants or interested observers (see previous chapter) at the time.

A second form of recommended reading is *genealogical* accounts where authors have produced a retrospective account of events (see previous chapter). Both accounting forms are an important source of knowledge and concepts that will add value to your decoding of political discourses, and both are relevant to discourse analysis so reading suggestions are drawn from both the early years of the Northern Ireland conflict to the present day.

The roots of republicanism

Northern Ireland: The Nervous Peace (2013)[51] is essential reading for a historical perspective on the Northern Ireland peace process. This book is also very useful for all chapters and is written with academic rigour combined with a practical insider understanding of life in Northern Ireland. Chapters One and Two outline the history of unionist culture and attitudes.

Unionist Politics and the Politics of Unionism since the Anglo-Irish Agreement (1997).[52] This is worth reading to gain detailed understanding of unionist politics and what republicanism represents to unionists.

Sinn Féin: A Hundred Turbulent Years (2002)[53] provides a comprehensive picture of the fortunes of Sinn Féin over a 100 years and charts the key events that helped to shape their political identity. This author has been both a political commentator and a politician in Northern Ireland.

In the Shadow of History: Sinn Féin, 1926–70 (2015)[54] focusses on the early history of Sinn Féin and is worth reading for the background detail on republican politics prior to the start of the conflict in Northern Ireland.

The Politics of Illusion (1997)[55] gives a historical account of how the two major strands of republicanism emerged. The author refers to social republicanism as a failed attempt to fuse two incompatible republican ideologies.

The IRA and Sinn Féin (1997)[56] is written by a British journalist who has reported on Northern Ireland since the summer of 1969. He has written several books but this work on the provisional movement brings an interesting perspective that covers all the themes of this chapter.

The republican relationship with physical force

IRA Tactics and Targets (1990)[57] is a practical way to understand their ideology and organization. The author is an American historian and expert on terrorism who brings an informative insight into IRA operations during their *Long War* with the British state. The book provides a useful context to understand the scale of political shifts made by republicans in the 1990s.

The Secret Army: The IRA (1998).[58] This book brings further insights into the special nature of Irish republican ideology and the belief, strongly held by some republicans, that the only means to a Republic is by physical violence. The discourse findings in this book challenge this position and indicate a pluralist approach to republican ideology across the republican movement.

The Long War: The IRA and Sinn Féin (1995)[59] argues that republican physical force is an offensive (rather than defensive) strategy to force a British withdrawal from Ireland and points to the legacy of the French revolution as a source of the republican construction of *enemy*.

The republican code and the Easter Rising

Post Nationalist Ireland: Politics, Culture and Philosophy (1997)[60] are a good source of ideas on the republican rituals to commemorate historic sacrifices. Republican stories of fallen heroes allow ordinary men and women to detach from reality and justify violence. This attachment to the past has been consistent in the discourse from the republican leadership to their grass roots to the present day.

The northern provisional movement

The Border: The Legacy of a Century of Anglo-Irish Politics (2019)[61] sets out a good analysis of Bloody Sunday and the impact on the south of Ireland. The author concludes that the hunger strikes signalled the start of a lengthy disengagement from the conflict by the Irish government and discusses the repercussions for the peace process.

Those Are Real Bullets Aren't They? (2001)[62] is written by two British journalists who give a detailed narrative of the events of Bloody Sunday. This is worth a read to gain an understanding of why this event was the tipping point for a major escalation in violence in Northern Ireland.

The Trouble with Guns (1998)[63] brings another perspective to the debate on the republican physical force tradition with a frank assessment that the provisional movement conducted calculated outrages to destabilize the state of Northern Ireland as a means to accelerate political change. This book is also a good insight into the development of provisional republicanism up to the Good Friday Agreement from a Catholic nationalist perspective.

Unfinished Business: The Politics of 'Dissident' Irish Republicanism (2019).[64] This book uses substantial interviews with different republican groups to examine the initial justification of the PIRA campaign in Northern Ireland and the competing narratives that now exist between provisionals and radical opponents.

The Politics of Illusion (1997)[65] is a good text to use with all chapters of this book, but there are key chapters with detail on the Official republicans (1970–1977) and the rise of the provisionals with their rediscovery of social republicanism.

From Armed Struggle to Political Struggle (2015).[66] Chapter Two is highly relevant to understanding the increasing militancy of provisionals in the 1970s. The interviews in this book bring a range of insights into the republican ability to fuse metaphors with valid grievances.

Northern Ireland: Conflict and Change (2002)[67] presents a comprehensive overview of the *Troubles* in Northern Ireland with reference to the Good Friday Agreement and the impact on the contemporary political situation. This is a good read to establish a strategic picture of Northern politics and the unique form of government in Belfast.

Republicans and hunger strikes

Ten Men Dead: The Story of the 1981 Hunger Strike (1987)[68] – a powerful insight into republican hunger strikers from a journalist's perspective which is supported by evidence from IRA volunteers. It also reveals the impact of the hunger strikes on the politicization of Northern nationalist communities.

Good Friday: The Death of Republicanism (2008) provides a detailed insight into the blanket protests and eventual hunger strikes. This is an essential read from a former republican prisoner.[69]
Blanketmen: The Untold Story of the H-Block Hunger Strike (2005).[70] This is an important book because it gives a detailed personal account from the original blanket protest to the republican hunger strike in 1981. The internal dynamics and politics between Sinn Féin and the IRA during the hunger strikes are discussed.

Republicanism and abstentionism

The Politics of Irish Freedom (1986).[71] The author, Gerry Adams, explains the nature of Sinn Féin's challenge to the republican principle of abstention. He outlines three republican traditions: militaristic, radical and constitutional, and reveals his political thinking at a time when a constitutional path would have been unthinkable for many republicans.
The Longest War (1990)[72] is another good source of information on abstentionism written in a context when the idea of changing a republican principle to enter constitutional politics was unthinkable.

Provisionals and republican unity

Spoiling for Peace (2015)[73] presents a detailed analysis of republican ideology and the compromises made by the republican leadership. The emergence of dissident republicanism is examined in the context of the Northern Ireland peace process.

Practical study task: Easter commemoration

This task is a step-by-step approach to conducting a piece of discourse analysis and will prepare you for a typical essay/assignment in politics, peace studies or conflict resolution. The task will enable you to apply the learning from this chapter to a specific extract of discourse.

Below is an extract from an address given by Martin McGuinness to republicans at an Easter commemoration. The date is 23 April 2000 and the venue is Dublin. To complete this task, use the following prompt questions to make your analysis of the forms of discourse and the purpose of the speech:

- *What do you notice about the date and venue of the commemoration and the purpose of the gathering?*
- *What do you know about the speechmaker and his political intentions towards his audience?*
- *Which forms of core discourses are embedded in the speech and what do you think their purpose is?*
- *Where are the roots of republicanism embedded in this speech?*
- *What do you notice about the relationship between war and peace discourses in the speech?*
- *Who are the key stakeholders for this speech? What is the nature of the power relations between the speaker and his other stakeholders?*

Extract from an Phoblacht: 23 April 2000

We are here to honour all those who died in the fight for our right to be a free and independent nation and recommit ourselves to the ideals for which they died. I want to pay tribute to the Volunteers of the Dublin brigade of Óglaigh na hÉireann who lie in these graves. They fought for justice, freedom and peace and we are rightly proud of each and every one of them. At this time too, we pay a special tribute to the republican PoWs and their families. The integrity of the prisoners and their families through many difficult years is a testimony of the determination of a people to be free. Partition, injustice, conflict and war dominated the political landscape throughout the last century. A dark century which against all odds came to an end on a ray of hope and optimism created by the leaders of republican and nationalist Ireland. The courage and imagination of an IRA leadership in calling a cessation gave space to those politicians whose responsibility it is to find a peaceful resolution to the conflict.

Notes

1. O'Brien, B. (1995). *The Long War: The IRA and Sinn Féin*, Dublin: O'Brien Press, p. 18.
2. Direct Rule was imposed by the British Government in 1972 and lifted in 1998.
3. McIntyre, A. (2008). *Good Friday: The Death of Irish Republicanism*, New York: Ausubo Press, p. 295.
4. IRA statement (1967), reported in *Republican News*.
5. Adams, G. (2016). '100th anniversary of the Easter Rising', *Irish Republican News*.
6. Wolfe Tone's proclamation, 1798.
7. Wolfe Tone advocated a non-sectarian society that welcomed religious, social and political diversity. His influence on Irish republicanism is commemorated annually and his ideas surfaced in Sinn Féin transitional and peace discourses as they steered republicans to inclusive politics.
8. '*Power to the people*' is an important principle that contributed to Sinn Féin politics in Northern Ireland in the 1970s and will be explored in more detail in Chapter Four.
9. Cicero was a Roman citizen who played an important role in promoting republican principles, 106–43, BC.
   For a more detailed explanation see Kearney, R. (1997). *Postnationalist Politics: Politics, Culture and Philosophy*, London: Routledge, p. 44.
10. For a more detailed explanation see O'Brien, B. (1995). *The Long War: The IRA and Sinn Féin*, Dublin: O'Brien Press, pp. 47–48.
11. Moody, T. W., McDowell, R. B., and Woods, C. J. (1998). *The Writings of Theobald Wolfe Tone, 1763–98*, Volume 1, Oxford: Oxford University Press.
12. Drover, G. (1995). *John Hume: Man of Peace*, London: Vista, p. 10.
13. Bobby Sands, his own diary, 1 March 1981, p. 1.
14. Citizens in Northern Ireland were disenfranchised and could not vote unless they rented or owned a property.
15. Tonge, J. (2002). *Northern Ireland: Conflict and Change*, Essex: Pearson Education Ltd, Chapter Seven.
16. McIntyre, A. (2008). *Good Friday: The Death of Irish Republicanism*, New York: Ausubo Press.
17. Cochrane, F. (2013). *Northern Ireland: The Reluctant Peace*, London: Yale University Press, Chapters Two and Three.
18. Seán MacStiofáin, *An Phoblacht*, April 1970. He was Chief of Staff for the Provisional IRA.
19. Adams, G. (1976). *The Long War*, Sinn Féin press Dublin, p. 3.
20. Bowyer Bell, J. (1998). *The Secret Army: The IRA*, Dublin: Poolbeg Press, p. 13.
21. Gerry Adams, Ard Fheis report, *Irish Republican News*, 2 March 2016.
22. *Ibid*.

23. This was essentially a democratic mandate for a thirty two county Irish republic and made the subsequent division of Ireland an outrage for republicans.
24. This was the First Dáil, 1919–1921. It was outlawed in 1919 but continued to meet in secret.
25. Extract from the first day of Bobby Sands diary, 1 March 1981. <https://www.pbs.org/wgbh/pages/frontline/shows/ira/readings/diary.html>.
26. McIntyre, A. (2008). *Good Friday: The Death of Irish Republicanism*, New York: Ausubo Press, p. 306.
27. Reed, D. (1984). *The Key to the British Revolution*, London: Larkin, p. 147.
28. <http://report.bloody-sunday-inquiry.org/> 15 June 2010.
29. McIntyre, A. (2008). *Good Friday: The Death of Irish Republicanism*, New York: Ausubo Press.
30. *An Phoblacht*, 30 March 1973, p. 1.
31. McIntyre, A. (1997). *Irish Republicans: Agents of Change?* Belfast: Queens University Press.
32. *Irish News*, 31 May 2004.
33. *An Phoblacht*, July 1970, p. 1.
34. Adams, G. (1976). *The Long War*, Belfast: Republican Press Centre.
35. Seamus Kerr, *Frontline*, 6 August 2001.
36. Beresford, D. (1987). *Ten Men Dead: The Story of the 1981 Irish Hunger Strike*, London: Grafton.
37. *An Phoblacht*, 10 October 1981, p. 13.
38. Since 1916, Irish republicans have argued that they are at war with the British state and this confers the status of prisoner of war if they are serving a prison sentence. In the 1980s the 'blanket men' refused to wear prison clothing because it was a label that criminalized them. There are good accounts of this in all the books cited in the suggested reading section of this chapter.
39. Margaret Thatcher was the British Prime Minister during the republican hunger strikes of 1980/1981. The strategy of the British government was not to negotiate with republicans.
40. *An Phoblacht*, 11 July 1981, p. 12.
41. *An Phoblacht*, 10 October 1981, p. 13.
42. Molloy, Francie, *Ard Fheis Report*, 1981, p. 13.
43. *An Phoblacht*, 5 September 1981, p. 20.
44. Gerry Adams, letter to John Hume, Sinn Féin/SDLP talks, Belfast, 1988.
45. There are references to *'sacred flame'* in O'Brien, B. (1995). *The Longest War: The IRA and Sinn Féin*, Dublin: O'Brien Press, p. 21.
46. Adams, A. *An Phoblacht*, 4 November 1981, p. 13.
47. *Ibid*.
48. Ard Fheis report, *Sinn Féin*, Dublin, 1986, p. 2.

49. McIntyre, A. (2008). *Good Friday: The Death of Irish Republicanism*, New York: Ausubo Press, p. 73.
50. Extracts from an oration by Marion Price, Republican Sinn Féin reported in *Irish Republican News*, 2001.
51. Cochrane, F. (2013). *Northern Ireland: The Nervous Peace*, London: Yale University Press.
52. Cochrane, F. (1997). *Unionist Politics and the Politics of Unionism since the Anglo-Irish Agreement*, Cork: Cork University Press.
53. Feeney, B. (2002). *Sinn Féin: A Hundred Turbulent Years*, Dublin: O'Brien Press.
54. Maillot, A. (2015). *In the Shadow of History: Sinn Féin, 1926–70*, Manchester: Manchester University Press.
55. Patterson, H. (1997). *The Politics of Illusion: A Political History of the IRA*, London: Serif.
56. Taylor, P. (1997). *Provos: The IRA and Sinn Féin*, London: Bloomsbury.
57. Bowyer Bell, J. (1990). *IRA: Tactics and Targets*, Dublin: Poolbeg Press.
58. Bowyer Bell, J. (1998). *The Secret Army: The IRA*, Dublin: Poolbeg Press.
59. O'Brien, B. (1995). *The Long War: The IRA and Sinn Féin*, Dublin: O'Brien Press.
60. Kearney. (1997). *Post Nationalist Ireland: Politics, Culture and Philosophy*, London: Routledge.
61. Ferriter, D. (2019). *The Border: The Legacy of a Century of Anglo-Irish Politics*, London: Profile Books.
62. Pringle, P., and Jacobsen, P. (2001). *Those Are Real Bullets Aren't They?* London: Fourth Estate Limited.
63. O' Doherty, M. (1998). *The Trouble with Guns: Republican Strategy and the Provisional IRA*, Belfast: Blackstaff Press.
64. McGlinchey, M. (2019). *Unfinished Business: The Politics of Irish Republicanism*, Manchester: Manchester University Press.
65. Patterson, H. (1997). *The Politics of Illusion: A Political History of the IRA*, London: Serif.
66. Spencer, G. (2015). *From Armed Struggle to Political Struggle: Republican Tradition and Transformation in Northern Ireland*, London: Bloomsbury.
67. Tonge, J. (2002). *Northern Ireland: Conflict and Change*, Essex: Pearson Education. For a clear explanation of 'special category status' see pp. 95–97 and the rationale for republican hunger strikes.
68. Beresford, D. (1987). *Ten Men Dead: The Story of the 1981 Irish Hunger Strike*, London: Grafton.
69. McIntyre, A. (2008). *Good Friday: The Death of Irish Republicanism*, New York: Ausubo Press.
70. O'Rawe, R. (2005). *Blanketmen: An Untold Story of the H-Block Hunger Strike*, Dublin: New Island.

71. Adams, G. (1986). *The Politics of Irish Freedom*, Brandon: Dingle.
72. Kelley, K. J. (1990). *The Longest War*, London: Zed Books.
73. Whiting, S. A. (2015). *Spoiling the Peace: The Threat of Dissident Republicans to the Peace in Northern Ireland*, Manchester: Manchester University Press.

Chapter 4

The political journey of Sinn Féin

Introduction

> Sinn Féin wants to lead the next government, our political ambitions go beyond the electoral success of the 1980s.[1]

The journey of provisional Sinn Féin from political activists, in the 1970s, to a mainstream constitutional party is an indicator of the scale of political change within Irish republicanism. This political journey can be tracked through their discourses, which grew in scale and complexity in parallel to the challenge they faced both within and outside the republican movement. Traditional republican discourses, which used republican history to legitimize their political philosophy, were supplemented with new colonized discourses. Colonized discourses allowed Sinn Féin to signal a pragmatic political approach to the traditional republican goal of a united Ireland. The research into republican discourse, which was outlined in Chapter Two, reveals a contrast between Sinn Féin's core and colonized discourses and bring insights to the debate over whether political shifts were tactical responses to external conditions or a radical philosophical departure from the republican code.

During the period between 1969 and 1998, Sinn Féin discourses reveal phases of political development interspersed with political vacuums as IRA military operations started to impact the credibility of Sinn Féin, the political wing of provisional republicanism. In the last chapter the historical legacy of republicanism was explored using historical and justification discourses which clearly signal that republicans see themselves as a radical political movement with physical force employed where necessary to achieve a political outcome. This makes the early development of

Sinn Féin, in Northern Ireland, interesting because they were carrying a historical legacy but attempting to politicize the grassroots and develop a social republicanism as a means to change society in Northern Ireland.

In the 1970s Sinn Féin's political activism was regarded, internally, as secondary to military operations and any form of constitutional politics was treated with great suspicion by many republicans because it was counter to their traditional principle of abstention. This meant any form of engagement in elections in Northern Ireland could be construed as a sign that republicans acknowledged the British state as a legal entity. The idea that republicans might engage in British politics was unthinkable at the time. The only form of acceptable governance in both North and South was a single republic that encompassed the entire land mass. The IRA Green Book clearly stated that the IRA were the direct representatives of the 1919 Irish Dáil and the only legal government of an Irish Republic:

> The Army are the legal and lawful army of the Irish Republic which has been forced underground by overwhelming forces.[2]

In this context, the political journey of Sinn Féin from republican activists to constitutional politicians is a fascinating study of leadership, political pragmatism and opportunism. A major surge in Sinn Féin political development followed the 1980/81 hunger strikes. Community support in elections became a new source of power for republicans. The term 'political mandate' was used to establish a different form of moral high ground that was ideologically different to republican radical politics. By 1987 new republican discourses emerged which were qualitatively different and a reflection of the influence Sinn Féin had within the republican movement. The following extract from the 83rd Ard Fheis, the annual republican conference, indicated an imminent challenge to traditional republican politics:

> The aim of our struggle is not only to remove the colonial system but also, and even more so, to develop the capacity to provide for the needs of real people, and to conduct our struggle in such a way that people increasingly participate in it.[3]

The cycles of political development and political vacuums continued throughout the 1980s. In 1987 Sinn Féin suffered reputational damage in the aftermath of the Enniskillen bomb in Northern Ireland, when an IRA bomb was detonated at a Remembrance Sunday ceremony and resulted in civilian casualties.[4] Sinn Féin had been in a discreet dialogue with Northern nationalist politicians and in the short term this work was impeded because John Hume, the leader of Social Democratic and Labour Party (SDLP), was an advocate of civil rights but not of violence. However, the Enniskillen bomb served as a catalyst for all stakeholders to continue working to develop pan-nationalist agenda for peace in Northern Ireland. By 1993, their work made a significant contribution to the Downing Street Declaration.[5]

From these early cycles of political development, IRA violence and political vacuums, the Sinn Féin leadership learned to adapt to changing situations and this is observable in new colonized discourses.

However, core discourses from the 1970s confirm that republicans believed their struggle for Irish freedom was best served by physical force and that an armed strategy would bring the British government to the negotiating table. The use of physical force was deemed, at the time, to be the most effective way to put pressure on the British state. In Northern Ireland, the scale of violence was a contributing factor to the mixed messages appearing in republican communications. In this statement, from 1972, the language implies a war situation despite the reference to peace, which, at the time, meant on republican terms:

> Vigorous IRA comeback as peace proposals are ignored. Foreign mercenaries of the British 1ˢᵗ Parachute Regiment searching Irish citizens on a street in Derry.[6]

Sinn Féin's political position was closely aligned to Irish republican philosophy and principles; on the surface there was a shared vision for both political activists and IRA volunteers. The straitjacket of principles of physical force tradition and abstentionism effectively constrained the potential transition of Sinn Féin into a credible political party. The more detailed examination of Sinn Féin discourses which is presented in this chapter reveals a gradual political pragmatism that brought international support, electoral success and a mandate to represent republicans in the government of Northern Ireland.

Sinn Féin's aspiration to lead the next government was clearly not hollow rhetoric and their journey from 1969 to 2019 illustrates a focused and determined will to gain political power and influence change from within the political system. At the time their political rhetoric was, however, unclear on whether they envisaged forming a pan-Irish government, the government in the north or a government in the republic. After the Good Friday Agreement, 1998, Sinn Féin discourses became more explicit that Northern Ireland was a political priority and will be discussed in Chapters Six and Seven. The scale of their political ambition is encapsulated by the career of the late Martin McGuinness, a senior republican who served as the Deputy First Minister of the Northern Ireland Assembly from 2007 to 2017.

For some republicans, the fact that the partition of Ireland continued to exist and yet one of their leaders was now part of the government in Northern Ireland was unconscionable. In the context of seismic political change, the role of warrior talk is clearly more complex than merely a historical legacy

Chapter purpose

This chapter maps a timeline of Sinn Féin's political development in Northern Ireland, from 1969 to 2019, against significant events and changing political conditions. Examples of core and colonized discourses will be used to analyse the complexity and plurality of Sinn Féin discourses as they initiated radical change and attempted to take the republican movement from a *Long War* with the British state to a *Long Peace* and the Good Friday Agreement (1998). Throughout this timeline, the content of republican warrior talk remained consistent, but the findings indicate adaptions were made to its role as a response to new situations and challenges.

From 1999 to 2019 there was a proliferation of Sinn Féin colonized discourses as all parties to the Good Friday Agreement continued to work on the implementation of its terms. A complex choreography of Sinn Féin discourses reflects the political aspirations of provisional republicanism and indicates their pragmatic departure from the traditional republican ideology as outlined in the previous chapter.

In this chapter, Provisional Sinn Féin will continue to be termed Sinn Féin to distinguish the organization from other republican groups. The provisional Irish Republican Army will be termed the IRA to distinguish them from other armed republican groups. Republican opposition to provisional republicanism is termed radical republicanism throughout this book and further explanations of different republican groupings will be given where appropriate.

Chapter structure

Sinn Féin political discourses (1969–1998)

1970s: Power to the people
1980s: Massive political victory
1990s: Armed only with political ideas

Sinn Féin political development (1999–2009)

An overview
Winning international support
Winning local support
The road to freedom
Sinn Féin strategies and republican unity
Radical republicanism

Sinn Féin political discourses (2009–2019)

Inclusive politics
An economic argument
Northern Ireland or New Ireland?
A new republic for the twenty-first century

Chapter summary
Suggested reading (chapter specific)
Practical study task: How to recognize core and colonized discourses

Sinn Féin political discourses (1969–1998)

1970s: Power to the people[7]

Early signals of Sinn Féin's political development can be seen in this extract from their recruiting material. Their intention was to politicize local republican communities with a vision of a just, fair and democratic society:

> To establish a reign of social justice based on Christian principles by a just distribution and effective control of the nation's wealth and resources, and to institute a system of government suited to the particular needs of the people.[8]

The political agenda was distinctly socialist, and their language aligned to the traditional republican values of democracy, justice and freedom, but in the context of increasing IRA activity their militaristic language sent out mixed messages. Their warrior talk masked the key political debates taking place within the republican movement as a whole, and not just in Northern Ireland. Sinn Féin, in the North, were developing their approach to socialist politics and attempting to interpret republican ideology and find a more pragmatic route to a united Ireland. There is no evidence of a planned strategy to abandon the republican goal, but they had clearly recognized the need to communicate their politics to a broader base of community support:

> It wasn't just about getting the Brits out of the country. It was about changing the whole socio-economic structures which led to our people living in servitude and poverty.[9]

A major problem for Sinn Féin was that the republican language of violent protest was also a feature of their 1970s political discourses. On 30 March 1973, Sinn Féin published their *Eire Nua* document, which presented a vision of self-governing communities that would give power to the people. They proposed an alternative structure for a new Irish republic with four provincial parliaments and a series of District and Community Councils to empower the people of Northern Ireland. In the same document, the IRA stated their conditions for peace, which included a date for British withdrawal and an amnesty for all political prisoners. The republican military wing was behaving as if they were at war and the political wing was developing political alternatives in preparation for Irish unity:

> Politics was a dirty word in those days. We actually believed that we could drive the British Army into the sea. We really thought victory was just around the corner.[10]

However, closer inspection of the *Eire Nua* document reveals an ideological tension within provisional republicanism between the political and military strategies. The IRA believed that military operations brought republicans the power to force a British withdrawal and the political traction to start negotiations on re-unification. In parallel, Sinn Féin was formulating political strategies that offered social, economic and political equality and which represented a route that would eventually take them towards electoral politics.

During the 1970s it is clear that traditional republican ideology was expressed through both military and political options. The historical republican position in relation to the British state was consistent and coherent for members of the republican movement but it was exclusive and unlikely to influence other communities in Northern Ireland. Gerry Adams was convinced that the political solution was to ensure that Catholic working-class communities were politicized as part of the republican struggle.[11] His ideas offered an alternative method of achieving a united Ireland by changing the political system of Northern Ireland from within. The following extract, from 1976, was a subtle signal from Gerry Adams that physical force had limitations:

> Revolutionary violence must be controlled and disciplined as a symbol of our people's resistance and the spearhead of their desire for a peaceful and just society.[12]

Sinn Féin's discourses reflected that the single most important hurdle to their political aspirations would be the need to enable a shift in the republican position on abstention. It would require a very strong case to persuade traditional republicans to accept electoralism as a practical alternative to achieving Irish unity through force. Sinn Féin activists were aware that republicans needed to develop new political strategies to capture the imagination of the grassroots in Northern Ireland. Gerry Adam's writing on *People's Assemblies* was significant because it focused on the importance of an organized and politicized working class. Writing as *Brownie*,[13] he discussed the idea of *Active Republicanism*. This language illustrates Sinn Féin's integration of warrior talk into their political messages. Given their position in the republican movement, the war cry was both directed at grassroots and a sign of solidarity:

> We fight for the people who find it hard to makes ends meet, whether they are small farmers being pushed off the land or factory workers being sold out by their Trade Union leaderships. They are our fight and out fight must be based among them.[14]

The extract above reflects the political space that Sinn Féin started to occupy within provisional republicanism. The statement signals a political strategy focused on developing communities, within Northern Ireland, into a powerful civil society. This was a fundamentally different philosophical position in comparison to the traditional republican goal of removing the British state and establishing a new Irish state across the whole island. This contrast marked the emergence of two strands of provisional republicanism, strands that have never been fully reconciled. The contradiction between armed rebellion against the British state to remove partition and the advocacy of a constitutional path to reform Northern Ireland became a highly emotive debate within the republican movement. The remark below is indication of what could be characterized as a rather dissembling style used by Gerry Adams in the 1970s. He developed a talent for advancing contentious political ideas and packaging them in traditional republican terms. In this statement, the blame for Sinn Féin political aspirations is with the British government:

> Wily Sassenachs manipulating Republicans into politics.[15]

In the 1970s Sinn Féin's emergent political thinking was clearly documented in *Republican News*, *An Phoblacht* and *Anderstown News*.[16] The growth of Sinn Féin cumann (committees) and the establishment of Republican Service Centres all indicated republican proactivity with their grassroots. However, the armed struggle and primacy of the IRA largely eclipsed their political discourses as illustrated in this statement:

> There was little appetite for political work of a more conventional kind. Sinn Fein's political programme is based on the defence of the nationalist people in the North. Although there are some innovative ideas on social, economic and cultural issues, and good proposals on alternative All-Ireland governmental structures, these were propagated only in a limited way through publicity machines.[17]

In the 1970s provisional republicans, with a strong influence from the IRA, communicated their strategy as the *3 Ds*. *Defence* was the protection of nationalist community; *Defiance* was civil disobedience; *Dissent* referred to the abstention of republicans from the Northern Ireland Assembly. The language of this strategy was used consistently and presented a clear mission to overthrow an undemocratic regime.

1980s: Massive political victory

In contrast to the experimental nature of Sinn Féin political development in the previous decade, their discourse of the 1980s communicated a very different political landscape and represented a major shift in their thinking on republican ideology:

> A decisive and important step in the political growth and development of the Republican Movement was taken last weekend, with the adoption of a positive approach to the participation in elections.[18]

Gerry Adams was careful to describe discussions on abstentionism as one aimed at 'opening another front', implying that republicans were still at war with the British. The use of warrior talk reflected the scale of internal debates and a recognition that republican principles and ideology were at stake:

> Whether one holds abstention as a principle or a tactic cannot be changed by a vote, regardless of how large the majority. We do not seek to change personal principles of any delegate here.[19]

The justification for Sinn Féin for contesting elections was still war-like and presented their political strategies as a means of supporting the armed struggle. Republican principles were sacrosanct and the language from Sinn Féin signalled their awareness that the provisional movement faced major ideological challenges. During the 1980s and 1990s Sinn Fein accelerated their challenge to the republican principles, physical force and abstentionism. Given the scale of change being proposed, it is unsurprising that the Sinn Féin leadership created new *transitional* discourses to keep the republican movement united. In reality, Sinn Féin was heading down the road of constitutional politics in Northern Ireland.

The road to electoral success was challenging. For example, in the wave of indignation following the Enniskillen bomb, 1987, Sinn Féin worked quickly to manage their reputational damage with their own grassroots.[20] The following extract indicates a pre-emptive political move to win back community support; notice the emphasis on living republicans rather than homage to dead heroes:

> A successful ideology of liberation has to develop from the reality of living people.[21]

Sinn Féin politics in the 1980s heralded a historic shift away from republican physical force tradition, culminating in IRA cessations in the 1990s. It is difficult to spot the moment that the IRA, as a dominant voice in republicanism, became marginalized because Sinn Féin were careful to present unarmed and armed strategies as one republican policy. To some republicans this erosion of IRA power was inexplicable when their war with the British state had not ended. By 1989 the ascendancy of Sinn Féin was clearly indicated by their internal messages. In this extract Gerry Adams was openly critical of IRA 'mistakes' but framed his remarks carefully:

> The base and the wider base have a right to question and do question those operations in which civilians are killed or injured.[22]

These words reveal an important ethos embedded into the republican principle of physical force, which legitimizes armed conflict if it is conducted for a noble cause. The rhetoric of *honourable conduct* and a *worthy enemy* is characteristic of republican historical and justification discourses. This statement by Gerry Adams is significant because he reminds IRA volunteers of the nobility of their cause. He implies that actions causing civilian casualties are not the behaviour of a noble army.

1990s: Armed only with political ideas

In the 1990s the political capital gained from republican hunger strikes enabled Sinn Féin to progress their electoral ambitions in Northern Ireland. Sinn Féin leaders continued to use warrior talk internally despite their advocacy for peace. Historical and justification discourses continued to be a common feature of Ard Fheis speeches:

> The history of Ireland and of British colonial involvement throughout the world tells us that the British government rarely listens to the force of argument. It understands only the argument of force. This is one of the reasons that armed struggle is a fact of life and death, in the Six Counties.[23]

In the 1980s Sinn Féin's electoral successes had given them the confidence to challenge the republican principle of abstention and they won support for Sinn Féin participation in local elections. A new form of discourse appeared which communicated an alternative route to Irish unity, one that was unarmed and based on phased transition and change:

> We have created a dynamic for change. We go into the next phase of our struggle armed only with our political ideas.[24]

The extract above illustrates the colonization of ideas from change theory and practice, a rapidly expanding field in the 1990s, and the outcome of wider societal and structural changes around the world.[25] Transitional discourses were focused on signalling and managing change; they frequently served as a mechanism for testing out new political strategies with other republicans.

Concepts such as transformational change and transformational leadership represented a new paradigm of the ways in which organizations and nations could become more democratic and citizens more empowered.[26] In the next extract, the language is chosen to reassure republicans that their noble struggle with the British state was still ongoing but there are subtle signals that republicans needed to adapt to their environment:

> We must all share in the daunting and massive task of interpreting and applying republicanism to changing and changed political conditions.[27]

Transitional discourses created a different form of continuity with the historic legacy of Irish republicanism and offered a middle way for republicans to adopt both unarmed and armed strategies.[28] This made Sinn Féin's internal communications during the 1990s an interesting choreography of transitional and transformational discourses: both were used to bridge the republican past with a new vision of the future. These forms of discourse will be examined in more detail in Chapters Six and Seven. In this context, Sinn Féin's continued use of republican core discourses and warrior talk was clearly a strategy to pre-empt internal opposition and avoid damaging splits. Colonized discourses were used to persuade, cajole and to a degree soften the harsh reality that republicans were being asked to abandon both their core principles and their historical ideology.

It is clear that warrior talk had a role to play in holding the republican movement together. An interesting paradox emerged for Sinn Féin in the 1990s. Their use of warrior talk in the public domain was a potential barrier to their political development and credibility as politicians. An invocation of warrior talk risked merely focusing all parties to the conflict in Northern Ireland – republicans, unionists and the British government – on the reality that they shared a history of violence.

In contrast, Sinn Féin colonized discourses provided clear evidence of their political investment in the future and the hope of a peaceful solution to the conflict in Northern Ireland. Their political strategy was pragmatic, community focused and ready to take advantage of the voting power that republican involvement in peace could bring. By 1998 Sinn Féin had a powerful retrospective narrative about the republican struggle and an equally powerful message about the future:

> In the last ten years, Sinn Féin's peace strategy has delivered the Hume/Adams talks, the Irish Peace Initiative, the IRA cessations, inclusive dialogue and the present opportunity for peace.[29]

The 1990s were a critical period for the broader republican movement, as Sinn Féin became the dominant voice for Irish republicanism in the North. Sinn Féin became more politically articulate and their colonization of terms such as 'reconciliation' and 'forgiveness' resonated with nationalist communities weary of conflict in Northern Ireland and ready to vote for an alternative to violence.

Sinn Féin political development (1999–2019)

An overview

> We will never allow the thirst for freedom to be quenched.[30]

This extract offers a rousing piece of warrior talk for a republican audience; the date is very interesting. The speech given by Gerry Adams was one month after the signing of the Good Friday Agreement; it sought to offer some reassurance to their republican opponents that Sinn Féin remained loyal to republican philosophy despite a major shift away the republican principles of physical force and abstentionism.

Sinn Féin discourses in this period were a reflection of the political progress they were making in Northern Ireland. The Good Friday Agreement showed that a republican peace strategy was advantageous for political credibility. Sinn Féin's continued use of core discourses with an occasional warrior tone demonstrated how they were managing the internal tensions through the traditional legitimacy and continuity of Irish republicanism. Republican history and past sacrifices continued to sustain the republican moral high ground but Sinn Féin were now signed up to a peace process.

Decommissioning weapons became a major political stumbling block for all parties to the Good Friday Agreement and the focus, from other stakeholders to the peace process, was on republicans to close down the IRA. This presented an enormous challenge for Sinn Féin and the discourse findings present clear evidence of their political skills working with internal and external stakeholders. Their discourses focused on the benefits of a political transition to Irish unity and the metaphor of a 'bridge' was used frequently to imply that republicans needed to reach out to unionists and recognize:

> The only show in town.[31]

Throughout this period Sinn Féin continued to cite the Good Friday Agreement as the moral imperative for peace in Northern Ireland. The political development of Sinn Féin after the Good Friday Agreement, and the impact of their strategies on the wider republican community, is revealed in the next section. Initially, the legitimacy of the peace process became a Sinn Féin mantra but during the next ten years they were forced to respond to internal and external challenges and this required new discourses. The result was multiple and, at times, conflicting messages which masked philosophical tensions within republicanism. In this period, several major discourse themes emerged.

Winning international support

The Sinn Féin leadership recognized that local political success was not enough, and republicans needed to secure and sustain international support to build their credibility as peacemakers in Northern Ireland. This comment by Gerry Adams in 2001, made to a republican audience, represents an interesting device to present a positive link between the peace process in Northern Ireland and other conflicts. It demonstrates a positive 'spin' on the Sinn Féin peace strategy that ignored the reality of a republican acquiescence to the continued presence of the British state in Northern Ireland:

> I recently travelled to South Africa and spoke to former President Nelson Mandela. Martin [McGuinness] is in the USA, in dialogue with political representatives there and Irish America. From South Africa and North America there are commitments and promises to support our work.[32]

Sinn Féin's political support for other international conflicts was also a good source of ideas and best practice in peace building and conflict resolution; this experience could be brought to negotiations with other political stakeholders in Northern Ireland. Transferable knowledge from other conflicts included the importance of inclusivity in talks, the progressive disarmament of paramilitaries and the establishment of institutions to support power sharing. The knowledge acquired by Sinn Féin in this period is clearly observable in their peace discourses and will be explored in detail in the next chapter.

This identification with international conflicts was an important way for Sinn Féin to dignify the armed struggle, especially when republicans moved towards decommissioning and met the requirements of the peace process. Republican volunteers faced the prospect that they were no longer needed. The change asked of them was far more existential than a shift of identity from a military to civilian status. The international perspective of Northern Ireland's peace process signalled that the IRA were freedom fighters who had served a crucial role in securing a peace treaty. Identification with other armed struggles in South Africa, Israel/Palestine and the Basque country (primarily in Spain) enabled Sinn Féin to claim a moral high ground in terms of human rights and the treatment of republican prisoners.

> In recent years, comrades from the ANC have constantly advised us that the revolutionary must always stay ahead of his or her opponents by seizing the strategic initiative. Clear and coherent strategy is a framework into which all forms of activism should be placed and organised. Strategy needs to be based on the reality of the existing situation. Strategy provides the armour for our ideology.[33]

In the extract above, the contact with the African National Congress legitimizes the term 'strategy' as a political tool for republicans. This is an interesting contrast to the traditional notion of ideology as the foundation of republican politics. Radical republicans perceived Sinn Féin's strategies as reactive to external circumstances and corrosive for Irish republicanism. It is interesting that the term 'armour' is used to present strategy as a positive tool and helps to explain Sinn Féin discourse production during this period.

Winning local support

The term 'electoral mandate' was used by Sinn Féin to persuade republicans that engagement with mainstream politics was a legitimate route to Irish unity, one which strengthened the republican position cause with both British and Irish governments. With an increasingly inclusive political strategy and greater emphasis on reconciling local communities in Northern Ireland, Sinn Féin believed they had a powerful moral high ground and were more likely to attract votes. This extract from a speech by Martin McGuinness advised that a strong electoral mandate would strengthen the republican negotiating position:

> The recent election results, in the north, were a massive endorsement of our politics, our vision for a united and free Ireland and of our strategy to achieve this. The role of the British government in Ireland has historically been a negative and divisive one and that needs to be brought to an end. That cannot happen soon enough for me. It will happen the sooner we educate, politicize and build the irrefutable and compelling rationale for Irish Freedom.[34]

This message is a clear example of the scale of change within provisional republicanism towards their relationship with the British government. The Sinn Féin manifesto (2002)[35] indicates that Gerry Adams and Martin McGuinness were moving the republican movement closer to a local socialist agenda in Northern Ireland. The focus on the traditional republican goal and ending of partition had started to fade a little in Sinn Féin discourses.

The primacy of the Good Friday Agreement became a mantra for Sinn Féin and shaped their responses for the next decade; this created dissent within the republican movement. In this period two immediate issues faced Sinn Féin republicans: IRA decommissioning and policing in Northern Ireland. Both issues presented Sinn Féin with major internal political challenges and this can be seen in language such as *The war is over*, *On the road to freedom* and *Building a nation*.[36] These examples are typical of their developing colonized discourses which attempted to address the republican agenda for a united Ireland as a final destination but through a journey of reconciliation and reform in Northern Ireland. The decommissioning of the IRA and the impact on the republican movement will be explored in the next chapter.

The road to freedom

Transitional and transformational discourses helped Sinn Féin to prepare and lead republicans towards involvement with the policing system in Northern Ireland. Sinn Féin was clear that the road to Irish freedom was paved by social, economic and political reform. A condition of the Good Friday Agreement included the reform of policing in Northern Ireland and this gave republicans an opportunity to engage in the process of reform and change. The security systems in Northern Ireland had been dominated by unionists and the British state since 1921. An Independent Commission on Policing, led by the British Conservative politician Chris Patten, was tasked to ensure that a new police service attracted people from both nationalist and unionist communities. The report was published in September 1999 with a series of structural and cultural changes planned to promote equality in the justice system.[37] At the time, a change of name and uniform was seen as the way to start the cultural transformation of the Royal Ulster Constabulary (RUC) with recruitment targets to achieve a balanced recruitment of police officers from both Catholic and Protestant backgrounds.

In 2005, Gerry Adams called for a special Ard Fheis to enable republicans to debate the issue of greater involvement in policing in Northern

Ireland. In his view, the police service needed to be more politically accountable. By 2007, Sinn Féin had joined the Northern Ireland Policing Board:

> Sinn Féin has taken up its position on the North's Policing Board for the first time this morning. What passed for policing here in the past must never repeated.[38]

This statement represented a major political shift for republicans. The Royal Ulster Constabulary had been renamed the Police Service of Northern Ireland (PSNI) in 2001 but a name change did not bring achieve the practical outcomes that Patten recommended.[39] Sinn Féin's presence on the PSNI Policing Board was communicated as a major political win that meant republicans now had a voice in the delivery of law and order in Northern Ireland. The Sinn Féin leadership saw this as an opportunity to address a major structural inequality and bring a republican slant to the long-standing issue of civil rights. For radical republicans this was another betrayal of republican philosophy and the historic sacrifices made by republican volunteers and veterans. From a radical republican perspective, provisional republicans who fought the British state were now policing their own communities on behalf of the British state.

Sinn Féin strategies and republican unity

In 2002 a 'Tirghra' was held in Dublin bringing together republicans from the North and South of Ireland to pay tribute to fallen volunteers of the IRA, republican activists and their families. The term Tirghra means 'Love of one's country' and key speeches at the event are a rich source of historical and justification discourses. In his address to over 2,000 republicans, Gerry Adams created a powerful storyboard of republican history that acknowledged the part played by the IRA in supporting the peace process in Northern Ireland:

> Republicans and nationalists hold the families of our republican dead in great esteem. It is because we are in your debt, 11 days from now, 86 years ago, the Irish Republic was proclaimed at the Easter Proclamation of 1916 and asserted in arms by republican men and women of that time. The IRA is not merely an army of soldiers; it is an army

of political activists. It takes bravery to wage war but it takes a special courage to sue for peace. The reality is that there would be no peace if it were not for the IRA.[40]

This extract is full of warrior talk, which is applied to both the republican armed struggle and a new world of peace. This Tirghra speech was rich in symbolism and portrayed as an act of celebration, thanksgiving and remembrance. The timing of this event indicates a political acuity within the Sinn Féin leadership that republicans needed reassurance that they were being taken in the right direction.

Historical and justification discourses continued to dominate speeches and were delivered in a reverential tone so familiar in republican gatherings. Warrior talk was used as a form of grieving for republicans and families who lost loved ones and comrades. Radical republicans regarded the Tirghra of 2002 as the political exploitation of dead republicans and a tactic to lay the republican past to rest with an elaborate ritual of closure, which masked the reality that Sinn Féin leadership wanted to press on with their political agenda for Northern Ireland.[41]

Radical republicanism

Republican opposition to the Good Friday Agreement was robust on the grounds that the terms were too much of a compromise with unionists and the British government. In the last chapter, the formation of Republican Sinn Féin in 1986 was introduced as a collective vote against the proposal to amend the republican principle of abstention. Republican Sinn Féin continued to use traditional warrior talk such as *war machine* and *military occupation* to articulate their political position in relation to the continued British presence in Northern Ireland.[42] A decade later, in the context of the Northern Ireland peace process, provisional republicans were described as traitors to the republican cause who have given unionists a mechanism to block Irish unity: the principle of consent embedded within the Good Friday Agreement stipulated that there would be no constitutional change in Northern Ireland without the consent of a majority of the population of Northern Ireland.[43]

The formation of Republican Sinn Féin marked an important split and clear opposition to the political strategies of Gerry Adams and Martin McGuinness. After the Good Friday Agreement, further splits occurred within provisional republicans and the outcome was new political and military groups, which initially coalesced around traditional republican ideology and principles. Over time, these groups became more diverse as different views were expressed about the use of violence as a political tool. All these groups are characterized by their allegiance to republican philosophy, ideology and principles and they universally adopt warrior talk in their communications. These groups and their discourses will be explored in more detail in Chapter Six.

In addition to the growth of new republican groups, three major scandals hit Sinn Féin in 2005: a raid at the Northern Rock bank, the murder of Robert McCartney[44] and accusations that senior Sinn Féin leaders were members of the IRA. The discourses used to repair the reputational damage were largely inclusive, transitional and focused on peace building. The Sinn Féin leadership stuck to their tried and tested formula of using the Good Friday Agreement to minimize the political damage but internally there was a clear message that effectively scapegoated their opponents:

> Twenty-five years ago, Margaret Thatcher couldn't criminalize us. The women prisoners in Armagh, the blanketmen and the hunger strikers wouldn't allow it. We won't allow anyone within republicanism to criminalise this party or this struggle.[45]

This was an interesting use of warrior talk because it appears to be a method of keeping order and enforcing discipline within the republican movement. In this extract there is a reference to a form of warrior talk which originated in the 1980s and was used to demonize other republicans. In a blink, Sinn Féin was able to draw on the past and compare the behaviour of British government with the behaviour of radical republicans. The moral tone of the extract was directed at republicans but, externally, it served to distance the Sinn Féin leadership from republican violence.

Gerry Adams and Martin McGuinness continued to use historical and justification discourses to maintain unity within the republican movement and as a show of loyalty to the traditions of Irish republicanism. They continued to use warrior talk drawn from 1916, the 1970s and the 1980s at commemorations, Easter gatherings and Ard Fheis conferences. Sinn Féin continued to uses phrases such as *guided by our patriot dead, final phase of our liberation, 1916 is becoming a reality, nothing will break us* and *a republic declared in arms.*

In the decade after the Good Friday Agreement, Sinn Féin managed to sustain their political influence in Northern Ireland despite challenges to their internal authority and military operations conducted by other IRA groups. A major political development within Sinn Féin can be observed in their enthusiasm for inclusive politics and dialogue with both unionists and other nationalists. Ideologically, this represented a 180-degree turn from their revolutionary politics of the 1970s.

Sinn Féin political discourses (2009–2019)

Inclusive politics

Sinn Féin's political shift to inclusive politics developed further in the period 2009–2019, to include a more robust argument for a united Ireland that was focussed on issues that faced communities both sides of the border. The fierce republican rhetoric of the 1980s and 1990s was tempered with sound economic reasoning for reunification that had appeal to a more diverse electorate.

An economic argument

Before the Good Friday Agreement, the inclusive republican politics of Sinn Féin were largely focused on building bridges with unionists and finding ways to create a fair and just society in Northern Ireland. The scale of their outreach to other stakeholders during the peace process can be observed in the proliferation of their peace discourses. These discourses were full of emotive language with terms such as 'forgiveness' and 'reconciliation' as republicans secured the moral high ground and attempted to persuade unionists to share power. The emergence and development of republican peace discourses will be explored in greater depth in the next chapter. Below is an extract of inclusive language from 2012, which reveals an interesting link with Wolfe Tone and skilful framing of reconciliation to republicans:

> Irish republicans come from a long and honorable tradition that seeks to unite Irish citizens. Tone captured its spirit when he wrote of a cordial union among the people of Ireland, to maintain that balance which is essential to the preservation of our liberties and the extension of our commerce.[46]

In the decade 2009–2019 Sinn Féin used their discourses to move from the emotive questions of reconciliation with historic enemies to a hard-nosed economic rationale for Irish unity. Their reasoning was more precise and dealt with issues that were attractive to voters across the political spectrum in Northern Ireland. Sinn Féin appeared to have been applying a number of strategies to keep Irish unity on the agenda. Below are some examples of their economic discourse:

> On this island there is now a considerable market of some six million people. Since the Good Friday Agreement, trade between North and South has steadily increased. Firms on both sides of the border do business with each other on a daily basis. Hundreds of thousands of people live in one jurisdiction while they shop, study or work in the other. Progress towards creating a truly all-Ireland economy is being made.[47]

> 'Many people now realise that is makes no sense to have two economies, two education system, two health systems, two tax codes, two currencies on one small island.'[48]

Northern Ireland or New Ireland?

An emphasis on inclusive politics was the road Sinn Féin had chosen, whether ideologically or as a political tactic. Their engagement with the peace process opened up new political opportunities to secure power but it closed down space for them to remain a radical movement. Their internal political credibility was put at risk when they became elected representatives, alongside unionists, in the new Northern Ireland Assembly on

1 July 1998. However, inclusive political strategies were starting to bring a level of influence for Sinn Féin across the island of Ireland and a development that would have been inconceivable in 1969. Their speeches increasingly positioned Sinn Féin as the only All-Ireland party with electoral success on both sides of the border:

> Every week, ministers, North and South, are working together, taking decisions affecting the lives of every person on this island. This is all-Ireland politics at work – and this after less than a year of us travelling along this road.[49]

The scale of Sinn Féin's political ambitions started to crystallize in their references to nation building and the creation of a 'New Republic'. The complexity of their socialist ambitions for Northern Ireland and their nationalist vision of a peaceful and political transition to a united Ireland made their discourses appear contradictory. In this extract, the emphasis on 'island' is a clear signal of Sinn Féin's All-Ireland agenda:

> We are nation builders. We are not motivated by self-interest or personal gain. We are determined and we are united. We are the engine driving historic, political, social and constitutional change on this island.[50]

By 2011, the language of 'New Republic' had appeared and signalled a level of confidence from Sinn Féin that constitutional politics could end partition and that building alliances with working-class unionists could be a practical way to use the principle of consent. With their political influence and infrastructure on both sides of the border, a political route to a united Ireland had appeared on the horizon. Warrior talk continued to appear as recycled language, for example the phrase 'other fronts' which had proved a useful tactic in the 1980s to signal change to the republican movement. The contradiction lies in the fact that Sinn Féin were now heavily committed to inclusive politics in Northern Ireland.

A new republic for the twenty-first century

The term 'New Republic' is very interesting because it implies a level of dissatisfaction with the existing government in the Irish republic but also a realization from Sinn Féin that a traditional republican conception of a republic was a barrier to attracting voters from unionist communities. New transformational discourses appeared to promote the reunification of Ireland as a benefit to all citizens:

> Imagine a new agreed Ireland.
> Imagine the unity of Orange and Green.[51]

The decade 2009–2019 is an interesting period in republican politics. Despite all their political achievements in Northern Ireland, across the Irish Republic and internationally, Sinn Féin continued to use historical discourses and warrior talk which, although slightly muted, still evoked memories and historical allegiances. In this extract the date is 2012 and the context is the Easter speech to republicans:

> The proclamation of 1916 continues to enthuse and motivate Irish republicans. Its message of freedom and equality, and of cherishing the children, is as relevant today as it was then.[52]

> Irish republicans come from a long and honourable republican and international tradition which seeks to unite Irish citizens and break the connection with England.[53]

Despite the traditional greetings and rhetoric, Sinn Féin remained focused on their mission in community politics and the transformation of society in Northern Ireland. The republican values of freedom, justice and democracy were an attractive message to working-class communities struggling in a decade of austerity imposed by a British government. Sinn Féin signalled very clearly that the next stage of the journey was to unite, bring peace and reconciliation to communities in Northern Ireland. The scale of the political journey of Sinn Féin can be seen in this response, in 2017, when the Democratic Unionist Party lost their majority in the Northern Ireland Assembly:

> The Assembly election presents all of us with a new opportunity to do things differently. I believe absolutely that Irish unity is the best outcome for all the people of this island. Sinn Féin will work to achieve that. But in the meantime, we need to co-operate with other progressives to create real changes in people's lives based on everyone's right to equality. This has to be our overarching strategy ahead.[54]

Chapter summary

This chapter has outlined the journey of Sinn Féin from radical political activists to mainstream politicians. A historical timeline has revealed a pattern of political development and political vacuums where new developments in Sinn Féin politics are revealed by their colonized discourses but are frequently packaged with republican core discourses and specifically warrior talk. The Good Friday Agreement (1998) had a significant impact on Sinn Féin discourses because it is raised the expectation of peace in Northern Ireland and the engagement of republicans with decommissioning.

The political journey of Sinn Féin, and specifically their engagement with constitutional politics in Northern Ireland, has brought them credibility with external observers and stakeholders. Internally, their continued use of warrior talk appears to be a signal to republicans that Sinn Féin's political strategies are not an abandonment of the core republican goal of Irish unity. In the context of a highly successful political presence in Northern Ireland, Sinn Féin's continued use of warrior talk is interesting because it draws attention to a violent past and risks drawing them into an ambiguous position on the peace process.

This purpose of this chapter was to map a timeline of Sinn Féin political development using republican discourses from the period 1969–2019. This has established the scale of their political journey prior to the Good Friday Agreement and their subsequent negotiations to secure IRA decommissioning. Over time, Sinn Féin leaders have navigated crises both internal to the republican movement and external, such as attacks from political detractors. Their colonized discourses have revealed the twists and turns of a unique political journey but the findings indicate that internal tensions between two core strands of provisional republicanism still exist. The 'means to an end' republican debate on Irish unity and a historical belief in the power of their political ideology, are not resolved. The level of opposition to Sinn Féin and their policies for Northern Ireland is small but vocal and violent.

From the analysis of Sinn Féin political development there appear to be a number of possible roles for warrior talk in their discourses. Warrior talk in Sinn Féin core discourses is not unexpected given that provisional republicans share the same history and philosophy as their radical republican opponents. Today, Sinn Féin use warrior talk at republican gatherings as an overture to settle the audience and a gesture of sacred remembrance. *The emphasis is on preserving the past.*

The warrior talk appearing in colonized Sinn Féin discourses is intriguing especially in the context of the Northern Ireland peace process. Colonized discourses have largely been adopted to influence both internal and external stakeholders to change and go forward. *The emphasis is building the future.*

In the next chapter, Sinn Féin's journey from their role in the provisional movement in Northern Ireland to political champions for peace and outreach to unionists will be explored using their emergent peace, transitional and transformational discourses. The following question will be addressed:

> How did Sinn Féin become political champions for the Northern Ireland peace process and what was the role of warrior talk in their journey from war to peace?

Suggested reading (chapter specific)

In this chapter the political development of Sinn Féin has been outlined from 1969 to 2019. There is a vast amount of literature on this topic and this section is a series of signposts to get you started with your reading. In the previous chapter it was suggested that you reflect on your specific interest and explore further. Some of the books suggested in the previous chapter are relevant to this chapter and where appropriate specific chapters will be referenced to expand your understanding of the Sinn Féin timeline.

There have been signposts in this chapter to the peace process, decommissioning, radical republicanism and republican unity. The suggested reading for these topics can be found in Chapters Five and Six. Chapter Five will explore Sinn Féin's role in the Northern Ireland peace process and their peace discourses. Chapter Six will explore the changing relationship between Sinn Féin and their republican opponents, and the role of their transitional discourses.

The New Politics of Sinn Féin (2007).[55] This book provides a clear analysis of the ideological origins of New Sinn Féin and the scale of departure from their republican roots. The author regards the Good Friday Agreement as a historic compromise that has damaged the unity of republicanism and created major contradictions for the provisionals.

New Sinn Féin: Irish Republicanism in the Twenty-First Century (2005).[56] The author points out that Sinn Féin's political development has eroded the radical qualities that shaped their early political journey. In her view, Sinn Féin's warrior talk could be seen as either outmoded rhetoric or a skilful use of language to signal their ideological lineage. In 2005 the writer concluded that warrior talk was a disadvantage and constraint to the political development of Sinn Féin because it implies a relationship with violence.

Unfinished Business: The Politics of 'Dissident' Irish Republicanism (2019).[57] This book contains some useful material on the Good Friday Agreement, decommissioning and policing; the author's views are drawn from significant research with *dissident republicans*. This will help you to gain a different and current perspective of provisional republicanism.

Good Friday: The Death of Republicanism (2008).[58] The author presents a republican view on a number of key themes, including the Good Friday Agreement, IRA decommissioning and policing in Northern Ireland. He concludes that the provisionals have not just switched tactics, they have abandoned Irish republicanism.

The Long War: The IRA and Sinn Féin (1995)[59] provides more detail on *People's Assemblies* as an alternative power structure for republicans in the 1970s and an account of how they jettisoned traditional republican thinking much earlier than some writers believed.

The Road to God Knows Where: Understanding Irish Republicanism (2005).[60] The author points out that Sinn Féin rarely conduct their internal changes in public and views contradictions in their discourse as indicators of the plurality of republican views. He concludes that the republican goal of a united Ireland has not been abandoned by any republican grouping, including Sinn Féin.

It is worth checking *From Armed Struggle to Political Struggle* (2015).[61] The author introduces a parallel journey approach to understanding Sinn Féin's political development. An inner journey communicates ideals; coupled with the certainty of armed struggle, it reassures other republicans. The outer journey is externally focused and reliant on engagement with other stakeholders and therefore the language is characterized by uncertainty and ambiguity.

Northern Ireland: Conflict and Change (2002). Chapter Five gives an excellent summary of the difference between nationalist and republican political views which will help the reader to understand the complexity of republican talks with John Hume and the SDLP.

Spoiling for Peace? The Threat of Dissident Republicans to Peace in Northern Ireland (2019).[62]

This book explores the contrast between republican purists and pragmatists, and the impact on the political development of Sinn Féin. The author conclude that there is largely academic consensus that Sinn Féin has changed its external identity from an IRA political wing to a mainstream political party. The book has a cautionary note and advises against polarizing the republican movement.

Practical study task: How to recognize core and colonized discourses

Choose three samples of discourse from this chapter. You could choose core or colonized discourses from different time periods or focus on a specific theme that you are interested in. The discourse model from Chapter Two will be needed to complete this exercise.

As you read, make some notes using the following prompt questions:

- *What are the similarities and differences between the three samples of discourse?*

- *What was the specific political context in which the discourses were created and applied?*
- *What do you notice about Sinn Féin politics and their use of language to influence different stakeholders? What surprises you about the language?*
- *How are the roots of Irish republicanism presented in Sinn Féin discourses after the Good Friday Agreement? Consider both core and colonized discourses.*
- *What have you learned about Sinn Féin's political development after the hunger strikes in 1981?*
- *How has provisional Sinn Féin changed republicanism in Northern Ireland?*
- *What are the key differences between provisional Sinn Féin and other republican groups?*

Now choose literature sources from the suggested reading section and read the material in a focused way to expand the ideas that you have already generated from your samples of discourse. Use the following prompt questions to analysis your responses above:

- *What is your understanding of the political development of Sinn Féin?*
- *What are the implications of their current political agenda for the republican movement?*
- *What have you learned about the political role of warrior talk?*

You now have a conceptual framework to help you start an essay, assignment or develop the rationale for further research.

Notes

1. Adams, G. Elected representatives conference, Monaghan, 26 October 2002.
2. O'Brien, B. (1995). *The Long War: The IRA and Sinn Féin*, Dublin: O'Brien Press, p. 351. Radical republican groups continue to use the Green Book (1977) to argue that the Provisional IRA gave up their role as inheritors of the Dáil, when they reneged on the principle of abstention and acknowledged the British state. The Green Book was a five-part strategy for guerrilla warfare and a manual used for training IRA volunteers. A more detailed explanation is in the glossary section at the front of the book.

3. *Ard Fheis Report* (1987). Dublin and Belfast: Sinn Féin, p. 2.
4. The ceremony was organized by the British Legion in honour of the war dead. The IRA is said to have claimed that the location of the explosion was a mistake as the actual target was a marching soldier: in fact the primary impact was on civilians, with eleven people killed and sixty three injured.
5. In 1993 the British and Irish Governments declared a Joint Declaration for Peace (the Downing Street Declaration) with an agenda for the removal of conflict from Northern Ireland. The Hume-Adams (SDLP and Sinn Féin) talks produced proposals on the principles of national self-determination.
6. *An Phoblacht*, 1972, p. 1. A delegation of IRA met the Northern Ireland Secretary for talks and proposed an end to violence in return for a British withdrawal.
7. The term 'power to the people' reflects the influence that Cicero's ideas had on Irish republicanism. Early thinking on the notion of a democracy is outlined in Chapter Three.
8. *An Phoblacht*, 29 October 1972, p. 8.
9. Tommy Gorman, Irish republican. Interview with the author, 12 September 2001.
10. Mallie, E., and McKittrick, D. (1997). *The Fight for Peace: The Inside Story of the Irish Peace Process*, London: Heineman, p. 135.
11. Adams, G. (1977). *An Phoblacht*, 2 October 1977 (writing as the 'Vindicator').
12. Adams, G. (1976). *The Long War*, Dublin and Belfast: Adams and Sinn Féin, p. 3.
13. Gerry Adams wrote under the name 'Brownie' in the 1970s.
14. Adams, G. (1976). *Republican News*, 1 May 1976, p. 4.
15. Adams, G. (1975). *Republican News*, 18 October 1976, p. 6. He was writing as 'Brownie' at the time.
16. *An Phoblacht*, published by Sinn Féin, was first printed in 1970 as a weekly newspaper and published in Dublin. It merged with Sinn Féin's Northern Ireland paper, *Republican News*, in 1979 and thereafter carried both names.
17. Adams, G. (1997). *Before the Dawn*, London: Mandarin, p. 263.
18. *An Phoblacht*, 10 October 1981, p. 13.
19. *Ard Fheis Report* (1984), p. 8.
20. The bomb at Enniskillen in 1987 created a critical disturbance in republican discourse. The political and military republican strategies were historically positioned as one ideology. Sinn Féin started to distance the party from violence and develop a more inclusive approach to their political strategies.
21. Adams, G., *An Phoblacht*, 28 January 1987, p. 4.
22. Ard Fheis report, 28 January 1989, p. 4.
23. Adams, G. (1989). 84th Ard Fheis, 28 January 1989. The statement was made in a period of time when Sinn Féin were having discussions with external stakeholders and starting to formulate a peace strategy. These forms of discourse were aimed at republicans.
24. 82nd Ard Fheis, 1986, p. 9.

The political journey of Sinn Féin　　　　　　　　　　　　　　　　　　　　　　99

25. A few examples include the fall of the Berlin Wall (1989) which ended the division of West and East Germany; the Oslo Accords (1993) that resulted in a peace treaty between Israelis and Palestinians; in South Africa, the regime of Apartheid ended.
26. New Labour discourse is a good example of transformational discourse. Tony Blair, a new British Prime Minister in 1997, brought a pragmatic attitude to socialist politics. Some of his transformational discourses can be seen in Sinn Féin speeches. See more detail in Chapter Seven.
27. 84th Ard Fheis report, 1989, p. 12.
28. Sinn Féin organizer Danny Morrison made a statement at the 1981 Ard Fheis which encouraged republicans to consider an '*Armalite and Ballot box*' approach to constitutional politics.
29. *For Real Change: Building a New Ireland*, Sinn Féin manifesto, 1998, p. 1.
30. *Irish News*, 4 May 1998.
31. Adams, G. Elected Representatives conference, 26 October 2002. In his speech, he admits '*this is not a perfect process. By its nature it has involved compromise.*'
32. Adams, G. *Republican News*, Belfast, 22 October 2001.
33. Declan Kearney, main address at Joe McGirl's commemorative weekend, reported in *RM Distribution*, 2 September 2002. Joe McGirl was a provisional republican.
34. McGuinness, M. (2001). Ard Fheis, reported in *Republican News*, 2 October 2001.
35. Sinn Féin manifesto (2002), Dublin and Belfast: Sinn Féin.
36. McGuinness, M. (2001). Ard Fheis, reported in *Republican News*, 2 October 2001.
37. Tonge, J. (2002). *Northern Ireland: Conflict and Change*, Harlow: Pearson Education.
38. Alex Maskey, Sinn Féin spokesman for policing issues, 31 May 2007.
39. To republicans, the Royal Ulster Constabulary was seen as the armed wing of unionists. A reorganization of policing was recommended by the Patten report (1999); it recommended a quota system to recruit more Catholic police in Northern Ireland.
40. Adams, G. (2002). Ard Fheis address, reported in *Republican News*, Dublin, 13 April 2002.
41. McIntyre, A. (2008). *Good Friday: The Death of Irish Republicanism*, New York: Ausubo.
42. Chapter Three has a brief explanation of the emergence of Republican Sinn Féin in response to changes to the republican principle of abstention.
43. Ruarirí Ó Brádaigh, leader of Republican Sinn Féin, reported in the Irish *News*, 16 May 1998.
44. Robert McCartney was a Belfast Catholic and supporter of Sinn Féin. He died of stab wounds and the Provisional IRA was blamed.
45. Adams, G. (2005). Ard Fheis reported in *Irish Republican News*, 5 March 2005.
46. Adams, G. (2012). Easter speech, County Cork, reported in *Irish Republican News*, 13 April 2012.
47. Adams, G. (2009). Ard Fheis, reported in Irish *Republican News*, 21 February 2009.

48. Adams, G. (2015). Ard Fheis speech, reported in *Irish Republican News*, 7 March 2015.
49. McGuinness, M. (2008). *An Phoblacht*, 6 March 2008.
50. Adams, G. (2012). Easter speech, reported in *Irish Republican News*, 13 April 2012.
51. Adams, G. (2017). Ard Fheis speech, reported in Irish *Republican News*, 14 April 2017.
52. Adams, G. (2012). Easter speech, reported in *Irish Republican News*.
53. *Ibid*.
54. McGuinness, M. 2017 speech reported in the *Irish Republican News*, 10 March 2017. This was a watershed election result for republicans which challenged the notion of a perpetual unionist majority in the North.
55. Bean, K. (2008). *The New Politics of Sinn Féin*, Liverpool: Liverpool University Press.
56. Maillot, A. (2005). *New Sinn Féin: Irish Republicanism in the Twenty-First Century*, Abingdon, Oxford: Routledge.
57. McGlinchey, M. (2019). *Unfinished Business: The Politics of Irish Republicanism*, Manchester: Manchester University Press. See Chapter Four (Good Friday Agreement), Chapter Three (decommissioning) and Chapter Six (policing).
58. McIntyre, A. (2008). *Good Friday: The Death of Irish Republicanism*, New York: Ausubo.
59. O'Brien, B. (1995). *The Long War: The IRA and Sinn Féin*, Dublin: O'Brien Press.
60. Smyth, J. (2005). 'The Road to God Knows Where: Understanding Irish Republicanism', *Capital and Class*, pp. 135–158.
61. Spencer, G. (2015). *From Armed Struggle to Political Struggle: Republican Tradition and Transformation in Northern Ireland*, London: Bloomsbury.
62. Whiting, S. A. (2015). *Spoiling the Peace: The Threat of Dissident Republicans to the peace in Northern Ireland*, Manchester: Manchester University Press.

Chapter 5

'War is a waste if we don't win the peace.'[1]

Introduction

> We want to be reconciled with you. We are concerned that you appreciate our commitment to reconciliation is on the basis of respect for your beliefs, your tradition and your hopes for the future.[2]

This extract is a good example of Sinn Féin peace discourse; it illustrates a significant shift to a more inclusive form of politics, and specifically addresses unionists. The use of the word *'we'* is highly symbolic because it represents a major change in republican ideology and implies a readiness to compromise with historic republican enemies. After a long history of war with the British state and a recent history engaged in local sectarian violence, republican peace discourses were a powerful contrast to their traditional warrior talk. The Good Friday Agreement (1998) brought challenges to the historic republican position on physical force because the agreement set out expectations that all parties would decommission their weapons and this included all armed groups irrespective of political affiliation.[3]

In the previous chapter, a chronological timeline of Sinn Féin colonized discourses was introduced to illustrate how Sinn Féin managed ideological challenges internally and sustained the political support of their grassroots. The term 'colonized' discourse was introduced in Chapter Two to illustrate the scale of adaptions made to the core discourses of Irish republicanism. The emergence of Sinn Féin peace discourses represented a significant shift from traditional republican forms of communication. Peace discourses appeared to have more of a therapeutic role that encouraged a republican separation from the past and a sense of redemption that is associated with an act of forgiveness. Sinn Féin peace discourses were a model of how to influence a wider range of external stakeholders and at the same time aim to retain an essential continuity with Irish republicanism. This was achieved through the invocation of warrior talk.

The purpose of warrior talk within peace discourses is intriguing, especially in the years when Sinn Féin were working hard to manage internal opposition to the decommissioning of the IRA. Today, Sinn Féin has a complex repertoire of core and colonized discourses which they adapt, create and renew in response to different stakeholders and emergent political conditions. The purpose of warrior talk, in the context of a peace, is likely to be a form of symbolic allegiance to Irish republicanism but the question is whether this is genuine or no more than a gesture.

For some republicans the peace process was deemed a *pacification process*,[4] more concerned with unionists forcing the issue of decommissioning weapons than dealing with the root causes of the conflict in Northern Ireland. Meanwhile, Sinn Féin's political rhetoric positioned its leaders as champions of social, economic and political reform in Northern Ireland. The development of their peace discourses signalled their transformation into peace builders and international experts in conflict resolution. However, the continued presence of the British state in Northern Ireland and the arguably illegal partition of Ireland meant that core republican goals had not been met. In the wake of the Good Friday Agreement, if republicans were going to authenticate their role as peacemakers then the IRA would have to abandon their armed struggle.

However, the Good Friday Agreement and decommissioning helped to position republicans as serious politicians and skilful negotiators.[5] Sinn Féin used the moral high ground of the Good Friday Agreement to press for the agreed reforms and also progress their ambitions for conflict resolution between the nationalist and unionist communities of Northern Ireland. The colonization of peace discourses from international conflicts became a recurring feature of Sinn Féin speeches and a language of reconciliation adapted for both internal and external audiences. Speeches to republicans, particularly at special occasions and annual gatherings, frequently presented peace as an alternative route to Irish unity.

In reality, the peace process drew provisional republicans further into their socialist mission in Northern Ireland and further away from the traditional agenda of ending partition. Transitional discourses enabled Sinn Féin to prepare the ground for new political strategies by presenting change as a dynamic process en route to Irish unity. Peace discourses became a trap because, by claiming the moral high ground of peace, anything short of a complete and lasting end to violence could be seen as failure. Radical republicans saw this danger and realized that compromise had brought the risk that the British government's continued presence in Northern Ireland might turn into a permanent destination rather than a staging post along the way. To radical republicans, transitional and peace discourses represented a weak substitute for the clear ideology which Irish republicanism already had. At the time of writing republican critics of the Good Friday Agreement point to the continued presence of the British state in Northern Ireland and mourn the manner in which provisional republicans have abandoned their republican heritage:

> Stormont remains a 'fundamentally undemocratic' assembly kept under the strict control of British imperialism, designed to give British rule in Ireland a democratic angle.[6]

The press statement that this extract comes from was made after republicans claimed a historic victory at the polls in Northern Ireland in 2017,[7] and it clearly indicates the political opposition of Republican Sinn Féin to the constitutional intentions of Sinn Féin. However, the divergence between provisional and radical republicanism cannot be understood fully as a simple binary: a more nuanced analysis is required to understand their differing political positions. There are a diversity of republican views on the Good Friday Agreement and decommissioning across both groupings, and commentators should be wary of the temptation to mark groups as peace makers and warriors, as heroes and villains or mainstream and dissident. These terms are divisive, reinforce stereotyping and constrain a deeper understanding of the politics of peace building and conflict resolution.

The focus of this book is on the role of warrior talk in the context of ending conflict and building a sustainable peace. Previous chapters have explored the history of Irish republicanism and the political legacy, which helped to shape events in Northern Ireland in the 1970s. The political development of the provisional movement has also been examined to demonstrate how Sinn Féin orchestrated major ideological changes in Irish republicanism and drew republicans into a peace process. The early discourses of Irish republicanism were radical, militant and with a rationale that was based on armed operations. Warrior talk emerged from this heritage so it unsurprising that war-like language remains in republican discourses. On their journey from political activists to constitutional politicians and later guardians of peace, Sinn Féin's public statements have retained their warrior talk. Today, Sinn Féin warrior talk appears at republican rituals and when the leadership face political challenge and feel the need to demonstrate their allegiance to the republican movement.

Chapter purpose

This chapter maps the emergence of Sinn Féin peace discourses between 1969 and 1998 and compares the findings with the development of their peace discourses from 1998 to 2019. The comparison between the two time periods punctuated by the Good Friday Agreement (1998) reveals a rapid development of colonized forms of Sinn Féin peace discourses, firstly to influence republicans to accept the Good Friday Agreement and later to promote the acceptance of IRA decommissioning. In both time periods Sinn Féin produced colonized discourses in response to a rapidly changing political environment and also to capitalize on their emerging political credibility as participants in a successful peace process. During the peace process, the relationship between Sinn Féin, IRA and the wider republican movement has remained under scrutiny and the potential for dangerous republican splits has remained high. In this context, the role of warrior talk co-existing with peace and transitional discourses presents an interesting puzzle for this chapter.

New republican groups were formed as a result of splits from the provisional movement in 1997, 2006, 2012 and 2016,[8] and their activities, have created dilemmas for Sinn Féin both in their external public relations and for the internal unity of the republican movement. An extract from a press interview, given in 1999, sums up the dilemma:

> There are lots of wobbles and there will continue to be wobbles in republican activism. That is the nature of the process. But I think it is time for republicans to hold their nerve.[9]

In this chapter, Provisional Sinn Féin will continue to be termed 'Sinn Féin'; 'IRA' refers to the Provisional Irish Republican Army as distinct from radical republican groups. The Good Friday Agreement and IRA decommissioning will be used as a political context for a study of Sinn Féin peace discourses. The treatment of these key events will be in outline only with a more detailed account presented in the next chapter and supported by a more in-depth examination of Sinn Féin transitional discourses.

Chapter structure

Sinn Féin peace discourses (1969–1998)

> *Sinn Féin ardently wants peace (1970s)*
> *Our search for peace (1980s)*
> *Our contribution to peace (1990s)*

Sinn Féin peace discourses (1999–2009)

> *The war is over*
> *Republican decommissioning*
> *Peace is under siege*

Sinn Féin peace discourses (2009–2019)

> *Building a nation*
> *International friends*
> *Journey rather than destination*

Chapter summary
Suggested reading (chapter specific)
Practical study task: 'Maskey lays a Somme wreath'

Sinn Féin peace discourses (1969–1998)

1970s: 'Sinn Féin ardently wants peace … based on justice'[10]

During the 1970s the public face of provisional republicans in Northern Ireland was usually embodied in the IRA, with Sinn Féin largely marginalized as the political wing. There is some evidence of Sinn Féin peace discourses and they were grounded in the core republican values of justice, freedom and democracy. Peace discourses presented a political argument for building peace and focused on an unjust system of government which marginalized Catholics:

> Peace can only be restored on the basis of civil and religious liberty.[11]

The statement above implies that structural changes and republican values were key to peace in Northern Ireland and that peace was a moral imperative for those who held power. From a republican perspective, peace was possible if the British were willing to negotiate and address the societal inequality in Northern Ireland. The message from republicans was clear. The route of peace in Northern Ireland was the establishment of a just society and the cessation of British violence:

> You stand indicted before the world for the wrongs you have done to Ireland. You send your troops to keep whatever you call the peace. You forget that peace must be based on justice; it cannot be founded in British bayonets.[12]

In the 1970s, during his time in prison, Gerry Adams wrote about the republican view of peace in Northern Ireland and communicated that the rationale for peace came from ordinary Irish people. He emphasized that republican conditions for peace were the creation of a just society in Northern Ireland:

> Republican violence has continued, and any call for peace, regardless of the sincerity of those involved which singles out republican violence and which ignores the nature of the society in which we live, is doomed to failure.[13]

In his essay *The Long War*,[14] Gerry Adams observed that Irish republicans do not view their strategies as fragmented into political work and military violence. He attempted to explain the nature of violence in Ireland and appeared to communicate a genuine desire for peace within ordinary Irish people. In his view the system of partition was not built for peace and he pointed out that sectarian violence in Northern Ireland had existed since partition. During the 1970s the reunification of Ireland remained a political aspiration for republicans but their warrior talk dominated communications and the embryonic Sinn Féin peace discourses remained largely hidden.

The following two extracts bring an interesting insight into the internal dynamics of the provisional movement facing Sinn Féin:

> Never to treat with the enemy, never to surrender to his mercy but to fight to the finish.[15]

> Sinn Féin should come under the Army Organisation at all levels. Sinn Féin should be radicalized under Army direction and agitate about social and economic issues.[16]

These extracts illustrate the militaristic nature of the provisional movement in the 1970s, and more importantly they tell us about the context in which Sinn Féin was operating at the time: the notion of shared responsibility for ending a conflict did not emerge in republican discourses until 1990s. In Northern Ireland, peace campaigns against terrorist violence were regarded with internal scepticism marking a republican fear of losing what was believed to be an honourable struggle.[17]

1980s: 'Our search for peace has to rise above the consequences of imperialist rule.'[18]

There is evidence of a critical shift in republican peace discourses in the 1980s. Sinn Féin moved republicans closer to inclusive politics and this is reflected in a more pragmatic approach to dealing with the British government. Sinn Féin grafted the language of peace onto traditional principles to persuade republicans that a change of strategy, away from armed struggle, was needed. Peace, rather than war, was positioned as route to societal change in Northern Ireland and, in time, Irish unity. This discourse shift was subtle but important because it signalled that Sinn Féin was planning a way to exit the *Long War*.

Sinn Fein's approach to peace required a more inclusive republican approach to dealing with other political parties engaged in conflict in Northern Ireland. This stance required new discourses that were fundamentally different from the physical force tradition of coercing the enemy to a negotiating table. During the 1980s Sinn Féin started to engage in productive relationships between republicans and other communities in Northern Ireland, including unionists. At the republican Ard Fheis in November 1984 Gerry Adams specifically spoke about the importance of working with others in a new Irish state:

> We assert that the loyalist people must be given, in common with all citizens, firm guarantees of their religious and civil liberties.[19]

While this statement appears on a superficial level to be fully inclusive, it simultaneously illustrates that republicans believed that they would achieve a united Ireland and a united Irish society as envisaged by Wolfe Tone. The extract above is interesting because it communicated magnanimity towards loyalists (and de facto unionists) in a political context of a majority unionist government that had held power, in Northern Ireland continuously from 1921 to 1969. In the 1980s republicans continued to draw their values from Wolfe Tone and assert that Irish unity would bring social, political and economic justice to all people irrespective of religious background.[20]

During the decade starting in 1980 Sinn Féin persevered with their inclusive agenda but continued to communicate the primacy of republican philosophy through their core discourses and warrior talk. The result was a mélange of mixed messages that communicated war and peace at the same time. Terms such as 'Ideology of Liberation' appeared in speeches to reinforce the commitment of Sinn Féin to communities in Northern Ireland: this signalled an important shift of focus in their political ambitions.²¹ Republican ideology was grounded in the notion of a new Irish state with no British involvement in Irish affairs. Sinn Féin now appeared to reach out to communities in Northern Ireland with the purpose of building peace. Peace discourses in the 1980s were quite subtle in nature with a gentle nod towards inclusive politics. During this time, the IRA was still engaged in their *Long War*.

A good example of mixed messages can be found in the *Scenario for Peace* (1987), which set out a peace strategy largely on republican terms and using traditional exclusive republican language. It failed to attract the attention it needed to be taken seriously but represented an early example of Sinn Féin articulating a peace strategy. The document was full of examples of early peace discourses, but they were masked by warrior talk and a combative tone. The document was published during a period of unremitting violence in Northern Ireland and this added to an external perception that Sinn Féin activists were involved in IRA campaigns:

> Sinn Féin seeks to create conditions which will lead to a permanent cessation of hostilities, an end to our long war and the development of a peaceful, united and independent Irish society. Such objectives will only be achieved when a British government adopts a strategy for decolonisation.²²

However, *Scenario for Peace* became an important foundation for greater co-operation between republican and nationalist politicians in Northern Ireland. In the same year, Sinn Féin leaders engaged in talks with John Hume, leader of the Social Democratic Labour Party (SDLP), and started to expand their political ambitions beyond the traditional narrative of republicanism. By 1992 a second Sinn Féin strategy document, *Towards a Lasting Peace in Northern Ireland*, revealed a change in emphasis on armed struggle and immediate British withdrawal, with a shift towards a constitutional position that was more likely to appeal to SDLP and nationalist communities.²³

In addition to their contact with nationalists, Sinn Féin also reached out to Protestants and this activity was openly reported to the annual republican Ard Fheis, 31 October 1987:

> Since our last Ard Fheis, I have had a series of discussions with a number of Northern Ireland Protestants. These discussions crystallised for me the need for republicans to understand the perceptions and fears of this section of our citizens.[24]

Traditional warrior talk can also be found in this speech and this is an important sign that the Sinn Féin leadership needed to keep republicans onside in view of the news that republicans had been in dialogue with unionists. Warrior talk allowed Sinn Féin to display their loyalty to the republican cause at a critical time for republican movement: it was a year since Republican Sinn Féin had split from the provisional movement. Contact with constitutional nationalists and unionists was discreet but it provided clear evidence that Sinn Féin leaders were advancing an inclusive political strategy. The internal message to republicans continued to place the responsibility for peace with the British government. The notion of collective responsibility for conflict resolution may have been growing but the rhetoric was still war-like.

On 8 November 1987 the IRA detonated a bomb at a Remembrance parade at Enniskillen. The attack was planned against military personnel, but the outcome was eleven dead civilians, sixty-three casualties and considerable outrage locally, nationally and internationally. The contrast between an embryonic Sinn Féin peace strategy and traditional republican warrior talk was too stark to prevent the external reputational damage. During this period Sinn Féin changed their tactics slightly and started to frame their peace strategy as another *front* in the republican struggle and – as such – a transition. Peace discourses supported by transitional discourses gave Sinn Féin a route through the complex internal dynamics of the provisional movement, at a time, when the possibility of a pan-national peace initiative was becoming feasible.

1990s: 'Our contribution to the peace process.'[25]

The language of inclusion, observed in Sinn Féin peace discourses of the 1980s, developed at a pace in the 1990s. This author's research findings indicate that Sinn Féin's colonization of peace discourses was becoming more explicit and practical – and they had global aspirations. Sinn Féin peace discourses grew in sophistication and representatives of the party actively engaged in talks with nationalists to secure a wider base of political support. The tone of Sinn Féin peace discourses towards unionists was also changing and this can be seen in the contrast between the next two extracts, from 1991 and 1997 respectively:

> The search for such agreement must, of course, involve northern Protestants and every effort must be made to get their agreement and involvement in the constitutional, financial and political arrangements needed to replace partition.[26]

> We recognise the fears of the unionist section of our people. We want peace with you. We want to share the island of Ireland with you on a democratic and equal basis. We want to see a pluralist Ireland that recognizes and celebrates the diversity of all the people of the island. We take no comfort from the fact that you live in fear about the future.[27]

The use of the word '*we*' in the second extract was highly symbolic and indicates the scale of change within Sinn Féin peace discourses. A new term 'Language of Invitation' emerged and reflected another shift in Sinn Féin's approach to republican ideology. Sinn Féin councillor Tom Hartley became a strong advocate for reconciliation:

> Republicans want no more suffering, no more victims. That is why we are irrevocably committed to the success of the peace process.[28]

Concepts drawn from the arena of conflict resolution appeared in Sinn Féin peace discourses. Conflict resolution theory brought a rational explanation, in contrast to the emotive language of republican struggle, why peace in Northern Ireland was both a mutual benefit and shared responsibility. The language of conflict resolution allowed republicans to combine their vision of radical societal change with the process of inclusive negotiations:

> It is clear that peace is not simply the absence of conflict. Rather, it is the existence of conditions in which the causes of the conflict have been eradicated.[29]

This statement was colonized from the work of Johan Galtung, a leading figure in conflict resolution and peace building.[30] Sinn Féin now had a legitimate platform to promote the notion of shared responsibility for peace building and this included the British and Irish governments.[31] Sinn Fein's colonization of conflict resolution discourses provided republicans with a powerful moral high ground but it also represented an important shift in their relationship with the British government. A shared responsibility for conflict resolution implied equity between all parties to the conflict. The traditional republican narrative of victim (republicans) and persecutor (British government), so frequently expressed by warrior talk seems incongruous alongside the Sinn Féin peace discourses in the 1990s.

There was colonization of terms such as 'forgiveness' and 'reconciliation' from the African National Congress (ANC) movement in South Africa. After thirty years of a guerrilla war, the ending of apartheid and the release of Nelson Mandela was an inspiration to Irish republicans. Sinn Féin discourses were clearly influenced by the work of the Truth and Reconciliation Commission established in South Africa in the 1990s.[32] Throughout that decade republican links with other international conflicts provided Sinn Féin with a variety of discourses to strengthen their political credibility both inside and outside Northern Ireland:

> The international experience of conflict resolution teaches us the way forward is through equality of treatment and inclusive negotiations without preconditions. The British government and the leaders of unionism know this also.[33]

By 1997, the political astuteness of Sinn Féin combined with their peace and transitional discourses paid dividends when they won 16.95 per cent of the vote in local elections in Northern Ireland. Their immediate response to the election result signalled a fundamental change in the republican relationship with physical force as a political tool. This statement, made in 1995, was directed at all stakeholders engaged in violence in Northern Ireland:

> Sinn Féin is totally committed to bringing about a complete and permanent removal of guns from Irish politics.[34]

Through their peace discourses Sinn Féin exploited the political gains of engagement with Northern nationalists and optimized international interest in resolving the conflict. The power of a republican-nationalist axis forced both Irish and British governments to take responsibility for resolving the conflict in Northern Ireland. The outcome was the Downing Street Declaration (1993) when the British government recognized the right of Northern Irish people to self-determination and the Irish government conceded their claims to jurisdiction in the North.

This document presented an internal dilemma for the Sinn Féin leadership because it made no reference to Irish unity.[35] In the months following the Downing Street Declaration, republicans were repeatedly pressed for an IRA surrender of weapons prior to peace talks. The complexity for Sinn Féin and their position within provisional republicanism was becoming highly complex and potentially dangerous. Despite the public trail of antagonistic communications between republicans and the British government, it is notable that behind the scenes the situation was very different.

An established backchannel between republicans and the British intelligence was busy working on a plan to end the political stalemate and push on with the peace process.[36] Below are two extracts from discreet exchanges between the leadership of the provisional movement and British government in 1993. The first is dated 22 February 1993, just days before IRA operations were staged in Warrington.[37] The second is a message from the British government, 17 July 1993, which is a response to a republican message of 10 May 1993:

> The conflict is over but we need your advice on how to bring it to a close. We wish to have an unannounced ceasefire in order to hold dialogue leading to peace. We cannot announce such a move as it will lead to confusion for the volunteers because the press will interpret is as surrender.
>
> There is one very important point, which needs to be answered to remove possible misunderstandings. Recent pronouncement, including the Bodenstown speech, seem to imply that unless your analysis of the way forward is accepted in a set time, the halt in violence will only be temporary. This is not acceptable. The reasons for not talking about a permanent cessation are understood, but the peace process cannot be conditional on the acceptance of any particular or single analysis.[38]

1994 proved to be a turning point in Northern Ireland. On 6 April 1994, the IRA announced a three-day temporary cessation of hostilities. Five months later, on 31 August, the IRA called a temporary cessation to all IRA military operations. The Combined Loyalist Military Command called their ceasefire on 13 October 1993.[39] Despite the ceasefires from republican and loyalist paramilitary organizations, the political complexity of managing internal and external expectations remained a challenge for Sinn Féin throughout the 1990s. The following extract is an interesting section from the Presidential Address (1994) which demonstrates how the leadership used their core and colonized discourses to encourage republicans to participate in the peace process in Northern Ireland:

> British imperialism created the problem in the first place and has maintained it ever since. If we are being told that Britain no longer has any selfish interests in Ireland and that the only problem today is the legacy of the past – the divisions among the people of Ireland – then it is obvious that this division can only be healed by agreement which earns the allegiance of all traditions, to quote again from my joint statements with John Hume.[40]

By 1995 Senator George Mitchell, in his role as the US Special Envoy to Northern Ireland, had become involved in cross party talks in Northern Ireland. He established the Mitchell Principles, which were six ground rules for all parties entering political negotiations.[41] The Mitchell Talks formed a precursor to the Good Friday Agreement (1998); they were supported by key players such Bill Clinton (US President), Tony Blair (British Prime Minister) and Bertie Ahern (Irish Taoiseach). This high level of support and some well-crafted political rhetoric brought a new dynamic to the peace process to Northern Ireland.[42]

Sinn Féin consistently argued that republicans supported the Mitchell Principles but a decision on decommissioning was entirely a matter for the IRA. This reasoning might appear disingenuous and, at the time, it cost the Sinn Féin leadership some hard-earned political credibility. This extract, from a speech given by Martin McGuinness to republicans in 1997, gives an insight into the external and internal pressures on both him and Gerry Adams:

> Some of the media and political leaders have launched a specific attack on the integrity of Sinn Féin, and particularly of this leadership. Seeking to marginalize and demonise us again. While they were busy using the same rhetoric as the late 1980s, Sinn Féin was taking risks for peace and laying the foundations for the peace process. When the IRA cessation collapsed, we did all in our power to rebuild the peace process. This Sinn Féin leadership is not giving up on our peace strategy.[43]

Decommissioning was a precondition for all parties joining the Mitchell Talks. Republicans wanted to address decommissioning as part of the peace talks to ensure all parties were under scrutiny, but it was clear that unionists were pressing for the IRA to comply first. The challenge for Sinn Féin leaders was how to comply with the Mitchell requirements and have a voice at the peace talks while, at the same time, to broker a historic shift with the IRA and keep the republican movement united. This political complexity was managed through colonized discourses and an increasing emphasis on transformational change as a route to Irish unity:

> The Ireland of the twenty-first century must be different from today's Ireland. It has to be transformed so that we can live together as equals. Sinn Féin is for reconciliation. This has been a consistent part of our strategy because a process of national reconciliation, a healing process is a very necessary part of uniting the people of this island.[44]

By 1998 the Good Friday Agreement set Sinn Féin on a political journey which would be very difficult to turn back from, and for the twenty years they continued to position republicans as 'peacemakers'.[45] This was a long way from their radical and violent politics in the 1970s. Sinn Féin's continued use of warrior talk is a puzzle. New form of warrior talks emerged which presented peace as another battlefront, or as a bridgehead to a more just society. Militaristic language continued to play a part in Sinn Féin discourses, but they clearly could not disguise a major turn towards constitutional politics or a highly publicized commitment to peace. The formation of new republican groups after the Good Friday Agreement was a clear indicator that the republican movement was not in full support of the terms of the agreement.

Sinn Féin peace discourses (1999–2009)

The war is over

The Good Friday Agreement was a document full of promises with scant detail on how the terms would be implemented practically. The political negotiations that followed were long and factious as republicans, nationalists and unionists attempted to build a consensus around how to create a new devolved Northern Ireland Assembly and establish an all-Ireland bodies. Decommissioning of paramilitary weapons was a big challenge and the major issue, leading to protracted negotiations. Unionists demanded that the IRA decommission first; republicans countered by pointing out that the Good Friday Agreement did not require decommissioning as a prerequisite to entering government in Northern Ireland.[46]

Republican decommissioning

In this period, Sinn Féin used their peace discourses to consolidate their role as peace makers: reference to the Good Friday Agreement was repeatedly used as the basis for republican moral high ground and as a tactic to challenge the behaviour of other stakeholders to the peace process:

> It is obvious to anyone interested in implementing the Good Friday Agreement that on policing, on demilitarisation, human rights, equality and justice, there remain significant gaps between what was agreed four years ago and what has been delivered so far.[47]

Through the numerous stops and starts of navigating the implementation of the Good Friday Agreement, Sinn Féin employed historical and justification discourses to manage republican reactions to allegations, from unionists, that the IRA could not be trusted to decommission their weapons. The response from Gerry Adams in this statement was traditional warrior talk:

> It's the same as it was in 1981, in 1968, as it was in 1916, the same as it was in any time in Irish history that people like you rose up and said we want our rights. They are trying to defeat us. The only difference is that this time they are not going to succeed.[48]

Republicans continued to argue that the issue of demilitarization was being handled in a one-sided manner, especially because the British Army and loyalist paramilitaries continued to retain their arms. Sinn Féin worked hard internally to influence the subsequent decommissioning of IRA weapons. During extensive negotiations between 2001 and 2005 Sinn Féin managed both the demands of unionists and the expectations of the IRA. This extract from an IRA statement (2002) reveals the scale of challenge that decommissioning brought for republicans:

> The IRA have decided that we will conclude the process to completely, and verifiably put all our arms beyond use and to enhance public confidence we agree to the presence of two clergymen as observers to this process. Ian Paisley demanded that our contribution be photographed and reduced to an act of humiliation. This was never possible.[49]

The pressing issue for provisional republicanism was now the question of how to persuade other republicans that the route to Irish unity, though it might take longer while Northern Ireland adjusted to the power-sharing terms of the Good Friday Agreement, was still in sight. Sinn Féin was focused on creating the conditions in Northern Ireland to sustain a just peace: reformed structures and systems were only one aspect of their agenda. The process of reconciliation and forgiveness across communities was seen as an important priority before further moves could be made towards the final republican goal of a united Ireland.

Peace is under siege

In 2005 the political gains from decommissioning were impacted a raid by the IRA on a branch of the Northern Rock Bank and the murder of a republican, Robert McCartney. There was short-term damage to Sinn Féin's political aspirations in Northern Ireland but, more importantly, there were longer-term implications for their credibility as peacemakers. Sinn Féin peace discourses appeared to place the blame for violence on others and language appeared to condemn other republicans, such as *peace is under siege* and *peace wreckers*.

The bank raid and the murder brought media attention back to the relationship between Sinn Féin leadership and the IRA and raised questions about why a military arm of republicanism was still active in a peace process. It was easy for unionist politicians to paint republicans as enemies of the peace process and use the opportunity to lead speculation that Gerry Adams and Martin McGuinness were IRA leaders. It is very interesting to observe the republican response when it was later established that IRA members were at fault. A typical military response was communicated:

> IRA volunteers fully understand that they are bound by rules and regulations and a code of conduct. There will be no tolerance of anyone who steps outside of these rules. Anyone who brings the IRA into disrepute will be held accountable.[50]

Leaders of both Sinn Féin and the IRA had a few tricky moments as they tried to keep the republican movement united and on track for decommissioning. New language appeared from Sinn Féin to repair the reputational damage of IRA operations such as *re-building the peace process, peace building is our struggle* and *we refuse to be criminalised*.[51] A form of adapted warrior talk was used to get back in control:

> We cannot allow republicanism to be diminished in this way. To do so would be a betrayal of our struggle, of our own personal commitment, of the hunger strikers and of those brave republicans who gave their lives and liberty for a noble and worthy cause.[52]

Throughout 2005 Sinn Féin was effectively managing two peace processes at the same time. Externally, they reiterated their political commitment to the Northern Ireland peace process; internally, they worked to keep the republican movement united.

Sinn Féin peace discourses (2009–2019)

Building a nation

This was a decade of changing rhetoric for Sinn Féin with an increase in transitional and transformational discourses. Decommissioning was finally completed on 28 July 2005: this removed any external objections to republicans sharing power with unionists in the government of Northern Ireland. However, the scale of ideological change for the republican movement had the potential to leave a deep scar in Irish republicanism and initiate a very damaging split. The traditional republican principles of physical force and abstention had been abandoned and republican volunteers stood down. Sinn Féin moved towards a new discourse of nation building, which envisaged an Irish nation state and, at the same time, emphasized that republicans had work to do in rebuilding Northern Ireland. With their transitional and transformational discourses they offered a vision of peace building first, followed by nation building. The extract below (2005) is typical of Sinn Féin discourse in this decade:

> National liberation struggles can have different phases. There is a time to resist, to stand up and to confront the enemy by arms if necessary. There is a time for war. There is also a time to engage, to reach out and put the war behind us. There is time for peace. There is a time for justice. There is a time for rebuilding. This is that time. This is the era of nation builders.[53]

This extract is a fascinating example of Sinn Féin's full spectrum of discourses and a clear summary of their history and future direction of travel. Historical discourse reminded the republican audience, in 2005, of the republican goal of liberation. Justification discourse legitimized the armed struggle and the peace discourse promised justice. For radical republicans, this style of Sinn Féin political rhetoric was hollow and insensitive.

International friends

Sinn Féin continued to use their peace discourses to sustain key political relationships with international stakeholders. Republicans maintained the support of Irish America and their long-established connections with other conflicts. The language of conflict resolution, which had appeared in the 1990s, was consolidated further with colonized language from a wider range of conflicts such as South Africa, the Basque Country and the Palestine Liberation Organization (PLO). Representatives from the African National Congress, Basque separatists and the PLO frequently appeared at key republican gatherings in a show of solidarity. This extract is the opening remarks from Gerry Adams at the 2011 Ard Fheis:

> Welcome to Friends of Sinn Féin from Canada and the USA. This is an emotive time for New York and we think of our friends who died in the attacks there. I want to welcome our international guests from South Africa and from the Basque country. A special welcome to Fady Abusidualghoul, our guest representing the Palestinian people.[54]

The nature of peace discourses became more emotional and focused on the impact of conflict on human beings rather than structures and systems. Transitional discourses played an important role in promoting forgiveness and reconciliation as a process of 'letting go' of past events. The lived experience of people in other conflicts brought practical ideas for Sinn Féin to adapt into their peace discourses, with visions of a better future. The word 'nation' was used liberally during this period.

In Northern Ireland, Sinn Féin continued to develop their inclusive political strategy towards unionists and to leverage the Good Friday Agreement to challenge the British and Irish governments:

> Politics in the north had for years been a scene of failed political initiative after failed political initiative. Within seven months of Sinn Féin joining the talk's process and after decades of failure, we had the Good Friday Agreement. However, the peace process nearly collapsed on a number of occasions due to the failure of the British government, under unionist pressure, to implement key elements of the agreement.[55]

The legitimacy of the Good Friday Agreement gave the Sinn Féin leadership confidence in their political strategies and their ability to negotiate with unionists. The result was a remarkable political collaboration between Sinn Féin and the DUP in a power-sharing government in Northern Ireland. In 2007 Ian Paisley had been appointed first minister of Northern Ireland working alongside an old enemy, Martin McGuinness, as deputy first minister. As Gerry Adams pointed out that year:

> The unimaginable – some would say unbelievable – has happened. Today, Sinn Féin ministers are placing equality at the heart of decision-making in the North for the first time.[56]

Sinn Féin continued to focus on their vision of rebuilding a nation but with a clear message that the partition of Ireland would be addressed *after* a period of reconciliation in Northern Ireland. Sinn Féin's political focus was on uniting communities in Northern Ireland, and this can be observed in a subtle shift to the term 'nation', rather than 'republic'.

> Sinn Féin has always been willing to put ourselves in other people's shoes, to understand their difficulties, and where this is possible to accommodate this in the national interest.[57]

Sinn Féin politicians now took up their seats in Stormont and were part of a government that radical republicans did not accept as legal. From a radical republican perspective, the British state still had power in Northern Ireland and there was no reassurance of Irish unity despite the political rhetoric from Sinn Féin. The evidence demonstrates that their concern was valid. British direct rule had been imposed on Northern Ireland from 1972 to 1998 and then five times in the period 2000–2019.[58]

For radical republicans, the ignominy of the relationship between Sinn Féin and the British government was evident in the famous handshake between Martin Mc Guinness and Queen Elizabeth II on 27 June 2012. A gesture of peace seen by millions of people across the world was also seen as a complete contradiction and total betrayal of Irish republicanism. For some, this handshake was a symbol that Irish republicans had accepted the sovereignty of the British government in Ireland.

Journey rather than destination

Sinn Féin political strategies were heavily invested in Northern Ireland and focused on bringing peace and reconciliation to all communities. Their vision of nation building was primarily to unify a culturally diverse society in Northern Ireland as a precursor to Irish re-unification. Sinn Féin continued to promote their values on conflict resolution and now employed a collective approach to forgiveness and reconciliation:

> The process of conflict resolution is far from over. Many families – republican and unionist – are still grieving and are still seeking answers regarding the deaths of their loved ones. They deserve the truth. Sinn Féin is committed to the truth recovery process that delivers for all victims and families.[59]

In the years 2009–2019, Sinn Féin was juggling with a political agenda of greater equality in the North and a commitment to a peaceful ending of partition. The extract below is a very clear message that Irish unity was on the back burner:

> The Assembly elections present all of us with a new opportunity to do things differently. I believe Irish unity is the best outcome for all the people of this land. Sinn Féin will work to achieve this. But in the meantime, we need to operate with other progressives to create real changes in people's lives based on everyone's right to equality. This has to be our overarching strategy in the time ahead.[60]

In this period, Sinn Féin's colonized discourses grew in sophistication. Transitional and transformational discourses gave them options to present the future as either a series of planned stages or a radical change for the better. These discourses allowed Sinn Féin to keep their promise to end partition but stay flexible in the approach by which this would be achieved. It is clear that peace discourses facilitated a new legitimacy for provisional republicans as constitutional politicians and opened up a political route for them to lobby for Ireland unity.

In parallel, Sinn Féin's transitional discourses created a breathing space to move from armed to unarmed strategies and to persuade the republican movement to remain unarmed. Transformational discourses opened up possibilities for a new society, a new nation and a new republic. Since the Good Friday Agreement, Sinn Féin had created an impressive range of discourses designed to manage external stakeholders and preserve unity across the republican movement.

The problem for Sinn Féin is that radical republicans did not believe that constitutional politics and the mantra of democratic mandate was the route to Irish unity. They were suspicious of a political system that could trap republicans into a state machine that they have been trying to overthrow for over a century. For some, Sinn Féin's ritualistic use of core discourses and warrior talk at republican gatherings has become a shallow gesture:

> The major question that historians will ask is not why Republicans surrendered but why they fought a futile Long War only to be brought back to accepting what was in offer in 1974.[61]

The relationship between Sinn Féin and radical republicans is an ongoing dilemma within the republican movement and merits further study. The emergence of transitional discourses provides some clues about how Sinn Féin leaders have managed internal dissent at key moments in the Northern Ireland peace process. The next chapter will focus on the emergence of radical republican groups since the 1980s, and the philosophical position they currently take in relation to Sinn Féin politics. The forms of warrior talk from both Sinn Féin and radical republicans will be examined to gain a greater understanding of the political issues and options facing republicans in both north and south of Ireland.

Chapter summary

The findings from the 1970s indicate that Sinn Féin peace discourses emerged in the form of social republicanism and bringing peace through justice for Catholic communities in the North. The provisional movement was dominated by the IRA and the republican goal to finally remove the British state from Ireland. The historical legacy of 1916 shaped the core discourses used during this period; warrior talk was a product of a militaristic culture with heroes, courageous acts and enemies.

In the 1980s there was a clear discursive shift towards inclusive politics, which signalled a republican political position that was considerably less war-like than in the previous decade. Sinn Féin communicated the possibility of peace with unionists but it was largely on republican terms. In short, republicans would drive out the British state, unite Ireland and create a republic that would respect the rights of unionists. Sinn Féin peace discourses changed during the 1980s as they started to appreciate that inclusive politics requires compromises from all parties and that their own supporters would need to be persuaded.

By the 1990s, Sinn Féin had colonized discourses from conflict resolution theory and international experiences of peace building. Their changing relationship with constitutional nationalists, unionists and the British government culminated in their role in the Good Friday Agreement. By

1998 republicans had signed up to a peace treaty that effectively tied them into a consent principle and the decommissioning of the IRA.

In the next decade (1999–2009) Sinn Féin became more vocal about peace in Northern Ireland and consolidated their position as constitutional politicians. This change of emphasis took republicans away from their primary goal of a united Ireland. The decommissioning of the IRA proved too much and previously loyal provisionals left to set up new groups or join established ones. In this period, transitional and transformational discourses developed further and indicated the effort that Sinn Féin made to keep the republican movement united. Peace discourses were developed further and used to persuade external stakeholders of republican trustworthiness and competence to share power with unionists in a new form of government in Northern Ireland.

By 2009 Sinn Féin had strong networks with international friends and supporters, a working relationship with nationalists and a place in the government of Northern Ireland alongside unionists. They clearly felt confident enough to extend their peace discourses to include a vision of 'one nation' based on justice, democracy and freedom. This vision was presented as a peaceful journey, but the warrior talk remained in speeches to other republicans.

Republican philosophy and principles integrate both armed struggle and political tactics and legitimize both options as a route to a peaceful settlement. This partially explains why the discourses of war and peace co-exist in republican discourses. In this study of peace discourses, it is clear that Sinn Féin gradually moved from a republican view, which asserts that war should be used to force a peace treaty with the enemy, to a willingness to compromise the republican goal.

It could be argued that Sinn Féin's peace development has eroded the republican project through major compromises and attempts to gain political credibility both nationally and internationally. In the journey from war to peace, Sinn Féin have moved away from the consistency of a traditional republican code and created a complex amalgam of transitional, peace and now transformational discourses. This phenomenon brings the spotlight back to the role of republican warrior talk and the place it has in the republican political aspirations in both Northern Ireland and the Irish Republic.

Sinn Féin's rhetoric of 'peace under siege' and 'armed for peace' is an interesting use of warrior talk to reach out to those republicans frustrated with the apparent abandonment of their core ideology. The continued use of war-like language to account for a peace strategy casts a shadow on the Sinn Féin leadership because it signals internal contradictions. Back in the 1970s, Gerry Adams wrote an essay from his prison cell. It made a strong case that peace in Northern Ireland could be achieved if there was social, economic and political justice for all citizens. His message is relevant today. Despite the focus on peace, the essay was called the *Long War* and points to an important paradox within Irish republicanism. The existence of warrior talk for both provisional and radical republicans means that they cannot fully retire from the past.

In the next chapter, the following question will be addressed:

> What was the impact on the republican movement of Sinn Féin's peace strategy in Northern Ireland and how were colonized discourses used to manage republican through the ideological change that the peace process brought?

Suggested reading (chapter specific)

War and peace discourses co-exist in republican discourses for good reason. The work of a number of writers brings further insights into this phenomenon.
Political Discourse and Conflict Resolution (2011).[62] This work has a number of chapters that are pertinent to the study of Sinn Féin peace discourses:

- *Finding consensus in the Republic of Ireland* discusses the nuances of political discourses in the Irish Republic and the impact on Sinn Féin and the IRA, both during the Troubles and the later peace process: pp. 16–31
- *The SDLP, political discourse and the peace process* explains how the 1980s dialogue between Gerry Adams and John Hume resulted in bringing other stakeholders into peace talks. This work paved

the way to the Downing Street Declaration and the Good Friday Agreement: pp. 77–92
- *Debating peace and conflict in Northern Ireland.* This chapter introduces some healthy doubt that discourses are never fully coherent or consistent and brings a reality check to the notion that conflicts can be resolved: pp. 208–223

The Nervous Peace (1996).[63] Here a journalist uses a collection of articles to map republican and loyalist ceasefires, 1994–1996, and gives an insight into the complexity of ceasefire process and the stakeholders involved. This material is also good preparation for the next chapter in this book.
Making Peace (1999).[64] US Senator George Mitchell writes about on his role as lead mediator in Northern Ireland's peace process. The book brings a very different perspective to peace talks, Sinn Féin's entry and the final stages of the Good Friday Agreement. Chapter Twelve gives an insight into the gives the political complexity facing Sinn Féin as they joined the talks: pp. 107–119.
The Long War: The IRA and Sinn Féin (1999)[65] is a good account of the republican journey from war to peace in Northern Ireland and gives a practical insight into the dynamics between Sinn Féin and the IRA. There is an interesting material on the IRA Green Book on p. 401.
From Armed Struggle to Political Struggle (2015).[66] Chapter Five, on peace, gives a good explanation of the peace process from early talks between Sinn Féin and SDLP through to the Good Friday Agreement, decommissioning and republican entry into government. pp. 139–224.
New Sinn Féin: Irish Republicanism in the Twenty-First Century (2005)[67] focusses on the critical change of identity for Sinn Féin from a party of activists to champions of peace. In 2005 the author concluded that the success of Sinn Féin would be in their ability to manage internal contradictions.
Northern Ireland: The Reluctant Peace (2013).[68] For a more detailed explanation of the post Good Friday Agreement years, read Chapter Seven 'The Incomplete Agreement', pp. 189–224, and Chapter Eight 'Delivery, Delivery, Delivery', pp. 225–254.
John Hume: Man of Peace (1995).[69] This book is worth a read to learn more about John Hume, leader of the SDLP and the man who contributed to

the peace process through his dialogue with Sinn Féin. The book gives an interesting account of the Hume-Adams talks and reveals the concerns that John Hume had about republican politics and a form of Irishness that excluded Protestants.

The Fight for Peace (1997) an important book charting the emergence of the peace process, in the early 1990s, through the Anglo-Irish Agreement, Downing Street Declaration and the IRA ceasefire (1994).[70] *Endgame in Northern Ireland* (2001) rounds off the narrative about the peace process.[71]

Practical study task: 'Maskey lays Somme wreath'[72]

Below is an extract from the republican newspaper *An Phoblacht*, dated 2002 and written by Fern Lane.
To complete the exercise, please follow the guidelines set out below:

- Review your notes from Chapters Three, Four and Five and summarize what you learned about reading political discourses
- Read this chapter on peace discourses and identify themes that help you to interpret the article on Alex Maskey below
- Check the suggested reading and literature sources for ideas on the implication of Alex Maskey laying a wreath at a British Legion remembrance event
- Now conduct a discourse analysis of the extract and make some conclusions about the deeper meaning of this behaviour from a senior republican

Extract from an Phoblacht 4 July 2002

> As symbolic acts go, this one could hardly have been any more, well, monumental.
>
> In laying a wreath to the dead of the Somme on Monday morning, Mayor Alex Maskey made a powerful case for Irish republicanism in its best and purest form, the form that seeks to disregard religion and ultimately, past antipathies, in the name of unity.

It is also a remarkable and graceful, individual act of reconciliation by a man who the British Army tried very hard to kill for twenty years or more. Mayor Mackey's act was important in a number of ways. Firstly, on behalf of republicanism, he acknowledged the scale of loss and grief experienced by the Protestant community at the Somme. Secondly, he took a vital first step in the process to enable the nationalist and republican communities in the Six Counties, and on the island of Ireland to acknowledge those members of their own families who, for very different reasons, fought and died on the British side.

He said, 'My objective is to seek to identify common ground for all of us in this generation.'

Mayor Maskey also said de-politicization of commemoration is key in establishing a form of ceremony that does not alienate almost the entire population and allows nationalist Ireland to recognize the sacrifices of previous generations whilst firmly rejecting the overarching political architecture which impelled them into such a sacrifice.

Notes

1. Adams, G. (2005). Ard Fheis speech, reported in *Irish Republican News*, 5 March 2005. Statements such as *'War is a waste'* and *'The peace process is our struggle'* communicated a republican commitment to peace but the language remained distinctly military.
2. *Ard Fheis Report* (1996). Dublin and Belfast: Sinn Féin, p. 11.
3. The Mitchell requirements for entering peace talks required a ceasefire, which the IRA complied with in 1997. Republicans have since pointed out that the rules were applied inconsistently.
4. Tommy Gorman, republican, interview with author, 12 September 2001.
5. Powell, J. (2014). *Talking to Terrorists: How to End Armed Conflicts*, London: Random House. Chapter Nine gives an insightful account of negotiating with the Sinn Féin team from a facilitator's perspective.
6. Republican Sinn Féin's press statement after the 2017 election, 9 March 2017, when unionists lost their overall control of Stormont for the first time since its creation.
7. Unionists lost their majority in government for the first time since 1921.
8. A few examples include Republican Sinn Féin, 32 County Sovereignty Movement and Real IRA, all 1997; éirígí, 2006; Saoradh, New IRA, 2016. More detail will be explored in the next chapter.
9. Adams, G. *Irish Republican News*, 8 July 1999, <http://irlnet.com>, accessed July 2000.

10. Adams, G. (1976). *The Long War*, Dublin and Belfast: Sinn Féin.
11. Sinn Féin press statement, *An Phoblacht*, April 1971.
12. Ó Conaill, D. (1970). *An Phlobacht*, 8 July 1970, p. 2. Dáithí Ó Conaill was a member of the Provisional IRA and the first Chief of Staff, Continuity IRA, 1986–1991.
13. *Ibid*, p. 6.
14. Adams, G. (1976). *The Long War*, Belfast: Republican Press Centre. This was an essay written when Gerry Adams was in prison in Long Kesh.
15. *An Phoblacht*, 2 April 1971, p. 8.
16. Extract from the IRA Green Book quoted in Taylor, P. (1997). *Provos: IRA and Sinn Féin*, London: Bloomsbury, p. 212.
17. Peace People, founded in 1976, was a grassroots movement with support from across the traditional divide between republicans and unionists. They launched several large-scale demonstrations against terrorist activity. Their work was viewed with suspicion from both republicans and unionists. Republican critics argued that peace marches took the attention away from reforming an unjust system that marginalized nationalist communities.
18. *Ard Fheis Report*, 1989, p. 10.
19. *Ibid*, p. 7.
20. Wolfe Tone's proclamation, 1798.
21. Adams, G. *Ideology of Liberation*, Ard Fheis address, 31 October 1987. He concluded that the '*big ideas*' of social republicanism also needed '*small ideas*' and more attention to what people really needed. It represents an interesting shift closer to community politics in Northern Ireland.
22. '*Scenario for Peace*', 1 May 1987, a discussion paper, published by Sinn Féin and accessible at <www.sinnfein.ie>.
23. '*Towards Lasting Peace*' (1994), Dublin: Sinn Féin, accessible at <www.sinnfein.ie>.
24. *Ard Fheis Report*, 31 October 1987.
25. *Irish News*, 6 May 2000.
26. Adams, G. (1991). *Ard Fheis Report*, October 1991, p. 9.
27. *Irish News*, October 1999, p. 2.
28. Hartley, T. (1995), speech to the republican Ard Fheis, February 1995, Linen Hall LIbrary, Belfast, archives, P. 9308A, assessed by the author, 1999. Hartley's discourse of invitation was reported in An Phoblacht 25 February 1995.
29. *Towards a Negotiated Settlement*, no. 2, p. 4, 19 December 1994. This was a second of three submissions to the British government sourced from archives in the Linen Hall Library, P.6210, March 1999.
30. Galtung, J. (1990). 'Cultural Violence', *Journal of Peace Research*, 27, no. 3, pp. 291–305.
31. Both governments demonstrated an ambivalent stance towards Northern Ireland.
32. McGuinness, M. (1997). Wolfe Tone Commemoration, published in *An Phoblacht*, 22 June 1997, p. 1, provides evidence of the relationship between Sinn Féin and the ANC.
33. *Ibid*.

34. *Towards a Negotiated Settlement*, Sinn Féin submission to the British government, no. 3, 16 January 1995 sourced from archives in the Linen Hall Library, Belfast, P.6210.
35. <https://www.dfa.ie/.../northernireland/peace-process--joint-declaration-1993>, accessed January 2019.
36. A speech by Peter Brooke, the UK government's Secretary of State for Northern Ireland, signalled a change in tone from the British government towards republicans. The statement that the British Government had 'no selfish or economic interest', in Northern Ireland helped to facilitate discreet communications between the Sinn Féin leadership through an established back channel.
37. Two bomb attacks were made in Warrington, in North West England, 26 February 1993 and 20 March 1993. These IRA operations were in the middle of negotiations on the detail of the Downing Street Declaration. IRA statements at the time put the blame on the British government.
38. This material was sourced in 2000, from archives in the Linen Hall Library, Belfast: call reference P5584.
39. This included Ulster Volunteer Force, Ulster Defence Association and Red Hand Commandos.
40. Adams, G. Presidential Address, reported in *Republican News /An Phoblacht*, 26 February 1994.
41. Mitchell, G. (1999). *Making Peace*, London: Random House, p. 35. Mitchell set out the following commitments and the detail below proved to be a challenge for all stakeholders to the peace talks:

- To democratic and exclusively peaceful means of resolving political issues;
- To the total disarmament of all paramilitary organizations;
- To agree that such disarmament must be verifiable to the satisfaction of an independent commission;
- To renounce for themselves, and to oppose any effort by others, to use force, or threaten to use force, to influence the course or the outcome of all-party negotiations;
- To agree to abide by the terms of any agreement reached in all-party negotiations and to resort to democratic and exclusively peaceful methods in trying to alter any aspect of that outcome with which they may disagree; and,
- To urge that 'punishment' killings and beatings stop and to take effective steps to prevent such actions.

42. An excellent chapter on the US involvement in the peace process can be found in Cochrane, F. (2013). *Northern Ireland: The Reluctant Peace*, London: Yale University Press, pp. 147–188.
43. McGuinness, M. Annual Wolfe Tone Commemoration, 22 June 1997. The IRA cessation was called on 25 June 1997.

44. Adams, G. Easter Address, Glasnevin Cemetery, Dublin, 4 April 1999.
45. *Transforming Hope into Reality*, Sinn Féin: Dublin and Belfast, 10 June 1996.
46. Tonge, J. (2002). *Northern Ireland: Conflict and Change*, Harlow: Pearson Education, pp. 182–197.
47. Adams, G. Keynote speech to a pre-election party conference, reported in *Irish Republican News*, 23 March 2002.
48. 'Peace process in profound crisis', address by Gerry Adams, reported in the *Irish News* round up, 16 May 2003.
49. O'Neill, P. IRA statement, *Irish Republican Publicity Bureau*, 2004, Dublin.
50. O'Neill, P. IRA statement, reported in the *Irish Republican News*, 25 February 2005.
51. Ard Fheis report, *Irish Republican News*, 4 March 2005.
52. McGuinness, M. (2005). Ard Fheis report, *Irish Republican News*, 4 March 2005.
53. Adams, G. 'Adams Welcomes IRA Statement', *Irish Republican News*, 28 July 2005.
54. Adams, G. (2011). Ard Fheis, *Irish Republican News*, 10 September 2011.
55. McGuinness, M. (2008). *Irish Republican News*, 28 March 2008.
56. Adams, G. (2008). Ard Fheis Presidential Address, reported in the *Irish Republican News*, 1 March 2008.
57. *Ibid.*
58. Direct rule from Westminster was (re) imposed on the following dates: 11 February–30 May 2000; 10 August 2001 (24-hour suspension); 22 September 2001 (24-hour suspension); 14 October 2002–7 May 2007.
59. Adams, G. Presidential address, *Irish Republican News*, 1 March 2008.
60. Adams, G. (2017). Press statement, 9 March 2017.
61. McIntyre, A. (2008). *Good Friday: The Death of Irish Republicanism*, New York: Ausubo, p. 295.
62. Haywood, K., and O'Donnell, C. (eds) (2011). *Political Discourse and Conflict Resolution*, London: Routledge.
63. McKittrick, D. (1996). *The Nervous Peace*, Belfast: Blackstaff.
64. Mitchell, G. (1999). *Making Peace*, London: Random House.
65. O'Brien, B. (1999). *The Long War: The IRA and Sinn Fein*, Dublin: O'Brien Press.
66. Spencer, G. (2015). *From Armed Struggle to Political Struggle: Republican Tradition and Transformation in Northern Ireland*, London: Bloomsbury.
67. Maillot, A. (2005). *New Sinn Féin: Irish Republicanism in the Twenty-First Century*, Abingdon: Routledge.
68. Cochrane, F. (2013). *Northern Ireland: The Reluctant Peace*, London: Yale University Press.
69. Drover, G. (1995). *John Hume: Man of Peace*, London: Vista.
70. Mallie, E., and McKittrick, D. (1997). *The Fight for Peace: The Inside Story of the Irish Peace Process*, London: Heinemann, p. 135.
71. Mallie, E., and McKittrick, D. (2001). *Endgame in Ireland*, London: Hodder and Stoughton.
72. Lane, F. (2002). Maskey lays Somme Wreath, *An Phoblacht*, 4 July 2002.

Chapter 6

'A greyhound trained to race'[1]

Introduction

> The IRA's decision to call a 'complete cessation of military operations' was built on the work of Sinn Féin, John Hume, Albert Reynolds and Irish America and developed in an inclusively based political initiative.[2]

In the 1990s, IRA cessations of their military operations reflected an acknowledgement by provisional republicans that armed struggle would not drive the British state out of Northern Ireland. Sinn Féin's engagement in a more inclusive style of politics with nationalists resulted in the Downing Street Declaration (1993) and the entry of republicans into peace talks in 1997.[3] A permanent IRA cessation, which came into force from 19 July1997, brought further evidence that Sinn Féin has persuaded a significant number of external stakeholders that republicans were serious about bringing peace to Northern Ireland. Internal opposition, from within the republican movement, exposed the level of concern at the scale of compromises made by the Sinn Féin negotiating team at the Mitchell talks. In retrospect, republican concerns were ideologically reasonable; when the conditions of the Good Friday Agreement were made public republicans found themselves committed to the principle of consent,[4] and an expectation of IRA decommissioning.

In the previous chapter, Sinn Féin's transitional and transformational discourses were briefly introduced to illustrate how the leadership managed the complex politics of brokering IRA cessations, representing republican political interests and managing internal opposition. At the time, IRA decommissioning represented a major challenge for republican, volunteers, prisoners and veterans. After years of military service they were being asked to abandon the republican armed struggle despite the fact that partition was still in place and the British Army was still armed and active in Northern Ireland. For some Irish republicans, the decommissioning process symbolized the nullification of a long history of radical politics and personal sacrifice. IRA decommissioning represented an act of appeasement towards the British government and a betrayal of core republican principles. Internally, Sinn Féin faced a full spectrum of political and emotional responses but managed to keep the republican movement together during the final negotiations for the Good Friday Agreement.

The last stage of decommissioning, in 2005, triggered some provisional republicans to split and form new-armed groups or join established ones. At the time, the purpose of these groups was very clear – the removal of the British state from Northern Ireland and the reunification of a divided Irish nation. For these breakaway groups, the traditional war with the British state was not over and their current warrior talk indicates that this remains their political position. The provisional republican movement was not significantly harmed by these splits during the period 2005–2006, because Sinn Féin had gained political leverage from decommissioning.

The origin of Sinn Féin's transitional discourses goes back to the 1970s, but it was in the 1990s that the term 'transition' appeared more frequently and signified that the leadership was taking a pragmatic view that the Good Friday Agreement would take republicans further into mainstream politics in Northern Ireland. For the next twenty years republican engagement with the peace process was, at times, overshadowed by the reputational risk of unsanctioned republican violence from breakaway groups. The Provisional IRA had decommissioned but not all republican groups had closed down their IRA operations.

Back in 1969, Cathal Goulding, Chief of Staff of the Official IRA, used a metaphor to explain his views on the presence of republican military capability and its impact on political development:

> It was like a greyhound trained to race – you have to let it race or it goes bad.[5]

This remark was made at a time when the Official IRA leadership was preparing a political route to Irish unity.[6] A strategy of political revolution in Northern Ireland was seen as a more effective route for republicans to develop into a stronger political organization to challenge the

British government. Crucially, this meant the Official IRA were looking for a way to let go of their long investment in armed struggle. Goulding's remark illustrates a rather dismissive attempt to explain the behaviour of the Provisional IRA in early 1970s and implies that they were engaging in violence for the sake of it. The remark does, however, illustrate how republicans traditionally manage those who question the strategies of their leadership. In the 1970s the term 'dissidents' was used by the Official IRA leadership to describe the activities of the Provisional IRA in Northern Ireland. The same term is now used by the current provisional leadership (Sinn Féin) to marginalize their republican opponents and appears to represent an internal dynamic conducted through warrior talk to isolate and control individuals and groups who challenge the authority of Sinn Féin. So, while transitional discourses were initially used to keep the republican movement united and been largely successful, a form of warrior talk is used to manage other republicans. This phenomenon will be explored in the context of the Northern Ireland peace process and the discourses of transition and transformation.

Republican decommissioning represented a deeply disturbing scenario for republican veterans and volunteers. Their identity was transformed overnight; they became redundant as freedom fighters and symbolically redundant as historic community protectors. The change of identity for republican prisoners was also traumatic as they moved from the status of prisoner of war to that of 'criminal'.[7]

Currently, there are numerous and highly diverse republican groups who attract the label of 'dissident' and they tend to be anyone who challenges Sinn Féin strategies. Despite the diversity of views within Irish republicanism, there is no substantive evidence to indicate that the core republican goal has changed but internal debates on the means to achieve this goal remain contentious to the present day. Current opponents of the Sinn Féin leadership believe they have come too far away from the original republican goal and that there is no going back. The worst-case scenario for all groups, including Sinn Féin, is that a united Ireland will never happen: this would mean that both republican political and military strategies would have failed.

In this chapter it will be important to look beyond Goulding's 'greyhound' metaphor and gain a deeper understanding of the Irish republican relationship with their principle of physical force. Sinn Féin transitional discourses will be studied and analysed in the context of the cyclical nature of republican splits. The term 'radical republicanism' will be used to describe republican groups and individuals who oppose Sinn Féin political strategies. The term 'Provisional Sinn Féin' will be used when it is important to understand the contrast between the two major strands of Irish republicanism operating within Northern Ireland. The terms 'provisional' and 'radical' are at this time not intended as polarizing terms, but a practical means to help the reader appreciate Irish republicanism as a complex political phenomenon.

Chapter purpose

This chapter will examine Sinn Féin transitional discourses in detail to illustrate the impact of the Good Friday Agreement, and subsequent decommissioning, on the dynamics of the republican movement. Both core and colonized discourse material will be used to understand how the Sinn Féin leadership managed the risk of republican splits during critical political decisions. New forms of Sinn Féin warrior talk, which demonizes other republicans, will be explored in the context of the complex dynamics between provisional and radical republicanism. The risk to Sinn Féin's political aspirations in Northern Ireland, and in the south, from a divided republican movement will be also considered.

The reputational damage of internal tensions between provisional and radical republicanism is illustrated by this carefully worded rebuke from Martin McGuinness, 2016:

> This means the opening of space where possible obstruction to political advancement is no longer from without but within, where Sinn Féin must now contend with other forms of republicanism seeking to influence the narrow ground of political policy.[8]

This extract reveals a more complex political situation than Goulding's 'greyhound' metaphor in 1969. The difference in the current political stances of provisional and radical republicans is about fundamental philosophical issues and based on concerns that Sinn Féin's political strategies are not congruent with the traditions of Irish republicanism. Radical republicans believe Sinn Féin have taken Irish republicanism into a constitutional position that maintains the status quo of a divided Ireland. The image of radical republicanism is largely misunderstood and frequently presented as violent and renegade. Radical republicanism appears to be a complex system of smaller groups dedicated to the republican cause but operating in different ways. Some groups are armed and engaged in violence and their role in the wider republican movement will be explored in this chapter.

In previous chapters, the political journey of provisional Sinn Féin from radical activists into constitutional politicians and peacemakers represented a remarkable achievement in managing complex change. A combination of core and colonized discourses helped them to navigate a political journey and several crises as they managed both the expectations of both external stakeholders and the internal dynamics of the republican movement. Sinn Féin's continued use of warrior talk remains a puzzle: a hollow gesture, management control or a genuine desire to respect the legacy of Irish republicanism?

Chapter structure

Sinn Féin transitional discourses (1969–1998)

1970s: Stages Theory
1980s: There are no short cuts
1990s: We cannot stand still

Impact of decommissioning on Irish republicanism

IRA cessations (1994 and 1997)
Decommissioning (2005)

Relationship between provisional and radical republicanism

Unfinished revolution
Legacy of republican splits

Sinn Féin transitional discourses (1999–2019)

The war is over
Reconciliation and transition
Greyhounds or patriots?

Chapter summary
Suggested reading (chapter specific)
Practical study task: Greyhounds or patriots?

Sinn Féin transitional discourses (1969–1998)

1970s: Stages theory[9]

Initial forms of Sinn Féin transitional discourses can be seen in an early transitional document *Eire Nua*[10] that set out a programme of social and economic reform based on co-operation within and between communities. *Eire Nua* (New Ireland) was a blueprint for a united Ireland based on the republican values of justice, freedom and equality. The provisional movement in Northern Ireland embraced the notion of community politics but a military strategy, led by the (Provisional) IRA, overtook any practical realization of Sinn Féin's transitional approach to changing the political landscape in Northern Ireland. All republican groups supported the notion of a social revolution driven by the working class, of all communities in Northern Ireland and shared the same philosophical roots and radical political ideology.[11]

However, the IRA believed that addressing injustice in Northern Ireland would require faster and more aggressive strategies to force a British withdrawal.

The statement below reflects the increasing frustration Cathal Goulding had with the provisional republican movement and the tension between what was, essentially, two republican armies operating in Northern Ireland in the 1970s:[12]

> Nothing could be more contrary to the revolutionary strategy of the Republican movement than the indiscriminate bombing and burning of certain elements.[13]

IRA military operations in Northern Ireland had two major objectives: the physical protection of republican communities and a planned campaign against a unionist government to force a response from the British state. The primary republican vision of a British withdrawal was overtaken by a surge in sectarian violence between nationalist and unionist communities. The scale of violence brought a highly charged and dangerous situation which put the unionist-controlled government under pressure. The provisional IRA, as they predicted, had triggered a military intervention from the British government. British troops were sent to Northern Ireland and republicans now had a noble cause to fight for. The British state stepped into its historic role of the 'enemy' of Irish republicanism. Sinn Féin continued to focus on political transition and the following statement from Gerry Adams, made in 1976, illustrates that he already believed that republicans could not stay at war indefinitely:

> Republicans must continue to examine their organisation, their tactics, their programmes and their achievements with objectivity, honesty and farsightedness.[14]

Gerry Adams took care with his words and the following statement illustrates his growing capability in developing creating discourses that opened up the space for flexible responses to challenge. The following is a response to questions about the relationship between Sinn Féin and the IRA:

> For there is absolutely no difference between a military tactic and a political tactic. Both are used simultaneously.[15]

In the 1970s, both military operations and political activism were shaped and communicated through historical and justification discourses and this ensured that Irish republican philosophy, ideology and principles remained a coherent and consistent message. During this period warrior talk was used by Sinn Féin and the IRA to convey the republican intent to drive the British out of Ireland. The volume and urgency of warrior talk drowned out transitional discourses and the notion that a united Ireland might be achieved through political transition was not seen as a priority.

1980s: 'There are no short cuts.'[16]

The concept of phases of republican struggle emerged in Sinn Féin discourse in the 1980s. Transitional discourses were used externally to win community support and build an infrastructure of activists and offices that could support the politicization of republican grass roots. The metaphor of a 'journey' was used more frequently, and to influence a wider body of republicans to accept a more inclusive approach to politics. Sinn Féin's vision of inclusive politics meant dialogue with a wider body of nationalists and unionists. However, early transitional discourses were delivered from a traditional republican position and unlikely to attract support from outside the republican movement. A good example of a gap between communication intent and its impact can be observed in this statement from Gerry Adams in 1984:

> There are no short cuts in the task of making a revolution. Only by painstakingly perfecting, education and structuring our organisation so that it becomes relevant to the people.[17]

In the 1980s, transitional discourses appeared to be a tactic to soften the traditional republican war-like stance and make republican politics more palatable to the outside world. The British media demonized the Sinn Féin leadership during this time and their efforts to communicate their political strategies to an external audience was lost, literally and symbolically.[18] However, their transitional discourses indicated that they had found a way to retain a sense of unity in the republican movement and this is reflected in the comment below:

> The process was presented as the struggle continuing by another means as opposed to a break with traditional republican methods and approach. There are lots of republicans, good republicans in the movement who do believe that this is the same struggle by another means.[19]

Gerry Adams and Martin McGuinness consistently pointed out the potential weakness of an isolated political position and developed transitional discourses as a counter argument to political challenges from other republicans. The following extract of Sinn Féin transitional discourse, from 1986, was written during a time of discreet talks between republicans and nationalist politicians:[20]

> Our experience teaches us that, as group, we are often more successful when we have a flexible approach. We are at our weakest when we are forced into a static political position where the more powerful forces of imperialism can be employed to isolate us.[21]

In the 1980s, it appears that Sinn Féin's transitional discourses were also used to manage ideological differences across the republican movement. The emergence of Provisional Sinn Féin and Provisional IRA had been the result of a major republican split in the 1970s and it is likely that the provisional leadership was sensitive to their recent history and wished to avoid internal divisions.

Transitional discourses gave Sinn Féin a mechanism to introduce constitutional politics as another phase in the republican struggle for Irish unity. It is important to remember that any engagement in constitutional politics in Northern Ireland meant, in practice, that republicans accepted the power of the British State and the legality of the 1921 partition. The language of Sinn Féin's transitional discourses became characterized by their practicality and reason and more importantly, they signalled a growing pragmatism about the republican relationship with the British state.

1990s: 'We cannot stand still. We need to keep making advances.'[22]

In the 1990s, Sinn Féin transitional discourses demonstrated a clear shift from the traditional message of Irish republicanism to inclusive political strategies towards other political parties and both Irish and British governments. Transitional discourses signalled not only changing political strategy but also a major challenge to republican ideology. Sinn Féin's transitional discourses were a good indicator of their growing responsiveness to external stakeholders and a growing unease within the republican movement.

Sinn Féin added more consensual language into their transitional discourses and included terms such as *'strategic concessions'*[23] to signify that the final phase of republican struggle had arrived. The appearance of the term 'concession' is fascinating and represents an early recognition that changes in republican ideology might be needed in order to end partition. IRA cessations in 1994 and 1997 were presented as concessions to the Northern Ireland peace process.

Radical republicans have since argued that both cessations were called without a binding agreement for the withdrawal of the British state and that the Sinn Féin rhetoric of 'phases' was simply a way of disguising the failure of republican political strategies in Northern Ireland.[24] It is clear that Sinn Féin transitional discourses had evolved to such a degree that their speeches communicated openly, a change in their attitude towards the British state:

> British withdrawal is based on an exercise of self-determination by the Irish people, as a whole, can best take place after a defined period of national reconciliation, the (transitional period).[25]

This proposal for a period of reconciliation, before a British withdrawal, was a complete break with Irish republican philosophy and principles. This new message from Sinn Féin was stark. Republicans were being asked to accept the state of Northern Ireland and continued partition of Ireland for an indefinite period of time. As early as 1987 (ten years before the Good Friday Agreement), Sinn Féin were proposing political concessions:

> We know and accept that the British government's departure must be preceded by a sustained period of peace and will arise out of negotiations involving different shades of Irish nationalism and unionism.[26]

In the 1990s, there was further colonization of language from the business world. In the previous chapter, there was evidence that discourses from change management were adapted and embedded in Sinn Féin peace discourses. At the time, theories of change management advocated a series of planned steps which required the engagement of key stakeholders as an effective approach to managerial change.[27] Sinn Féin's transitional discourses took a discursive turn towards a managerial approach and started to communicate a staged approach to a united Ireland, which encouraged people to accept change en route. This was an interesting shift from the language of radical political action.

The importance of collective responsibility for societal and structural change remained a key feature of transitional discourses throughout the 1990s and a stark contrast to the traditional republican stance that the British government was responsible for addressing injustice and inequality in Northern Ireland. Sinn Féin leadership speeches continued to emphasize the importance of engaging people in political change as a series of planned stages, rather than one radical jump:

> Such a transitional process could provide a pragmatic route to republicans' ultimate goal but only if the dynamic for change was stronger to the resistance to it.[28]
>
> Change must be managed and the anchor of change is dialogue.[29]
>
> We must realise, as never before, our interdependence on each other.[30]

It is interesting that warrior talk continued to have a role in the 1990s. The term '*another battle front*'[31] had been a discursive tactic used by Sinn Féin, in the 1980s, to sanction republican hunger strikes in prison. Initially seen as a distraction from IRA military operations, the hunger strikes were deemed to be an alternative front in the republican fight for a united Ireland. Military terms such as 'struggle', 'battle' and 'alternative fronts' may appear incongruous alongside peace and transitional discourses but Sinn Féin were preparing the republican movement for the Good Friday Agreement, and the inevitable demands for decommissioning.

Impact of decommissioning on Irish republicanism

The republican principle of physical force came under threat in the 1990s through the recommendations of the Downing Street Declaration (1993) and later, the Good Friday Agreement (1998). The Sinn Féin peace strategy, and the growing pan-national relationship with John Hume of the Social Democratic Labour Party, helped to facilitate republicans into a political role in the peace process. With the promise of peace came a political expectation of an end to violence for both republican and loyalist paramilitaries, and their path to decommissioning was lengthy and complex. Both republican and unionist leaders were looking for the political leverage of 'silencing the guns' but both had internal stakeholders to manage and this brought a game of brinkmanship on who would decommission first. Republican decommissioning was announced on 28 July 2005 and represented change on a major scale for republicans.

IRA cessations (1994 and 1997)

Sinn Féin's peace strategy, in practice, delivered very little progress on Irish unity or a definitive timescale for the exit of the British state from Northern Ireland. Ironically the Good Friday Agreement, and specifically the consent principle enshrined within it, created the conditions for the continuing presence of the British government in Northern Ireland politics. The lack of political progress on Irish unity and the demand for IRA decommissioning were two major signs for republicans, that their leadership was trading away their radical political heritage.

The terms of the Mitchell Principles required a commitment to total disarmament by all parties prior to joining the peace talks. A study of both Sinn Féin and IRA messages prior to the republican ceasefire, 31 August 1994, indicates that content was the same but the style of delivery very different. IRA communications were brief statements using core republican discourses. The delivery was in the style of a military brief and a sharp contrast to Sinn Féin's longer political speeches with colonized discourses and rhetoric. However, the substantive content of cessation and decommissioning statements from Sinn Féin and the IRA was the same. This IRA statement is an interesting public display of support for Sinn Féin:

> Recognising the potential of the current situation and in order to enhance the democratic peace and underline our commitment to its success, the leadership of Óglaigh na hÉireann have decided at midnight, Wednesday, 31 August, there will be a complete cessation of military operations.[32]

This statement uses the term 'cessation' and was deemed by republicans to be a temporary lull in hostilities to aid political negotiations. The response from unionists was immediate condemnation and a demand for a permanent ceasefire. In the context of the republican principle of physical force, a permanent ceasefire without a British withdrawal from Northern Ireland was inconceivable. To republicans a cessation was a test of the motives of both unionists and the British government. IRA tactics, at the time, were similar to armed conflicts across the world in that paramilitary violence was seen as a negotiating tool to force the opponent to agree to talks. With this reasoning, military tactics become a means to address the symmetry of the conflict, negotiate and change the power relations.

The cessation of July 1994 lasted until February 1996 and was brought to a dramatic end with a major explosion at Canary Wharf, in London. This event proved that the IRA could maintain a cessation, but it also indicated their state of readiness to launch major attacks in England. By 19 July 1997, a permanent cessation became the precursor to the final decommissioning of the Provisional IRA in 2005.

Decommissioning (2005)

> No informer throughout the course of the conflict has been able to deal such a blow to the military capacity of the IRA as its own leadership have.[33]

This extract illustrates a sense of betrayal felt within the republican movement. It is clear that Sinn Féin recognized that republican decommissioning before a British withdrawal would cause difficulties internally and risk more republican splits. In the terms of the Good Friday Agreement, IRA decommissioning was not a prerequisite to Sinn Féin's participation in government and this made life for Gerry Adams and Martin McGuinness more challenging. The response below indicates how tense inner debates became:

> When I say that we want to bring an end to physical force republicanism, that clearly means bringing an end to the organisation or the vehicle of physical force republicanism.[34]

Sinn Féin developed more transitional discourses to navigate the growing discord within the republican movement but also resorted to core discourses to demonstrate their allegiance to Irish republicanism. Despite the fact that they had taken a constitutional route to Irish unity, they continued to adopt warrior talk to communicate to republicans. The reference to republican ideology in the following extract is interesting, given that a republican acceptance of the consent principle was in reality an abandonment of their republican ideology:

> If we, as Irish republicans, are to understand anything about the struggle for freedom and independence, and if we are to advance and achieve our republican objective, we must have a firm sense of who we are. This has to be rooted in our Republican ideology.[35]

Republicans critical of Sinn Féin's political strategies argue that Irish republicans already have a clear ideology and a clear sense of who they are. From a radical republican perspective, the act of decommissioning rewrites republican ideology and criminalizes republicans. Five years after the Good Friday Agreement, Sinn Féin were in a challenging situation because their external credibility with international supporters was at risk if they could not deliver on decommissioning.

Gerry Adams and Martin McGuiness were keenly aware that challenges to their leadership were fuelled by an internal perception that the terms of the Good Friday Agreement would not be implemented favourably for republicans. Several speeches from the period 2001–2005 reveal a combination of core discourses to signal solidarity and transitional discourses to signal change:

> It is okay to be against this move but what we have to be is united and strategic and looking to the future and committed to our republican cause. It is big because it does cause pain to republicans.
>
> Republicans, as agents of change, are prepared to loosen up and free up a movement, which can resolve all the issues that need to be resolved.[36]
>
> Tony Blair said decommissioning was a symbol. He's more right than he can know. To Unionists, decommissioning is a symbol of victory over the IRA; to republicans, decommissioning is a symbol of surrender.[37]

It is now clear that Sinn Féin transitional discourses were used as a bridge between past and future, between sacred republican principles and future political strategies. In both extracts quoted above, Gerry Adams reached out to republicans and acknowledged the scale of change being asked of them. In 2005, the final act of republican decommissioning was completed; it delivered a boost to Sinn Féin's international reputation and their political support in Northern Ireland. The downside of decommissioning is that the provisional republicans were now committed to the peace process and any return to violence was likely to have serious consequences for their political aspirations in Northern Ireland. The scale of change for Irish republicanism was signalled clearly in 2001:

> The IRA is committed to our republican objectives and to the establishment of a united Ireland based on justice, equality and freedom. No one should doubt the difficulties these initiatives caused for our volunteers, our supporters and us. Our motivation is clear. This unprecedented move is to save the peace process and to persuade others of our genuine intentions.[38]

Behind the scenes, both the IRA and Sinn Féin pushed on with decommissioning, albeit in their unique styles. Below are two statements from republicans; the first statement is from the IRA and the second from Sinn Féin. The IRA focus on British rule whereas Sinn Féin focus on reaching out to republican volunteers and veterans: it provides an interesting example of their transitional discourse at the time:

> We believe there is now an alternative way to achieve this and to end British rule in our country.[39]

Let me give a clear signal here: the Army is going to deliver on its commitments on the armed struggle. Republicans are going to hear that in the news. Republicans may feel a sense of deflation. There is nobody going to be cheering.[40]

After the Good Friday Agreement, cessations and finally decommissioning there was a subtle change in Sinn Féin's transitional discourses. For the provisional movement, the republican war was over and their focus was now on leveraging their successes politically at the ballot box. From a pragmatic viewpoint, a democratic mandate in Northern Ireland and political success in the south meant that a constitutional route to Irish unity was conceivable. In the meantime, Sinn Féin had political work to do reforming society in Northern Ireland and their transitional discourses adapted to reflect their ambitions in mainstream politics. The result was the emergence of new radical republican groups ready to take up the unfinished business of the republican cause.

Relationship between provisional and radical republicanism

The statement below is a sample of warrior talk; it was part of a longer speech using transitional discourses to influence a republican audience. The context is two years after the Good Friday Agreement:[41]

> We are Irish Republicans. We will always be Irish Republicans. We are unrepentant about the right of the people of this island to freedom.[42]

It is interesting that the mantra 'We are Irish Republicans' was used at a time when the emergence of new republican groups indicated that the republican movement was not united nor completely influenced by Sinn Féin transitional rhetoric. For some republicans, transitional discourses did not address their political concerns that the Good Friday Agreement was a dangerous precedent for Irish republicanism.

Sinn Féin leaders continued to use 'We are Irish Republicans' for the next twenty years as a counter to criticism from radical republicans. A combination of republican core discourses, warrior talk and transitional discourses emerges as a default strategy for the Sinn Féin leadership to manage the provisional republican movement. The emergence of more republican armed groups after 2005, despite the decommissioning of the Provisional IRA, brought more challenges for Sinn Féin and polarized further their relationship with radical republicanism.

Unfinished revolution[43]

On 18 April 2019, Lyra McKee, a journalist, was shot by a masked sniper as she observed rioting in the Creggan area of Derry.[44] A few days later, the New IRA released a statement admitting to the crime, apologized and described it as a 'mistake'. This extract from a press interview illustrates New IRA's allegiance to Irish republican principles and a continued belief in the legitimacy of physical force:

> You think this is madness? There will be madness as long as there is an armed occupation in Ireland. Go back to what the IRA did in the 1970s. Condemning the IRA is nothing new.[45]

New IRA is one of several armed republican groups who reject republican decommissioning and the political strategies of provisional republicanism. New IRA discourses are predominantly warrior talk drawing on historical justifications for armed struggle and a mission to disrupt the normalization of Northern Ireland.[46]

Discourse findings from both provisional and radical republicans confirm that they share the same historic goal of unifying Ireland. The main source of disagreement is the continued influence of the British government in Northern Ireland.[47] The timing and nature of a British withdrawal is still not resolved despite the IRA decommissioning in 2005. This is a major sticking point between provisional republicans who see constitutional politics as a long-term strategy and radical republicans who consider any republican involvement in a Northern Ireland government to be a form of betrayal. Despite their allegiance to core republican principles and ideology, not all radical groups support an armed struggle. Several groups present a reasoned argument that Sinn Féin's commitment to peace does not deliver a clear plan for Irish unity. Sinn Féin's counter argument is that they represent the only 'All Ireland' political party and now in a strong position to unite Ireland through political means.[48]

After 2005, two key events accelerated the development of new radical groups: the involvement of Sinn Féin in Northern Ireland policing and the impact of Brexit on the border between the North and South. Both events were a sharp reminder for all republicans that Northern Ireland continues to remain part of the UK. These extracts from New IRA press statements in 2019 deliver a specific and war-like message:

> We fully accept we cannot defeat the British militarily, or even drive them away from Ireland but we will continue to fight for as long as they remain there. Our actions serve one purpose. They let the world know there is ongoing conflict in Northern Ireland.[49]

The history behind the development of radical republican groups is essential to an understanding of the scale and form of their opposition to Sinn Féin's political strategies and to assess the reputational risk of further violence for the republican project in Northern Ireland.

Legacy of republican splits

Irish republicanism has a long history of splits and these generally arise from different perceptions of how to achieve a united Ireland. It is important to recognize that republican splits are not simply a disagreement on whether the republican struggle is armed or unarmed. Irish republicanism is characterized by a spectrum of political views that co-exist and adapt according to political conditions. Internal disagreements and splits are not a new republican phenomenon, but they generate new discourses and narratives to study. The following section is an overview of key republican splits since 1969 to gain an understanding of the current tensions between provisional republicanism and radical republicanism. It is not an exhaustive list and further references will be provided in the suggested reading section in this chapter.

The provisional split (1969)

In the 1970s, the emergence of the provisional movement was the result of a split from 'official' republicanism by a group of republicans politicized by the scale of social injustice experienced by Catholics in Northern Ireland. At the time Gerry Adams, a member of Provisional Sinn Féin although developing political ideas, was liberal with his warrior talk using terms such as 'Republican War Machine'[50] to communicate his view that the impetus and energy for political change came from people at war. At the time, the new provisional movement presented revolutionary violence as a political project:

> Our duty is clear, it is to live up to the courage, the determination of martyred comrades in the struggle to achieve the ideals for which they died.[51]

This early violent history of provisional republicanism is important because it highlights a paradox facing the current Sinn Féin leadership. Their political aspirations for a united Irish nation are tinged with their links to a violent history and warrior talk has a part to play in the production of that image. Another paradox lies in the political success of Provisional Sinn Féin, which has taken them away from their radical roots of 1969. The political space for radical republican thinking and action is now taken up by their republican opponents.

Republican Sinn Féin (1986)

In the 1980s, the formation of Republican Sinn Féin represented the next major split and was the result of internal disagreement on an amendment to the principle of abstention which would allow Provisional Sinn Féin to take up seats if they won in local elections in North Ireland.[52] Republican Sinn Féin discourses have consistently maintained their position on abstention. The following statements by Republican Sinn Féin, from 2001, 2008 and 2017, provide clear evidence of their political consistency:

> Now thanks to the Provisional Movement's switch from revolution to reform, The British government's normalisation policy is in place. Nationalists and former Republicans have been bought, alike and have been pacified and placated.[53]

> Republican Sinn Féin has sought to address the root cause of conflict in Ireland, namely the cancerous British presence. The Provos have tried to silence opposition to the Stormont sell out of 1998.[54]

> It was a setback for republicans and the Irish working class. Stormont remains a 'fundamentally undemocratic assembly' kept under the strict control of British imperialism, designed to give British rule in Ireland a democratic mantle.[55]

This statement was released after a major election success for provisional Sinn Féin in 2017 which ended the unionist control of the government of Northern Ireland and clarifies that Republican Sinn Féin are shaped by traditional republican ideology and principles. For them, the struggle is not over and, therefore, the political work must go on.

Continuity IRA (1986)

This is an armed group formed at the same time as Republican Sinn Féin and committed to the republican principles of abstention and physical force. This republican group also attracts the label 'dissident' but claims that their organization holds the 'continuity' of Irish republicanism and sees their role is to keep a sacred link with the Easter Rising of 1916. Continuity IRA did not become active until 1994, when it emerged as a protest against the Provisional IRA cessations of the same year. Their current military operations are designed to oppose the 'normalization' of Northern Ireland and to disrupt Sinn Féin's political strategies. Continuity IRA have continued to have a role in community policing and the following extract, from 2006, gives an insight into their perceptions of their role:

> We are not putting ourselves forward to police nationalist districts but if contacted by the people we will take action against known drug dealers, burglars and rapists. These people have been warned.[56]

Continuity IRA has largely stayed separate from other armed republican groups and did not join a later merger of armed groups in 2012.

32 County Sovereignty Movement (1997)

This group is similar to Republican Sinn Féin in their complete rejection of any republican engagement with the British state. Their political legitimacy comes from the Easter Rising (1916) and this extract is a sample of their discourse in 2016:

> The past year has highlighted the extent to which the six county state remains an outpost of British oppression. We have seen continuing harassment of Republican families, the return of the supergrass system, internment and inhumane treatment of Republican prisoners in British jails. The narrative that is being peddled by the establishment is one of Republican violence and a refusal to engage politically with the Stormont regime. Republicans have consistently pointed to the British presence as the source of conflict. The only legitimate basis for engaging in discussion is to talk about the removal of the occupation.[57]

This statement is important because it confirms the betrayal that 32 County members felt during the Mitchell talks and Good Friday Agreement.[58] This group asserts that Sinn Féin are now working with the enemies of Irish republicanism and cited the terms of the Good Friday Agreement, which included provisions for the fair treatment of paramilitary prisoners, both loyalists and republicans.

Real IRA (1997)

This republican group objected to Mitchell Principles and felt betrayed that provisional leadership was willing to compromise the armed struggle in order to enter peace talks. In the eyes of Real IRA volunteers, decommissioning before a British withdrawal is a direct contravention of the republican principle of physical force.[59] The irony of this stance cannot be overlooked. The provisional movement took republicans into an armed struggle against the British state in the 1970s. By the 1990s, provisional republicans were signalling an end to the armed struggle and crucially this was before a British withdrawal. This irony is not lost on the Real IRA:

> Once again, Óglaigh na hÉireann declares the right of the Irish people to the ownership of Ireland. We call on all volunteers loyal to the Irish Republic to unite to uphold the Republic and establish a permanent national parliament representative of all the people.[60]

A bombing operation by the Real IRA in Omagh in 1998 became the catalyst that spurred key stakeholders of the Good Friday talks to press on with the final negotiations and create the momentum to close down the space for all armed groups, loyalist or republican, to operate in Northern Ireland.[61]

éirígí ('Arisen', 2006)

This group was formed by republican activists disillusioned with Sinn Féin's move away from a purist view of a united Irish republic. Its adherents blame the provisional leadership for accepting a process of normalizing Northern Ireland, which, in radical republican eyes, is an illegal state. This group engages in grass roots campaigning, is opposed to the Good Friday Agreement, policing reform and the role that provisional republicans have taken in the government of Northern Ireland:

> It is a true honour to be here in the heart of Republican West Belfast among the heroes of Ireland – among the martyred soldiers of Ireland from this and previous generations who are buried here in the hallowed grounds of this cemetery. It is our firm belief that we will have to fight if we are to successfully achieve our primary objectives of removing the British presence from Ireland.[62]

Despite the warrior talk in this statement, there is no clear evidence that *éirígí* have any paramilitary links.

Community-policing groups

In the 1970s, the Provisional IRA were drawn into community protection, initially against loyalist paramilitary attacks. Their military operations extended to the Royal Ulster Constabulary, as representatives of a unionist government, and British soldiers, as representatives of the British state. To republicans this represented a war 'on all fronts' so it is unsurprising that a community-policing role became a legacy for the Provisional IRA throughout the 1970s and 1980s. By the end of the 1990s the Mitchell talks created several conditions for the conduct of multi-party peace negotiations. All paramilitaries were asked to cease their operations to create a climate for peace talks. These conditions specifically mentioned the 'policing activities' of paramilitary groups and included punishment beatings, killings and kneecapping.[63]

Currently there are a number of groups, both republican and loyalist, who continue to police antisocial behaviour and drug dealing within their communities in Northern Ireland. Since the 1970s this protection has been an alternative to policing from the state-sanctioned official system. Some armed republican groups continue to exert community control through violent methods and, although their operations are largely covert, their presence in Northern Ireland remains a threat to the peace process and Sinn Féin's political credibility. Ironically, the survival of these groups depends on community support and compliance. A good example is Republican Action Against Drugs (RAAD), formed in 2008, who argue that their purpose is to highlight concerns about the use of drugs amongst young people. They claim to be proactive in their fight against drugs and imply the police have lost control:

> There is no political agenda within our organization. The organization is now rightly or wrongly, considered by many to be at the cutting edge of eradicating drug-dealing in the North West.[64]

Currently, RAAD activity has a number of implications for peace in Northern Ireland. The scale of violence is perceived, externally, to be excessive and points to a military-style organization with an arsenal.

A merger of armed republicans (2012)

On 26 July 2012, a statement from a new group calling itself the Irish Republican Army announced a merger between a numbers of militant republican groups that were united in their condemnation of the decommissioning of Provisional IRA in 2005. Some of these groups had created niches for themselves such as RAAD with its emphasis on policing drug culture while others were dedicated to the republican struggle and the final removal of the British state. The merger brought together Real IRA, RAAD and a group called Óglaigh na hÉireann:⁶⁵

> A re-grouping of previously distinct breakaway IRA groups is being described as the most significant development within physical force republicanism since the Provisional IRA split in 1997. The transition was helped by the fact that a majority of the new IRA's leadership previously held roles within the Provisional IRA. The IRA's mandate for armed struggle derives from Britain's denial of the fundamental right to of the Irish people to national self – determination and sovereignty.⁶⁶

This merger marked an important recognition amongst these republican groups that their previous fragmentation was eroding their capability and capacity to conduct operations and signal opposition to the normalization of Northern Ireland. Out of this militant grouping has emerged the New IRA, in 2016, which was an amalgam of Real IRA, RAAD and a few individuals. Continuity IRA continues to operate as a separate entity.

Saoradh (2016)

Saoradh does not contest elections and sees the Stormont government as illegal. Their political legitimacy is derived from the historical republican position that the British state illegally occupies Ireland. Saoradh members are committed to the 1916 proclamation and the principles enshrined within it. They are primarily focused on representing the working class to overthrow a capitalist system. This extract from 2017 sums up their position:

> Saoradh activists would expect nothing less than the attacks on them by the state and her proxies. This has been part of the Freedom Struggle since it began. Saoradh, the Irish Republican Prisoners Welfare Association and the Republican Movement in Belfast are not going away, regardless of the state utilizing tactics that have failed for generations. To our enemies we once again say simply – do you worst, it won't be enough.⁶⁷

This republican group espouses far-left politics and is alleged to have connections with the New IRA.

Republican independents

Finally, it is important to acknowledge the political views of republicans who have left the provisional movement but chosen not to align with a specific group and who continue to challenge Sinn Féin political strategies. These individuals tend to be IRA veterans, academics and writers who question the benefit of the Good Friday Agreement but do not subscribe to the continuation of armed struggle.[68] The following extract reveals how some republican individuals view the current state of Irish republicanism:

> The IRA was a manifestation of insurrectional energy within the nationalist community at that time, a reaction to how the British behaved there. The difference between what was on offer in 1974 and what was accepted in 1998 did not justify the loss of one single life.[69]

The diverse nature of radical republicanism is more complex than a range of views on physical force. Several republican groups have emerged in responses to localized issues, for example, Republican Action Against Drugs in Derry, and Saoradh with a network of local offices in Derry, Belfast, Dungannon and Newry. However, they all share ideological concerns about the route that Sinn Féin has taken in Northern Ireland but express it in a multitude of different ways, from political campaigns to military-style operations and community violence. Many of these groups have members in prison so a pattern of republican rebellion, seen in provisional republicanism in the 1970s is being repeated in 2019.

The problem is that violence, or the threat of violence, from armed groups draws attention away from the political nature of the republican cause and legitimate nationalist concerns about the ongoing political, social and economic impact of partition. The forming and reforming of IRA groups, post decommissioning, is an interesting phenomenon, which cannot simply be explained by Goulding's analysis of 'greyhounds'. Republican violence in Northern Ireland traps Irish republicanism in the past and this presents a dilemma for Sinn Féin and their political aspirations for transformational change. The continued existence of armed republican groups, although small scale and fragmented, indicates that Sinn Féin transitional discourses were only partially successful.

Sinn Féin transitional discourses (1999–2019)

The war is over

The use of transitional discourses to maintain republican unity appeared to change after the Good Friday Agreement and in response to the emergence of newly armed republican groups. The extract below, from 2000, is an interesting combination of peace and transitional discourses communicated through Sinn Féin warrior talk:

> Who said it was going to be easy? Peace requires justice. Everyone here also knows, or should know, that such changes will be resisted by those who cling to the old order, the old agenda. There is no comfort for the faint-hearted or weak-willed. But then we know that people like ourselves who want to see a total transformation of society on this island cannot be faint-hearted or weak-willed.[70]

In the aftermath of the Good Friday Agreement and during the negotiations on decommissioning, it appears that Sinn Féin consciously employed warrior talk as a device to resonate with republican values. This device may have seemed to be a practical strategy at the time, but it now appears as a series of mixed messages coming from the Sinn Féin leadership as they steered the republican movement through seismic change. Sinn Féin's transitional discourses illustrate tensions between their role in constitutional politics, the demands of government service and need to stay close to their own grassroots.

In the previous chapter on peace discourses, Sinn Féin warrior talk described peace using military terms such as '*alternative front*',[71] '*bridgehead*',[72] and '*armed for peace*',[73] which were clearly meant for other republicans. In the years following the Good Friday Agreement, Sinn Féin transitional discourses also carried a subtle militaristic message despite their assertion that the republican war was over:

'A greyhound trained to race'

> The people's army must make way for the people's party. If the IRA ceases to exist, it will liberate the embattled peace process, invigorate nationalists and republicans, put unionists on the back foot and focus minds on the only political show in town: fighting peacefully and democratically to secure the bridgehead of the Good Friday Agreement.[74]

The use of warrior talk is directed at other republicans to persuade them to accept decommissioning and in that context a practical communication device. However, a language of war was used to legitimize a republican strategy to secure peace. The contradictions in this speech are a good example of how republican warrior talk has been adapted to serve different political agendas.

Reconciliation and transition

In the 1990s, Sinn Féin peace discourses colonized language from the field of conflict resolution and this pattern continued in their transitional discourses. The importance of forgiveness and reconciliation was positioned as a key phase in the republican journey to one Irish nation. In this extract from 2002 the Provisional IRA statement is referring to a republican military operation in 1972:

> On the anniversary of this tragic event, we address all of the deaths and injuries of non-combatants caused by us. We offer our sincere apologies and condolences to their families.
>
> The future will not be found in denying collective failures and mistakes or closing minds and hearts to the plight of those who have been hurt.[75]

Conflict resolution in Northern Ireland was presented as a transitional process which would take time and patience with other stakeholders. The extract below, from 2011, represents a clear message from Sinn Féin that their priority was to work with unionists to heal the past as a step towards a united Ireland:

> This means Republicans reaching out to unionists. We need to be patient and to seek common ground on which we can celebrate our difference as diversity. This is a personal priority for me, and for Sinn Féin.[76]

Sinn Féin transitional discourses presented reconciliation across different communities in Northern Ireland as the route to social, political and economic justice. In Northern Ireland. This was an important shift away from blaming unionists or the British government for past grievances and injustice. Through their discourses, Sinn Féin committed republicans to a transitional agenda which gave primacy to solving issues in Northern Ireland.

The Sinn Féin leadership was convinced that addressing structural reform could be achieved more effectively from inside the political system with republicans as members of the Northern Ireland Assembly. Ard Fheis speeches started to sound less war-like and closer to party political broadcasts as Sinn Féin navigated a political route that included the reform of Northern Ireland and, at the same time, the notion of a societal transformation. New transformational discourses emerged which communicated grand republican visions with a substantial degree of ambiguity around Sinn Féin's political priorities – Northern Ireland or united Ireland.

Greyhounds or patriots?

By 2008, the activities of radical republican groups had started to impact the credibility of Sinn Féin in the media.[77] The two extracts below display a rare glimpse into the reactions of the Sinn Féin leadership to the actions of armed radical groups and a noticeable shift in the response from the provisional leadership:

> I am amused at the efforts that are being made by people to drag the IRA of whatever description back into the equation. Any attempt to drag them back onto the stage is a big mistake.[78]

> The IRA has no responsibility for the tiny number of former republicans who have embraced criminal activity. We repudiate this activity and denounce those involved.[79]

Sinn Féin leadership clearly recognized the risk of further republican violence to their credibility as peacemakers and constitutional politicians. There was an interesting development in the language directed at radical republican groups and an example of the marginalization of republican opponents:

> We must truly act as nation builders and peacemakers. All Republicans have an obligation to participate in this task. This means, first of all, firmly rejecting sectarianism, bigotry and violence in all its forms - no matter what its source and no matter what its target.[80]

> Armed actions by republican militants were "acts of futility" which would not damage the power-sharing Six County administration. A tiny number of people who are committed to violence, their strategy is really about trying to divide Sinn Féin from our unionist government. They want to bring down the government, they want to destroy the peace process, they want to plunge us back into the past and there is no support in the community for that.[81]

There is no pretence of republican unity in these remarks from Martin McGuinness in 2012 and 2016. In both extracts he was directing his remarks at radical republican groups and his language reflects a growing demonization of radical republicanism as Sinn Féin tactically sought to distance themselves from increasing republican violence across Northern Ireland.[82]

Chapter summary

In this chapter, extracts of Sinn Féin transitional discourses have been used to illustrate the impact of the Good Friday Agreement and IRA decommissioning on the republican movement. Through the transitional discourses, Sinn Féin leaders engineered a major shift from the exclusive goal of traditional Irish republicanism to a more inclusive message of reconciliation, renewal and reform in Northern Ireland. The republican movement was persuaded to embrace constitutional politics and accept that armed struggle was no longer a route to a united Ireland. The prize of a democratic mandate to govern in Northern Ireland was clearly a political goal for Sinn Féin leaders and their transitional discourses were used to help republicans come to terms with the reality that the IRA volunteers were no longer required.

Transitional discourses emerged in two phases and those developed prior to the Good Friday Agreement helped to hold the republican movement together by presenting political strategies as a new phase of the republican struggle. After the Good Friday Agreement the reality of the terms that republicans had signed up to became a major source of tension within the republican movement. The act of decommissioning was a step too far and an exodus of republicans resulted in new radical groups, both political and armed, forming in protest. Transitional discourses shifted slightly after decommissioning, with a greater emphasis on conflict resolution and establishing structures and processes that would bring peace and unity to Northern Ireland. The engagement of Sinn Féin with policing in Northern Ireland was the final straw for some radical groups who became increasingly militant.

Sinn Féin warrior talk continued to appear at republican gatherings, rituals and commemorations, largely to signal loyalty with the Irish republican cause. For some republicans, this appropriation of a sacred tradition of honouring republican heroism and sacrifice was a sign of complete hypocrisy on the part of the provisional leadership. In addition, there was a subtle rise in the use of terms such as 'dissidents' and 'spoilers' appearing in the media which applied a collective label to a wider spectrum of republicans, which included academics, political activists, ex-prisoners, current prisoners and hunger strikers.

A summary of radical republicanism has revealed that not all groups are armed, and this makes Sinn Féin's demonization of other republicans appear counterproductive within their bigger picture for Irish republicanism. It is difficult to envisage how Sinn Féin can achieve their transformational vision for Northern Ireland or the republican goal of a united Ireland when their warrior talk serves as reminder of conflict and violence. The continued presence of Sinn Féin warrior talk in speeches remains a paradox, especially in the constitutional world that they now inhabit. A return to armed struggle that involves Sinn Féin would be political suicide. However, the continued existence of radical groups is a reminder that provisional republicanism has failed to secure a united Ireland. The operational activity of armed republican groups is both a threat to Sinn Féin's political aspirations and now a daily reminder that Northern Ireland is not at peace.

In the next chapter, the focus will change to Sinn Féin transformational discourses to provide more understanding of the role of their warrior talk and the following question is a signpost to Chapter Eight:

> What is the role of Sinn Féin's transformational discourses in the peace process and what part do they play in republican political aspirations for Irish unity? What is the current relevance for Sinn Féin's warrior talk and their ambition to bring transformational change to Northern Ireland?

Suggested reading (chapter specific)

In this chapter, Sinn Féin's transitional discourses have been used to explore the impact of the Good Friday Agreement and IRA decommissioning on the unity of the republican movement. Irish republicanism is a complex, dynamic and evolving phenomenon and there is a vast amount of literature on the issues which arose in this chapter. The suggested readings are signposts to more detailed reading and they will enable you to focus on topics that interest you. Or help to prepare for an assignment.

Taking to the Enemy: Violent Extremism, Sacred Values and What It Means to Be Human (2010).[83] A very practical source which explains why it is possible to research violent groups without sharing their convictions. The key is to understand their origins, culture and the human drivers that shape their actions. The author covers a range of international conflicts, but his practical experiences demonstrate the common denominators of political violence and the imagined kinship it brings.

Organizational Culture (1998).[84] If you are interested in the cultural aspects of change in organizations, this book covers different models of change with practical case studies from outside politics and conflict resolution. The first edition was written in 1995 and reflects the context in which Gerry Adams and Martin McGuinness were drawing on ideas to manage ideological change within republicanism. The author has since written extensively on the subject of changing identities and power.

Ending Wars (2008)[85] is an important read, especially Chapter Four on 'Resistance to the Peace', pp. 101–125.

Identity: Contemporary Identity Politics and the Struggle for Recognition (2019).[86] This book brings an important insight into the importance of identity in political and social change. This material has significant relevance to the impact of decommissioning on republicans when their identity as warriors with a noble cause came under threat. The labels of 'dissident' and 'spoilers' represent further attacks on identity.

Beyond Confrontation (1996)[87] is important if you are interested in the notion of interdependent relationships across organizations and groups and how members learn to manage conflict. Interdependence is a mental lens where short-term self-interest is subjugated for longer-term outcomes and this concept provides some insights into transitional discourses.

The Trouble with Guns: Republican Strategy and the Provisional IRA (1998).[88] This book was also recommended in Chapter Three. There is a very good analysis of the constraints of armed struggle at a time when IRA decommissioning was an option for provisional republicans, pp. 156–200.

Endgame in Ireland (2002).[89] For a good section on the trauma for republicans on decommissioning read pp. 200–202. This book was written during the period of time after the Good Friday Agreement and before decommissioning in 2005.

Unfinished Business: The Politics of 'Dissident' Irish Republicanism (2019).[90] This book provides a detailed explanation of different radical republican groups and sheds light on the complexity of the dynamic between provisional and radical republicanism.

Good Friday: The Death of Irish Republicanism (2008)[91] delivers insights into how radical republicans view the political strategies of Sinn Féin, pp. 3–21 and 293–310, and a pragmatic conclusion that it is no longer a traditional ideology that shapes republicanism but political expediency.

A Secret History of the IRA (2002).[92] A highly informative book which gives insights into the republican relationship with republican principles and physical force.

Talking to Terrorists: How to End Armed Conflicts (2014).[93] An interesting section on how governments talk to terrorists will give you insights into why dehumanizing radical groups, armed or unarmed, is counterproductive in conflict resolution: pp. 109–134.

Language of War, Language of Peace (2015).[94] The context is the Middle East, but this book gives a clear and practical illustration of how the language of war can erode a peace process. There are good examples of parallels with the Northern Ireland peace process and Sinn Féin warrior talk

From Armed Struggle to Political Struggle (2015).[95] Chapter Six is helpful to develop your thinking on the potential threat to peace, from armed republican groups, in Northern Ireland.

Spoiling for Peace: The Threat of Dissident Republicans to the Peace in Northern Ireland (2015).[96]

The author explains why republican splits have a cyclical nature and that they reflect forms of dissention necessary to a dynamic political entity. An understanding of the differences between republicans is essential to their 'splits'. The term 'spoiler' is developed in Chapter Seven, pp. 162–183.

'The Discourse of Defence': 'Dissident' Irish Republicanism and the 'Propaganda War' (2012).[97]

This paper provides additional material on the attitude of provisional republican towards the continued activity, in Northern Ireland, of armed republican groups.

Practical study task: Greyhounds or patriots?

This task will help you to analyse further the 'greyhound trained to race' statement made by Cathal Goulding in 1969, and to understand the challenges, which currently face the Sinn Féin leadership in their political aspirations in Northern Ireland and in their aim to facilitate the creation of an independent Irish nation. The roots of the physical force tradition in Irish republicanism were introduced in Chapter Three. Chapters Four and Five mapped the journey of Sinn Féin into elected politicians in Northern Ireland and stakeholders of the peace process. To radical republicans, the provisional movement had transformed into constitutional nationalists and betrayed the republican cause. The extract below is from 2019; it is an important source of understanding the dynamics between provisional and radical republicanism.

Here are a few guidelines:

- Read the extract and check previous chapters for relevant literature sources to understand the history and current context for the New IRA statement below
- Reflect on core republican and Sinn Féin colonized discourses (see Chapter Two) and check the chapter summaries for ideas
- Now you are ready to start critically analysing the extract in more detail
- Make some notes on both your findings and learning from the exercise
- Record any themes or ideas that interest you in case you decide to write an assignment

Extract from Easter statement, 2010

'New IRA vows to continue struggle'[98]

The leadership of the Irish Republican Army extends fraternal greetings to Republican activists and to our supporters and friends at home and abroad. We salute the Volunteers of the Irish Republican Army and applaud their discipline, determination and continuing steadfast commitment to the cause for which those we commemorate have given their lives. We also send solidarity to our imprisoned comrades and their families.

On this anniversary of the 1916 Easter Rising, we especially remember our patriot dead. We commemorate the freedom fighters of all generations who gave their lives for Irish Freedom.

Responsibility for the ongoing conflict rests firmly on the shoulders of the British Government. While the British occupation persists particularly those who implement its policies via Stormont, the Irish people are denied their right to national self-determination and sovereignty. Faced with this reality we remain committed to bringing the British government's undemocratic rule of the occupied part of our country to an end.

Notes

1. Patterson, H. (1997). *The Politics of Illusion: A Political History of the IRA*, London: Serif, p. 150.
2. *Irish News round-up* 2 July 1999. This is a good example of transitional discourse because it acknowledges the past but focusses on a political future. In this statement, Sinn Féin claimed the effectiveness of their inclusive politics and closed down the space for armed struggle. In this example, their transitional discourses were respectful of the IRA but presented a wholly political vision of the future.
3. See endnote 41 in Chapter Five. Senator George Mitchell made some clear rules for entry into peace talks.
4. In the Good Friday Agreement, the principle of consent stated that partition could not be ended without the consent of the majority from the people of Northern Ireland. Republican critics of Sinn Féin argued this gave unionists a veto to block Irish unity.
5. Patterson, H. (1997). *The Politics of Illusion: A Political History of the IRA*, London: Serif, p. 15.
6. Official Irish Republican Army (OIRA) emerged in 1969 with a mission to remove Northern Ireland from the United Kingdom and create a workers' republic across the whole island. Their political stance acknowledged that Ireland could not be unified until Protestants and Catholics in the North were at peace.
7. See Chapter Three and Four for sections on the 'Blanket protest' and republican hunger strikes.
8. McGuinness, M. (2016). *Irish Republican News*, 26 May 2016.
9. Stages Theory was a key ideological position for 'Official' republicans who wanted to remove the sectarian politics between unionists and nationalists that existed across the whole of Ireland. They saw the issues as a class struggle between a united working class against unjust government and a ruling class. Sectarianism in Northern Ireland spilled over into violent clashes in Northern Ireland in the 1970s.
10. The Irish Left Archive: Provisional Sinn Féin, Éire Nua Document, January 1971.
11. See Chapter Three for more detail.
12. Provisional IRA and Provisional Sinn Féin were labelled 'dissidents' because of their armed response to sectarian violence and British military presence.
13. Kelley, K. (1990). *The Longest War*, London: Zed Books, p. 89.

14. Adams, G. (1976). *The Long War*, Dublin: Sinn Féin press, p. 3.
15. Adams, G. (1976). *Republican News*, 1 May 1976, p. 5. This was in response to questions about the relationship between Sinn Féin and the IRA.
16. 80th Ard Fheis report, 4 November 1984.
17. *Ibid.*
18. During the period 1988–1994, the British government imposed a broadcasting ban on Sinn Féin leaders. It was lifted two weeks after an IRA cessation, on 31 August 1994.
19. A reflection from a republican about the use of '*phase of struggle*' to explain changes in republican strategy. Unnamed republican source, interviewed by the author, September 2001.
20. Talks were initially between John Hume, leader of SDLP, and Gerry Adams, Sinn Féin.
21. 82nd Ard Fheis report, *An Phoblacht*, 1986, p. 9.
22. Martin McGuinness, *An Phoblacht*, 23 April 1998. He went on to say the republican movement had undergone the political education of a lifetime within a four/five year time period.
23. McLaughlin, M. (1998). *Belfast Telegraph*, 18 April 1998.
24. McIntyre, A. (2008). *Good Friday: The Death of Irish Republicanism*, New York: Ausubo Press.
25. 'Charter for Justice and Peace in Northern Ireland' (1995) Belfast and Dublin: Sinn Féin, pp. 1–3.
26. *Scenario for Peace*, 1 May 1987, a discussion paper, published by Sinn Féin. <www.sinnfein.ie> accessed July 2019.
27. Balogun, J., and Hope Hailey, V. (2008). *Exploring Strategic Change*, Harlow: Pearson, third edition.
    This is a seminal text and a good introduction to change management.
28. Adams, G. (1998). Presidential Address, *An Phoblacht*, 18 April 1998. This is a colonization from a change model known as a Force Field Analysis, introduced by Kurt Lewin in 1938; it became more well known in the 1990s and currently still widely used in strategic planning.
29. Adams, G. *Belfast Telegraph*, 13 May 1998, P.13.
30. Adams, G. *Irish News*, 19 May 1998.
31. An early example of '*another front*' appeared during the 1981 republican hunger strikes. Sinn Féin sought to legitimate the action of republican prisoners as part of the armed struggle. Later the term was used to persuade republicans to accept an amendment on abstention and IRA decommissioning.
32. IRA cessation, *Republican News*, 31 August 1994. This was welcome news in the USA.
33. McIntyre, A. (2008). *Good Friday: The Death of Irish Republicanism*, New York: Ausubo Press, p. 75.

34. Adams, G. A speech to the republican movement, *Irish Republican News*, 29 September 2003.
35. Adams, G. (2000). Full speech reported in *Republican News*, 1 August 2000.
36. Adams, G. (2001). *Irish Republican News*, 24 October 2001.
37. Ward, C. *Irish People*, 15 February 2001.
38. P. O'Neil, Flash statement, 18:45 hours, 23 October 2001. Standard signature in an IRA statement.
39. Provisional IRA statement to signal the stand down, *Irish Republican News*, 28 July 2005.
40. Adams, A. (2005). A speech to Sinn Féin leaders and elected representatives, Mullaghbawn, South Armagh, reported in *Irish Republican News*, 23 September 2005.
41. The Good Friday Agreement was a framework document with very little operational detail. It is a good example of constructive ambiguity designed to encourage to dialogue between different political stakeholders. In practice, the talks on decommissioning, policing, prisoners and a variety of contentious issues was lengthy and brutal.
42. Adams, G. (2000). *Irish Republican News*, 24 January 2000, p. 1.
43. '*Welcome to the Unfinished Revolution*' is taken from a speech by Brian Kenna, Saoradh chairperson at their Ard Fheis, 2019.
44. A Catholic priest, Father Martin Magill, gave a public lecture to the politicians sitting in the front rows at Lyra McKee's funeral and this included British and Irish Prime ministers. Within forty-eight hours, talks were resumed to restore devolved powers to Stormont.
45. John Mooney, interview with New IRA, *Sunday Times*, 28 April 2019.
46. 'Normalization' is a term used to challenge the political strategies of Sinn Féin because it appears that republicans condone Stormont policies which effectively 'normalize' the state of Northern Ireland. Some radical groups want to disrupt this process to show the world that the conditions that caused the conflict still exist.
47. Under the terms of the Good Friday Agreement, Northern Ireland was still part of UK. The intervention of the British government was deemed at '*arms length*'. In practice, the power-sharing model has created tensions between the main parties, Democratic Unionist Party and Sinn Féin with the result that direct rule from London has been imposed.
48. In the Northern Ireland Assembly elections held in 2017 unionists lost their majority for the first time since 1921. On 8 February 2020 Sinn Féin won an unprecedented number of seats (37) in a General Election in the Irish Republic, vying with Fianna Fail (38) and Fine Gael (35). Sinn Féin are arguably moving towards a democratic mandate for Irish Unity.
49. John Mooney, interview with New IRA, *Sunday Times*, 28 April 2019.
50. Adams, G. (1976). *The Long War*, Dublin: Sinn Féin press, p. 3.

51. Army Council Statement, *An Phoblacht*, 17 November 1972. The Army Council is the ruling body of the IRA.
52. This is covered in more detail in Chapter Four, where the political development of Sinn Féin is mapped, 1969–2019.
53. Cathleen Knowles McGuirk, Vice president, Republican Sinn Féin, *Republican News*, 6 September 2001 <http://freespeech.org/republicansf/boden00.htm>, accessed January 2020.
54. McGuinness, M. (2008). Irish *Republican News*, 6 May 2008.
55. Republican Sinn Féin election vote that reduced the power of the DUP, March 2017.
56. Continuity IRA statement, published in *Irish Republican News*, 20 October 2000.
57. Gary Donnelly, Easter Message of the 32 County Sovereignty Movement, Irish *Republican News*, 13 March 2012.
58. Republicans refer to the '32 Counties' instead of the Irish Republic and the '6 Counties' instead of Northern Ireland. This reflects their assertion that Northern Ireland is an illegal state.
59. Republican principles are translated into procedures in a manual called the Green Book. IRA. The glossary has an explanation of the importance of this manual to IRA volunteers are trained using this book.
60. Real IRA issued a '*call to arms*' and condemned the Northern Ireland Executive, *Irish Times* 20 January 2000.
61. British and Irish governments, plus some lobbying from Senator Mitchell and the Clinton administration, brought pressure to bear on republicans and unionists to bring the negotiations to a close and produce a document.
62. Dáithí Mac an Mhaistir, *éirígí*, 1916 Commemoration speech, *Irish Republican News*, 13 March 2012.
63. Senator George Mitchell was specific in his conditions and included mention of kneecapping, which was a punishment given to alleged perpetrators of street crime and violence. The person deemed to have committed a crime was dealt with by the IRA rather than involving the RUC. This practice continues.
64. Interview with RAAD representative, *Derry Journal*, August 2009.
65. Óglaigh na hÉireann (ONH) was another armed group with affiliation to the Republican Network for Unity, a political party formed in 2007. ONH were a separate group to others using the name Irish Republican Army.
66. Flash statement, IRA Army Council, *Irish Republican News*, 26 July 2012.
67. *Irish Republican News*, 2 August 2017.
68. <http://indiamond6.ulib.iupui.edu:81/republicancountry.html and Pensive Quill blog>, <https://www.thepensivequill.com/>, accessed 29 February 2020.
69. McIntyre, A. (2019). *Belfast Telegraph*, 29 April 2019. 1974 refers to the Sunningdale Agreement which drafted proposals for a power-sharing Northern Ireland executive and a Council of Ireland. The British government would retain power over law and order and finance.

70. Gerry Adams, Presidential address, 94th Ard Fheis, 8 April 2000.
71. '*Bridgehead to peace*' is a military term used by Sinn Féin in an effort to influence IRA volunteers to comply with the Good Friday Agreement. This term was used in speeches frequently in 2005 and examples can be found in *Irish Republican News* throughout this turbulent year as the IRA prepared to decommission.
72. '*Armed for Peace*' is another example of Sinn Féin using military terms to persuade republicans to accept IRA decommissioning. It appears on multiple occasions in *Irish Republican News* during 2005.
73. *Irish Republican News*, 2 October 2005, p. 1.
74. O Muilleoir, M. *Irish Republican News*, 2005.
75. IRA statement, 16 July 2002. The language reflects Sinn Féin peace discourses and is another example of internal co-operation between the Provisional IRA and Provisional Sinn Féin.
76. Adams, G. (2011). Ard Fheis, reported by *Irish Republican News*, 10 September 2011.
77. The Northern Bank raid, a murder and an accusation that Gerry Adams and Martin McGuinness were IRA leaders were significant challenges in 2007. There are further details in Chapters Four and Five.
78. Martin McGuinness, *Irish Republican News*, 8 May 2008.
79. IRA Easter message, 2006, reported in *Irish Republican News*, 13 April 2006.
80. Martin McGuinness, Easter speech, Drumboe, County Donegal, *Irish Republican News*, 13 April 2012.
81. McGuinness, M. 'Clashing Agendas for Nationalists, 100 Years on', *Irish Republican News*, 26 March 2016.
82. Timeline of dissident republican activity, BBC NI report, 10 September 2019. Details of reported incidents in Northern Ireland involving armed republican groups from 2009 to 2019.
83. Atran, S. (2010). *Talking to the Enemy: Violent Extremism, Sacred Values and What It Means to Be Human*, London: Allen Lane, Penguin Books.
84. Brown, D. A. (1998). *Organisational Culture*, London: Financial Times Management.
85. Cochrane, F. (2008). *Ending Wars*, Cambridge: Polity Press.
86. Fukuyama, F. (2019). *Identity: Contemporary Identity Politics and the Struggle for Recognition*, London: Profile Books.
87. Haus, C. (1996). *Beyond Confrontation: Transforming World Culture*, Paris: Praeger.
88. O'Doherty, M. (1998). *The Trouble with Guns, Republican Strategy and the Provisional IRA*, Belfast: Blackstaff Press.
89. Mallie, E., and McKittrick, D. (2001). *Endgame in Ireland*, London: Hodder and Stoughton.
90. McGlinchey, M. (2019). *Unfinished Business: The Politics of Irish Republicanism*, Manchester: Manchester University Press.

91. McIntyre, A. (2008). *Good Friday: The Death of Irish Republicanism*, New York: Ausubo.
92. Moloney, E. (2002). *A Secret History of the IRA*, London: Faber.
93. Powell, J. (2014). *Talking to Terrorists: How to End Armed Conflicts*, London: Random House.
94. Shehadeh, R. (2015). *Language of War, Language of Peace*, London: Profile books.
95. Spencer, G. (2015). *From Armed Struggle to Political Struggle: Republican Tradition and Transformation in Northern Ireland*, London: Bloomsbury.
96. Whiting, S. A. (2015). *Spoiling the Peace: The Threat of Dissident Republicans to the Peace in Northern Ireland*, Manchester: Manchester University Press.
97. Whiting, S. A. (2012). 'The Discourse of Defence: "Dissident" Irish Republicanism and the Propaganda War', *Terrorism and Political Violence*, 24, no. 3, pp. 483–503.
98. Easter Statement, New IRA, *Irish Republican News*, 17 April 2020.

Chapter 7

Transformational discourses and warrior talk

Introduction

> We are on the road to freedom. If we go forward together, firmly united and in great numbers, we will complete our historic task – a united Ireland and a New Republic.[1]

A transformational vision has been a consistent feature of the Irish republican narrative for over 100 years, articulated as an independent Irish nation shaped by republican values. After the Easter Rising (1916) and subsequent partition of Ireland (1921) Irish republicans had clear goals to fight for: to remove the British government out of Northern Ireland and to end partition. Transformation meant the reunification of a nation divided by a border that republicans considered illegal and the creation of a new form of society that would address injustice and inequality. In short, republican transformational discourses are not a new phenomenon, but the manner in which Sinn Féin has developed them has changed.

Evidence from previous chapters concluded that republican core discourses, both 'historical' and 'justification',[2] were used to promote and sustain the consistency and legitimacy of the republican cause. Warrior talk was a form of language used by republican leaders to unite and focus republicans on their vision of transforming Ireland. In Northern Ireland, republican warrior talk proved to be a powerful communication tool for all republicans irrespective of their political stance on the Good Friday Agreement (1998). Provisional republicans continue to use warrior talk at key events, annual rituals and funerals.

Provisional Sinn Féin started to develop a repertoire of colonized discourses in the 1970s which, although embryonic, acted as a test bed for political strategies that would later influence the republican movement to accept ideological change.³ By the 1990s Sinn Féin's colonized discourses evolved further and indicated a political agility which enabled their leaders to move republicans towards constitutional politics in Northern Ireland. Colonized peace discourses paved the way for republicans to join all-party peace talks in Northern Ireland and colonized transitional discourses ensured the majority of the republican movement stayed united. Peace discourses had appeal with external stakeholders, especially the Irish diaspora in the US, because the language signalled that republicans wanted peace in Northern Ireland. Core discourses focused on the historic republican agenda but colonized discourses reflected a more externally driven political agenda. By the end of the 1990s the scale of responsiveness by Sinn Féin to external demands had become a contentious issue internally and the key cause of fragmentation within the republican movement.

Another form of Sinn Féin colonized discourses emerged after the Good Friday Agreement (1998) which, in this book, are termed *transformational* because they represent a fundamentally different political approach to ending partition and reuniting Ireland. Sinn Féin's transformational discourses represented a significantly different political stance and a commitment to a united Ireland but on terms that were a complete break with established republican ideology and principles.

An ongoing tension remains within Irish republicanism between a purist view of the British state and the pragmatic view, expressed by the Sinn Féin leadership, that a political route to Irish unity will involve the British state. Between these two positions is a full spectrum of political views and opinions on the ethics of constitutional politics and the efficacy of continued physical force. Sinn Féin's aspiration of a democratic mandate, on both sides of the border, commits modern republicans fully to a constitutional route and their election successes in 2017 (Northern Ireland) and 2019 (Irish Republic) proved that they could leverage their position as the only All Ireland Republican Party.⁴

The role of Sinn Féin's transformational discourses is to communicate a republican vision of a united Ireland which is achieved through political support from across different communities: unionists, nationalists and republicans. Transformational discourses frequently use the terms 'union', 'nation' and 'republic' interchangeably depending on the audience at the time. The following extract of transformational discourse communicates that partition will be ended through a democratic process and the collective will of people on both sides of the border:

> Everyone, whether nationalist or unionist, republican or loyalist, or none of these, has to have the space in which to discuss their view of the events of 100 years ago, and their consequences. But crucially, it must not be about the past. That would be a huge mistake. The conversation about partition must be about the future. About the next five years - 10 years - 100 years.[5]

Sinn Fein's use of the term 'transformation' elevates the republican vision beyond the traditional message and creates another form of moral high ground with appeal for a wider base of voters. The attraction of Sinn Féin's transformational discourses resides in the notion that people from different backgrounds might collaborate to let go of the past and create a new 'nation' together. This grand vision is tempered with a political pragmatism that has become a signature of the Sinn Féin leadership:

> Irish republicans come from a long and honourable republican and internationalist tradition, which seeks to unite Irish citizens and break the connection with England. This is Sinn Féin's starting point – a belief in a new union – a cordial union of all the people on this island.[6]

In this extract from 2012, the audience is reminded of Wolfe Tone's instructions on creating a union between *Catholic, Protestant and Dissenter*.[7] The term 'union' is used in a specific way and avoids the reality that the Good Friday Agreement gave unionists the power to veto a reunification of Ireland. The reference to Wolfe Tone is a tactic used by Gerry Adams to acknowledge the legacy of Irish republicanism and at the same time, dignify the republican vision of 'union' across Ireland. The term 'union' started to co-exist with the term 'republic' as Sinn Féin subtly adapted their transformational discourses to make republican politics more appealing to a wider electorate.

Previous chapters have focused on the role of warrior talk within the changing scenario of Sinn Féin's political development. The relationship between their transformational discourses and republican warrior talk represents the most curious paradox in Sinn Féin colonized discourses so far. Social transformation implies a systematic reconfiguration of structures, values and behaviours and represents a shift to a new paradigm of thinking. The continued use of warrior talk keeps republicans attached to past events and closes down the space for sustainable peace.

Chapter purpose

This chapter explores the emergence of Sinn Féin transformational discourses following the Good Friday Agreement and to understand their role in facilitating a political republican route to a united Ireland. The political and military strategies of radical republican groups will be explored in the context of Sinn Féin's 'transformational' agenda on both sides of the border. The ambiguity and political agility of transformational discourses will be studied to understand more fully Sinn Féin's commitment to constitutional politics.

A brief outline of theory on peace, conflict resolution and conflict transformation will be used to analyse the political purpose of Sinn Féin transformational discourses. Finally, the role of discourses such as 'dissidents' and 'terrorists' will be examined to understand a fundamental paradox facing Sinn Féin and their espoused political vision of sustainable, peaceful transformation in Northern Ireland.

Chapter structure

Emergence of Sinn Féin transformational discourses
Transitional and transformational discourses
Theory and practice:

War and peace
Conflict and violence

Approaches to conflict
Conflict resolution
Conflict transformation

Current dilemmas and Sinn Féin leadership
Dissidents or spoilers?
What is the purpose of Sinn Féin Transformational discourses?

International credibility
Constitutional politics
Community agenda
Appropriation of republican heroes

Sinn Féin and their transformation

Chapter summary
Suggested reading (chapter specific)
Practical study task 1: Assignment writing
Practical study task 2: My experience of warrior talk

Emergence of Sinn Féin transformational discourses

> In recent times other political parties have begun to accept that the logic of the republican position is popular with many of the plain people of this island.[8]

Transformational discourses are a reflection of a complex political agenda for Sinn Féin, which includes an aspiration to take a lead in government both sides of the border and finally facilitate Irish unity. Sinn Féin's historic allegiance to the goal of Irish unity continues to shape their political ambitions but their approach is now fully constitutional. Transformational discourses developed further after the provisional IRA decommissioned their weapons in 2005. In that year, Gerry Adams published a new book, *The New Ireland: A Vision for the Future*,[9] which set out his vision for the future direction of Irish republicanism. This extract is from a speech at the book launch:

> If Irish republicanism is to be relevant to modern Ireland, it needs to be defined and redefined. Beyond the Agreement, which is essentially an accommodation, Irish republicanism has a new vision of a new society, a New Ireland that is democratic.[10]

The term 'accommodation' is interesting because it appears to present the republican role in the Good Friday Agreement as a positive step and a modernization of republicanism. The final decommissioning of Provisional IRA (2005) represented much more than a political accommodation for republicans but a major ideological change. The act of decommissioning had practical, emotional and psychological implications, and impacted a diverse group of people including republican politicians, activists, veterans, volunteers and families. A long history of republican armed struggle for Irish unity had commanded loyalty from several generations, within families, and now the IRA were being asked to stand down and destroy weapons before the withdrawal of the British state. It was for many republicans a deep psychological shock.[11]

Sinn Féin leadership was temporarily freed from their relationship with republican violence but this was later replaced by the emergence of new armed radical republican groups. Sinn Féin's relationship with violence in the past coupled with the continued presence of armed republicans in Northern Ireland potentially trapped them in a political vacuum of 'no going back' but equally an indistinct vision of the future.

Transformational discourses after 2005 provided an additional form of communication that brought a more focused message about how the transformation of society in Northern Ireland could be achieved through both structural changes and conflict reconciliation processes. Through their transformational discourse, Sinn Féin leadership revealed a longer-term political vision for the future, which included a new society in Northern Ireland as the precursor to a united Irish nation:

> Imagine an end to the divisions
> Imagine a new agreed Ireland
> Imagine the unity of Orange and Green
> Imagine a fair society
> Our vision is based on equality.[12]

While republican power-sharing with unionists in the Northern Ireland Assembly was communicated by Sinn Féin as a win for democracy, the continued existence of Northern Ireland was an injury some republicans could not tolerate. Sinn Féin's response was to build a stronger inclusive message within their transformational discourses to influence both republican and unionist communities. An economic argument also appeared which challenged the logic of a division between two small states:

> The fact is that we live on a small island. It is too small for us to stand alone and aloof from each other. Our destiny is intertwined. Our freedoms are inextricably bound up together.[13]

Transformational discourses were also used to communicate a moral imperative for everyone to embrace change including republicans, nationalists and unionists, British and Irish governments. The notion of transforming societies became a powerful moral high ground that had the potential to elevate the republican cause beyond historic grievances. On closer examination, however, Sinn Féin appeared to use their transformational discourses interchangeably to mean a united society in Northern Ireland and a united Irish nation. Even the term 'nation' rather than 'republic' started to appear more frequently and a signal that Sinn Féin were directing their attention externally on the strategies and relationships that would bring them a democratic mandate to push for the ending of partition.

A major issue for Sinn Féin's transformational discourses is that they were by nature ambiguous with language that created the space for multiple interpretations, as illustrated by this statement in 2005:

> Let us join with other parties and share our vision of a New Ireland. Let us ask them to walk with us; to work with us; to move forward with us toward the republican and democratic goals of unity, freedom and equality. Anyone who wants to win a struggle has to have a dream. The dream that things can be different.[14]

This statement also illustrates that transformational discourses offer hope and especially, in times of conflict, chaos and crisis. A vision that a crisis can be transformed into positive change in the future is an attractive political prospect and appeals to human values. In the context of Northern Ireland, Sinn Féin transformational discourses appeared as a device to counter criticisms of their political strategies before and after the Good Friday agreement and IRA decommissioning. A good example is the discourse of *New Republic*,[15] which acknowledged the historic republican goal of reunification but on closer inspection, revealed that the primary Sinn Féin goal was actually social reform in Northern Ireland.

Community politics now dominated Sinn Féin's political strategies and the goal of a united Ireland was quietly moved to second place. The extract below illustrates how the term 'New Republic' emerged as a bridge between Sinn Féin's republican legacy and their future ambitions:

> The key to building a new republic, democratically shaped by the people is to start now. All of us who believe in a just society, in a real republic; we need to make our beliefs relevant to more and more people. We need to be about empowerment. Struggles aren't won by single actions. Or by iconic leaders. Though they have a role. They are won by people, taking individual actions, which accumulate into irreversible change.[16]

A 'New Republic' as conceived by Sinn Féin, could be interpreted as smart political rhetoric to persuade other republicans to support the transformation of Northern Ireland as a means to advance the republican goal. In 2002, Gerry Adams made a remark to Sinn Féin elected representatives that the party wanted to *lead the next government*.[17] At the time, it appeared a clear vision but now begs the question as to which government: Northern Ireland, a 'New Republic' or a 'New Nation'. Transformational discourses are by nature an ambiguous phenomenon leaving space for political 'wriggle' room. The following statement, delivered at a time of significant internal opposition to the Sinn Féin leadership, represents an interesting shift in tone:

Defining republicanism today means redefining our republicanism for today's Ireland. Those who established Sinn Féin, 100 years ago; those who fought on the streets of this city in 1916 and later the might of the British Empire; and those who raised the flag of resistance in each subsequent generation, did so in circumstances that differed and changed as the years rolled by. This is not 1905, this is 2005.[18]

Prior to the Good Friday Agreement, Sinn Féin transitional discourses had been key to persuading republicans to accept that Northern Ireland would continue to exist until a majority of the electorate gave consent. Transitional discourses reduced a seismic ideological change to a final historic journey towards Irish unity. The journey had a number of stages and republicans were asked to be patient and trust that a republic was achievable through political means. Transformational discourses went further and provided a vision of Irish unity through political means but contained a new message that implied Irish republicanism would also need to change.

Transitional and transformational discourses

Transitional and transformational discourses had a different purpose but were used to complement each other and focus on the future unlike core discourses with their attachment to the past. Transitional discourses communicated a goal and a series of practical steps to achieve that goal. Transformational discourses created an aspiration rather than a clearly defined set of stages. Both forms of discourse promoted a political and peaceful route to a united Ireland.

The interplay between transitional and transformational discourses enabled Sinn Féin leadership to retain a moral high ground for the republican cause and remain the dominant voice of the republican movement. From 1998, the use of Sinn Féin transitional and transformational discourses was prolific and frequently signalled a strategic change to the republican movement. These discourses were multipurpose and promoted

Sinn Féin's role part in changing the political landscape of Northern Ireland.

The crucial difference between transition and transformation can be likened to building a bridge across a river. During a transition, the bridge is a solid structure to ensure everyone crosses safely. Traditional models of change are frequently linear and characterized by phases, stages and steps, which can be measured and evaluated. A transformation is characterized by a whole system change and this includes structures and stakeholders. The bridge is no longer needed because the world has changed and an alternative method of transporting people has been invented, or indeed the reason for crossing the river is now defunct.

It is unsurprising that republican opponents of Sinn Féin might view their transformational rhetoric as a cynical political ruse to disguise the constitutional route being taken:

> Sinn Féin will not be deflected from the historic work we are engaged in. We are nation builders. We have set ourselves high standards. We are the engine driving historical, political, social and constitutional change on this island. We need a mighty movement across this land to reach our goal of freedom and unity.[19]

This study of Sinn Fein's transformational discourses would be incomplete without reference to some definitions of war, peace, conflict and violence. The notion of transforming a conflict has emerged from a number of disciplines and includes both theory and practice from social and political sciences. In addition, there is considerable overlap between peace and conflict studies with the field of organizational development. The scale of macro conflicts across the world is in plain sight. At a micro level, conflict in work environments may not have reached a state of war but the dynamics follow similar patterns but are less visible.

Theory and practice: Conflict transformation and sustainable peace

This brief outline of theory from peace and conflict studies will include:

- *War and peace*
- *Conflict and violence*
- *Approaches to conflict*
- *Conflict resolution*
- *Conflict transformation*

War and peace

A war is generally defined as a state of armed conflict between groups.[20] It could be argued that this definition makes the republican claim of war with the British state a valid description, given the Easter Rising (1916) when both parties were armed. This is an important distinction because the notion of a legitimate war has shaped republican discourses to the present day. The term 'war' instantly polarizes opponents into good or evil and influences external perceptions of the situation. The polarizing effect of the language of war with terms such as 'the enemy' heightens emotional reactions. The result is polarization, which reduces complex histories, political dynamics and human experiences to a simplistic duality of 'self' and 'other'. The process of splitting is a psychological projection, which can take place between individuals, groups and nations.

The splitting process is open to further distortion when the label of 'enemy' is applied because it invokes images of threat, stories of violence and the language of war. A good example is the Irish republican attachment to their noble war. The leaders of the Easter Rising were executed for treason by the British government. From an Irish republican perspective, this was a struggle for freedom from British rule in the form of an armed insurrection and radical protests. For Irish republicans, the executions reframed their armed insurrection into war and were instrumental in sustaining their warrior talk, as a political default position, for the next 100 years.

The terms conflict and war are used interchangeably in accounts of the Northern Ireland 'Troubles' but there is a key difference in the way republicans and unionists use language to account for violence. Republican history is one of war with the British and this account is sustained through the heroic stories and warrior talk. Other stakeholders, including unionists, nationalists and the British government, generally refer to the 'Troubles' as a conflict. This distinction reveals a lot about how republicans view their armed struggle and sheds some light on their rituals of commemoration.

Schmockler (1988)[21] argues that warrior talk perpetuates an image of a warrior elite and the language is characterized by a passionate certainty. Warrior stories frequently represent a world where the warrior is of higher status and uses their courage to prevent the victimization of others. This explanation is important to understanding the ethos of the IRA and their internal military discipline as mandated in their Green Book.[22] Warrior talk confers an identity and dignity for republican volunteers, which protects them from the criminalization narratives used by their opponents.

Galtung (1996)[23] made a significant contribution to the definition of peace, which previously had been presented as an absence of war. Galtung introduced the concept of 'negative peace', which meant stopping the violence, and 'positive peace' which addressed the root causes of the conflict through practical systematic changes. Stable positive peace is therefore more than a peace treaty: it is a collective will between all parties to change and operate differently. In practice, this means structural relationships within and between groups need to change to allow new behaviours and attitudes to develop. An example is the Good Friday Agreement (1998) which initiated a new model of power sharing. It ensured republicans had a constitutional role in a new Northern Ireland Assembly but also required a shift in attitude from leaders Martin McGuinness (Sinn Féin) and Ian Paisley (Democratic Unionist Party) to model positive peace in the Northern Ireland Assembly.[24]

A peace process is not a single event such as the signing of a treaty. Peace making and peace building are processes whereby antagonists come to trust each other enough to create new structures and adopt new attitudes. Trust

Transformational discourses and warrior talk 185

not only involves politicians and designated negotiators but grass roots and communities who have been impacted by violence. In Chapter Five, the practical study task, 'Maskey lays a wreath', is a practical example of positive peace building in 2002, four years after the Good Friday Agreement.

Conflict and violence

In addition to his contribution to peace studies, Galtung (1996)[25] differentiated between different forms of violence. He pointed out that violence did not necessarily manifest as armed conflict or war. This means that violence is not simply a physical act but a complex chemistry of diverse human needs, interests and behaviours which can result in acts of non-physical violence as well as the more obvious physical violence. Galtung's model is another useful tool to analyse the role of warrior talk in different settings:

- Direct violence: killing, maiming, rape
- Structural violence: repressive regimes, injustice, disenfranchisement, exploitation
- Cultural violence: religious beliefs and language to deny or debase the values or identity of another or justify structural violence
- Behavioural violence: domestic abuse, coercion and bullying

The language of conflict and the language of war frequently cross over irrespective of the context. A violent dispute between neighbours over land could mean critical access to water or it could be about a minor issue over parking. The escalation to direct physical violence is not always predictable and rarely proportionate to the situation.

The causes of a conflict might be a combination of a number of factors including historic grievances, denial of human needs, power struggles and incompatibility of stakeholder's interests. The sudden shift of a conflict situation into violent confrontation is generally when the subjective aspect of an existing conflict starts to escalate. In 1969, in Northern Ireland, the civil rights movement was created to redress structural inequalities. Political and social injustice for Catholic communities contributed to the conditions for conflict but it was the subjective, human responses that turned a latent conflict into a violent confrontation. The alignment of the structural, social and human aspects of conflict is vital to a sustainable peace process but politicians are rarely able to achieve this when faced with competing and complex agendas.

Current conceptual models of conflict have been influenced by ideas from social theory and the notion that relationships within a conflict are generally based on the power dynamic between individuals and groups. A power relationship that is, or appears to be, asymmetric has the potential for civil unrest and violent protest. Jabri[26] argues that conflict is a social phenomenon and a product of societies and the politics that establishes their identities. Identity politics is a modern political phenomenon where group identity is a primary driver to address inequality and (re-)establish a symmetrical power dynamic. Identification with a group is a powerful human instinct and a humiliated group seeking a restitution of its dignity can be a powerful force. The emotional volume increases when a disadvantaged or disempowered group starts to protest. Concepts such as *identity* and *identity politics*[27] are a significant avenue in the study of human conflict and provide another explanation for why and how warrior talk emerges. Rational discussion about the structural conditions experienced by disadvantaged group is frequently overtaken by a human propensity for conflict and violence as competing identities defend their positions.[28]

In the 1970s in Northern Ireland the time frame between peaceful protest, sectarian clashes and British military intervention was very short. To the outside world, it appeared to be a sudden descent into community violence, which masked the structural inequality between different communities across Northern Ireland.

Approaches to conflict

The range of approaches to conflict may appear complex but this is a reflection of a conceptual development which is drawn from a range of ideas from organizational behaviour, social and political sciences. The theory of peace and conflict studies is also informed by good practice developed by those working in the field in conflicts. The result is a practical framework show below:

- Conflict prevention, where actions are taken to prevent escalation into violence
- Conflict settlement, a negotiating process to end violent behaviour and reach a peace agreement
- Conflict resolution, involving addressing the root causes of the conflict and seeking new and lasting relationships with opposing groups
- Conflict transformation, addressing the wider social and political context of the conflict and bringing positive social and political change

Each of these approaches can be initiated independently or combined as part of a long-term strategy depending on the scale of the conflict and level of violence involved. In practice, the political positions and interests of opposing parties dominate peace processes and the momentum may stall as past grievances trap stakeholders into a historical dynamic. This makes trust-building very challenging and negotiations tend to get bogged down with procedural issues and power relationships rather than addressing the causes of the conflict.

Conflict resolution

The field of conflict resolution has also emerged from a number of sources ranging from a behavioural approach (Lewin, 1948)[29] to the notion of mutual gain from theories of negotiation (Fisher and Ury, 1981).[30] This early work was a precursor to the practice of problem-solving as a route out of a conflict (Burton, 1990)[31] that argues that the denial of human needs was the ultimate source of all conflicts. Human needs range from access to basic needs such as water, food and physical safety to sociological and psychological needs for respect and dignity. Burton's contribution to conflict resolution encouraged a multi-disciplinary approach to conflict resolution and this resulted in a practical approach which is used today.

The notion of addressing conflict over scarcity of resources and control over resources remains significant because it involves an ostensibly objective approach, and the results of conflict resolution are measurable. Funders of governmental agencies and charitable organizations engaged in conflict resolution and peace building have stakeholders with targets and evidence-based performance measures. This power dynamic tends to favour a problem-solving approach.

Burton's approach introduced the role of a third party into the conflict resolution. In theory, a third party brings a 'neutral' position to the negotiations. In practice, it is very difficult for a third party to be completely neutral irrespective of professional skill or the size of the negotiating team.[32] However, a third party can be an advantage especially when tensions exist between the conflicting parties. A subtle disadvantage is that a third party quickly becomes an authority figure and key stakeholders (whether present or represented) are effectively disempowered. This has implications for peace building and how the original causes of the conflict are systematically addressed.

In the context of Northern Ireland, a practical example is the Mitchell peace talks which were well-chaired and allowed unionists, republicans and nationalist to have a voice. The outcome of third-party intervention resulted in a framework treaty which is still in place, but it did not resolve the human issues between unionists and republicans. In practice, the negotiations were in the hands of a political elite who focused on historic positions and demands. Despite the high-profile nature of the negotiations and the political rhetoric emerging, it is clear that historical positions both shaped and stalled peace talks. A sustainable conflict resolution lay in the nature of future relationships between unionist, nationalist and republican communities.

The work of Keashly and Fisher (1990)[33] brought a sharper focus on the human aspects of conflict resolution. They reasoned that conflict is a highly subjective social process centred on the interests of different groups. In practice, a subjective approach to conflict resolution starts from the basis of interests rather than positions. By establishing a common ground in interests, negotiations start from a positive note, which encourages the sharing needs and problem-solving.[34] When negotiations start with stakeholder positions, the process can become sidetracked, as positions entrench and this is frequently manifested in protracted discussions on the protocols of the negotiation rather than the substantive content.[35]

A variation on a subjective perspective to conflict resolution was introduced by Lederach (1995)[36] who believed a new approach was needed to ensure a bottom up process which empowered grass roots and communities.[37] Lederach's work challenged the established conflict resolution mantra of achieving 'common ground' because it represented a process of trading within confines of the status quo (interests, needs and positions) rather than creating a new paradigm for the future. Lederach used his own experience of development work to promote a new perspective, which acknowledged that grassroots and communities possessed the human and cultural resources essential to transforming attitudes and behaviours post-conflict.

Finally, Jabri (1996) was also critical of conflict resolution approaches because she believed that the notion of resolution was flawed if the outcomes did not fully address the social conditions that lead to conflict.[38] The benefit of Jabri's approach is that it transcended the objective/subjective debate within the field of conflict resolution and promoted a more transformational approach.

Conflict transformation

The field of conflict transformation shares similar roots with theories of transformational change and transformational leadership.[39] The notion of a transformation in a conflict scenario emerged in response to criticisms of conflict resolution, which tended to polarize human experiences as objective or subjective. In reality, human beings operate within complex political and social systems and the application of binary conflict models may limit a comprehensive analysis. By contrast, conflict transformation is an integrative approach, which balances both objective and subjective aspects of the conflict with its root causes and power dynamics.

Haus (1996) provided a practical definition of transformation when he talked about the paradigm shifts which occur when people start to question the principles of the previous paradigm. The evidence for a transformational change is clear because there is no voluntary or active return to an old paradigm unless coercion is used. Coercion may manifest as direct violence from stakeholders who do not agree with the terms of peace, or more subtle indirect forms, to induce compliance. A basic linguistic indicator of a transformation is people start to define themselves as 'we'. This process from 'I' to 'we' may start as political rhetoric, which inevitably fails unless there is a paradigm shift of thinking matched by actions and behaviours.[40] Haus's views on interdependence and empowerment offered a more flexible and sustainable approach to sustaining peace. In practical terms, this means a shift away from a purely militaristic view of national and community security to one of collaboration on social, economic and environmental issues.

Systems theory, and specifically the work of Checkland (1981),[41] made an important contribution to the practical understanding of conflict transformation. Interdependence across parts of a larger system, combined with collaborative behaviours and language, improves the quality of relationships across the whole system. Instead of resisting change, people learn to adapt and become better able to handle challenges as they occur. Transformation frequently occurs when a social or political system comes into crisis and adjustments are made to systematically address a range of causes. Adjustments might include a reconfiguration of structures, processes and rules but a transformation also requires change to assumptions, attitudes and behaviours. Frequently, the political stakeholders who negotiate a peace treaty focus on structural and power issues, for example, what is the new form of governance and what are the rules of engagement. From the outset, some peace processes are not destined to become a conflict transformation or a sustainable outcome for all parties.

Conflict transformation is about creating a new paradigm not a reworking of old fault lines: that is a very challenging prospect for both republicans and unionists in Northern Ireland. With a long history of division, asymmetrical power dynamics and sectarian violence, a societal transformation is not simply about addressing injustice but a major shift in deeply embedded attitudes. Attitudes and behaviours are shaped by language and Jabri's work on war discourses is highly relevant to the study of conflict transformation.[42] War discourses have provided Irish republicanism with ideological continuity for over a century. If we apply Jabri's logic, then language institutionalizes war from one generation to the next by reinforcing old identities. By contrast, transformational change requires an acceptance of new identities and the possibility of peaceful co-existence of multiple identities.

Current dilemmas and Sinn Féin leadership

> I am an Irish republican. Make no mistake about it – I will always remember and commemorate our patriot dead – each of our fallen comrades who gave their lives for Irish freedom.[43]

A major dilemma for Sinn Féin is an inability to fully let go of their military past. The remark above from Michelle O'Neil,[44] current Deputy First Minister at Stormont, is very interesting example of the political challenges that arise with an aspiration for transformational change. At the time of her remark, Michelle O'Neil was asked if there was a contradiction in Sinn Féin's outreach programme with unionist communities and her attendance at a commemoration for IRA volunteers. Her response was very important because it illustrated a key dilemma for Sinn Féin going forward. The reference to 'fallen comrades' was a mark of respect but equally a source of unease for those who do not believe that republicans have renounced their armed struggle. This example of the commemorative role of republican warrior talk represents a powerful tradition but it also brings media attention back to republican violence.

The continued presence of armed republican groups contributes to a sense of unease for communities across Northern Ireland and there is evidence that the reputational risk of further violence is highly probable.[45] In the context of Sinn Fein's aspirations to transform society in Northern Ireland, as a precursor to Irish unity, the use of warrior talk appears counterproductive.

The political environment for provisional republicanism is potentially more complex than at any time since their formation in 1969. While Sinn Féin can claim political success in the removal of a unionist majority from the Northern Ireland Assembly in 2017, the outcome cannot be described as transformational. Republican political gains further polarize their relationships with unionists, making the business of power-sharing more fractious and the Northern Ireland Assembly more vulnerable to the imposition of direct rule.[46] In the following extract there is an interesting use of both examples of both transformational and transitional discourses to sustain the republican moral high ground and reach out to a wider nationalist voting community:

> The Assembly election presents all of us with a new opportunity to do things differently. I believe absolutely that Irish unity is the best outcome for the people of this island. There is a need to co-operate with other progressives to create real changes in people's lives based on everyone's right to equality. This has to be our overarching strategy in the time ahead. That means we need a discourse on how we manage the transition from where we are now to an end to partition.[47]

This example of transformational discourse from the Sinn Féin leadership portrayed exciting visions of the future that masked the scale of compromises they had made during the peace talks. The current Sinn Féin leader, Michelle O'Neil, has picked up a complicated legacy between political strategies that trap republicans into a system still dominated by the British government and the military activity of radical republicans: this takes Irish republicanism back to an old pattern of internal splits.

The journey of Sinn Féin to their current position in mainstream politics has been enabled by discursive strategies that both signal change and mask reality. The existential problem for Sinn Féin and their future political strategies lies in their continued use of warrior talk. The following extract, from 2019, is an interesting insight into how Sinn Féin currently formulate the republican priorities:

> After many years of struggle, we have created the basis for peaceful and democratic means to pursue our goal of National Self-Determination. No one can seriously deny that change has been delivered and that the Orange state of 1969 no longer exists. We have new battles to fight in the context of Brexit.[48]

The current role of Sinn Féin warrior talk and their transformational discourses can be more fully understood through the lens of radical republicanism. The repugnance of radical groups to the terms of the Good

Friday Agreement and IRA decommissioning is expressed clearly in their warrior talk:

> We believe the fundamental source of conflict in Ireland remains the violation of Irish Sovereignty through the occupation of the six counties. As such all our actions, positions and future endeavours are underpinned by the reality of the occupation.[49]

In this context, transformational discourses pose problems for the consistency of the republican message because they counter the traditional historical narrative that runs through Irish republicanism. Sinn Féin transformational discourses may provide a powerful vision of the future and win votes but their transformational rhetoric does not reflect the inner working of the republican movement. A transformation is a paradigm shift, which involves all stakeholders and implies that no one gets left behind or is excluded. Sinn Féin successfully secured a place in the peace process and now have a growing political mandate for Irish unity but appear to be unable to stabilize the internal dynamics of the republican movement.

In the aftermath of decommissioning and the subsequent rise in radical republican groups there was a changing tone to the message from Sinn Féin leaders to other republicans. The transitional language used to persuade the republican movement to support a constitutional route to Irish unity appeared to recede and replaced with a new form of 'dissident' discourse. This was a very important development which not only fixes the dynamics of the republican movement into a predictable cycle of military/ political splits, but it undermines Sinn Féin's political aspiration to achieve a major transformation into one Irish nation.

Dissidents or spoilers?

> When assembled at the gravesides of 'fallen comrades' around Ireland, radical republicans are listening to the same message, at the same gravesides, as they did as members of the Provisional Movement of the 1970s and 1980s.[50]

This comment is a profound observation (2019) because despite the transformational rhetoric from Sinn Fein, the reality is that provisional republicans have chosen a constitutional route and accepted that the British state will continue to intervene and that this involvement will continue for an indeterminate time period.

In the previous chapter, the phenomenon of republican splits in Northern Ireland was presented as a timeline starting in 1969 when provisional republicans split from the dominant 'official' republican organization. It is clear that transitional and transformational discourses were used by the Sinn Féin leadership as a tactic to preserve unity in the republican movement. However, given the number of radical republican groups currently operating in Northern Ireland, transitional discourses have been only moderately successful. An added complication for Sinn Féin is that their transformational discourses signal a future political agenda for that is even further away from the traditional republican ideology. The transformation to one Irish nation is a vision that is not necessarily shared by people who regard themselves as British.

During the decade after decommissioning, the discourses of '*dissident*', '*peace wrecker*', and '*terrorist*' emerged from Sinn Féin leaders to account for the activities of radical republican groups.[51] These labels were used to alienate, marginalize and later demonize opponents of provisional republicanism. An insight into this behaviour can be drawn from peace studies where the term 'spoiler' is used to describe the resistance of individuals or groups opposed to a negotiated peace settlement.[52]

Spoiler groups disagree with political compromise, especially one agreed by politicians, elites and third parties. Spoilers are an important part of a conflict because they are signalling a gap between political rhetoric and the reality. The rhetoric of a 'negotiated settlement', with promises to address the root causes of the conflict, may partially resolve the issues but the asymmetrical nature of the conflict frequently remains. The response from spoiler groups is to revert back to traditional methods, radical action and armed struggle to get their message heard.[53] The statement below from a republican group called 'Saordadh' illuminates a radical response to police raids on their community offices:

> What the state does today on Irish Republicans, it will not hesitate to use tomorrow on the rest of society. You may not share our opinion, you may be diametrically opposed to it, as is your right, but you must understand, the denial of our rights today will be the denial of your rights tomorrow.[54]

For transformational change to be achieved and sustained, it is essential that the views of spoiler groups be acknowledged and understood. This does not mean that violence is condoned. The danger is that if spoiler groups get left behind or marginalized, the dynamics of the conflict remain fixed and polarized. The language of dissidents, terrorists and peace wreckers immediately labels an individual or group as enemies of a peace and contributes to a flawed assumption that 'anti peace' means 'pro war'. This statement from Martin McGuinness in 2016 illustrates the point:

> The tiny number of people out there who are committed to violence, their strategy is really about trying to divide Sinn Féin from our unionist government. The best antidote for the activities of these people is for us to stick together and for the community to support the police services both north and south.[55]

This is a very interesting example of polarizing language because it retains a triangular dynamic between provisional republicans, unionist government and radical republicans. A new republican enemy has been created out of a diverse grouping known as radical republicanism. This may be a political tactic to help Sinn Féin to distance from republican violence but it is unlikely to transform the internal dynamics of the republican movement.

Sinn Féin have made significant progress in their inclusive agenda with unionists and managed to keep republicans centre stage and credible in the peace process. They appear less successful within the republican movement. Dissident discourses represent another, more subtle form of Sinn Féin warrior talk which is directed at other republicans and a potential flaw in their strategy of transforming society in Northern Ireland.

What is the purpose of Sinn Féin transformational discourses?

All forms of Sinn Féin discourses serve a political purpose – to secure a united Ireland – and over time this has included the republican legacy, their justification for armed struggle and later a pragmatic rationale for constitutional politics. The labels applied to Irish republicanism such as provisional, radical or official are reflections of fierce internal debates about the means to achieve the republican goal. Despite their principle of legitimate physical force, Irish republicanism is fundamentally a political project based on the notion that a unification of Ireland will address the inequalities and injustice created the partition of 1921.

In Northern Ireland, from 1969 onwards, republican discourses changed as provisional Sinn Féin became more politically active and ambitious. Colonized discourses emerged to steer republicans towards a more pragmatic approach to Irish unity and to promote a republican commitment to peace in Northern Ireland. This chapter has been focused on Sinn Féin transformational discourses and considered their purpose in the context of conflict resolution and transformation. At the time of writing, the Sinn Féin leadership faces political opposition from vocal republican opponents and the added complication of republican armed groups still operating in Northern Ireland. This complexity has created a number of issues for the future, challenging their transformational rhetoric.

International credibility

Sinn Féin has significant international networks with leaders and peacemakers in other conflicts, and both political and financial support from Irish America. Sinn Féin's peace and transformational discourses have helped them to create a positive image outside Northern Ireland. Since the Good Friday Agreement, Gerry Adams and Martin McGuinness have been viewed as experienced strategists and politicians by a number of external stakeholders to the peace process, including members of the British government.[56] External stakeholders may be political allies, funders or powerful leaders and they all have expectations of how their resources are being used.[57]

Transformational discourses focus on the future and imply a whole system change to address the issues of the past. Transformation means learning to be different and learning to collaborate to create a new society. The language is highly emotive, motivational but short on detail. The psychological contract between voters and political leaders is rooted in a temporary bond of trust that election promises will be met. Provisional republicans are faced with a harsh reality that, despite their hard work in establishing the Good Friday Agreement (1998), there are no immediate signs of a British withdrawal.

Politicians across the world understand the need for constructive ambiguity or 'wriggle room' and have their own form of transformational discourses to persuade others to follow them. It appears that the message of transformation is an appeal to both external stakeholders and republican grass roots with a sustained message that Sinn Féin has not abandoned the republican goal.

Constitutional politics

In Northern Ireland, Sinn Féin has used their transformational discourses to win votes and persuade a growing base of nationalists to support a republican agenda. The vision of transforming communities in Northern Ireland is a powerful moral high ground but it needs the power of an electoral mandate, on both sides of the border, to drive political change. The irony is that Sinn Féin's commitment to constitutional politics has taken them away from republican principles and opened up the space for radical republican groups to operate. Some radical republican groups not only disagree with Sinn Féin strategies but also refute the power of the provisional leadership to represent the republican cause in Northern Ireland. The tension for Sinn Féin between their republican past and their commitment to a constitutional future is not easily resolved. This tension is revealed in speeches where core and colonized discourses are used interchangeably to appeal to a diverse spectrum of republican views.

Sinn Féin leaders are reaching a tipping point where their constitutional position in Northern Ireland is so well developed that it makes their use of core discourses appear disingenuous. The fiery warrior talk of the 1970s and 1980s is a complete antithesis to the political rhetoric of peace and transformation. The internal dynamics of the republican movement are complex and rarely on display but Sinn Féin's response to radical republicans raises important issues for the future.

Currently, Sinn Féin uses 'dissident' discourses to distance them from republican violence in Northern Ireland. This could be viewed as a political tactic to protect the external reputation of provisional republicanism.

However, the existence of radical republicanism is a clear sign that Sinn Féin has not won full support or respect for their strategies. The term 'dissident' has a polarizing effect and when is used to marginalize opponents it can quickly become highly emotive creating the toxic conditions for further conflict. This form of coercion and control of dissenting groups is a leadership option, but it is risks further internal division and disrupts the Sinn Féin vision of political transformation to an Irish nation. In practical terms, the reputational damage for Sinn Féin of being linked to IRA activity could have a serious impact on their polling results, in both Northern Ireland and the Irish Republic.

Community agenda

In the 1970s, provisional republicans (Sinn Féin and IRA) prided themselves on their relationship with republican and nationalist communities. The IRA operated as a defence force in the face of sectarian violence and the interventions of the British Army. A second and highly significant role was republican community policing, at a time when the Royal Ulster Constabulary was seen as a unionist organization and not to be trusted. In parallel, Sinn Féin was gaining ground by building their political strategies, skills and infrastructure for what was to become a successful republican political party.

In 2007, Sinn Féin joined the Northern Ireland Policing Board. In the context of conflict resolution and transformation, this was an extension of power-sharing and meant republicans were in a position to influence the reform of policing across Northern Ireland. This resulted in both structural and cultural reforms designed to support the peace process, but it had serious consequences for the republican movement. The idea of republicans on a policing board was highly contentious internally and impacted the credibility of the provisional leadership. Sinn Féin remain on the policing board but have, to a large extent, lost control of their communities to armed groups such as Continuity IRA, the New IRA and Republican Action Against Drugs. This creates a perception that Sinn Féin are distant from their grassroots and now part of a political elite. Their current political rhetoric of societal transformation is at odds with the scale of republican violence in Belfast and Derry. From a traditional republican perspective, Sinn Féin is seen as operating within a security system that maintains the state of Northern Ireland. In retrospect, a structural change in policing in Northern Ireland was initiated with good intentions but failed to deliver the level of attitudinal and behavioural change needed to support a transformational change in the way all communities in Northern Ireland are policed.

Appropriation of republican heroes

Sinn Féin has an ongoing attachment to republican warrior talk. In previous chapters, extracts of discourse have been cited from the 1970s, 1980s and 1990s to illustrate the republican stance on the commemoration of republican heroism and loyal service. Despite the peace process and signing of the Good Friday Agreement, Sinn Féin have continued to use their warrior talk at annual conferences, Easter speeches and funeral orations.[58] It could be argued that this demonstrates a respectful tradition and is a benign gesture. However, the political context has changed dramatically and Sinn Fein's stated agenda for transformational change appears hollow when compared with their warrior talk.

Today, warrior talk represents a traumatic past not a glorious revolution. The Good Friday Agreement left unionists and the British government still in control of Northern Ireland. Warrior talk conjures up a relentless, endless and harsh narrative of republican struggle. The memorials for dead heroes appear less heroic and more tragic. The republican struggle to transform Irish society has not been achieved and yet it has extracted a heavy price. For some republicans, commemoration is a sacred act not a political tool:

> Bobby did not die for cross-border bodies with executive powers. He did not die for nationalists to be equal British citizens within the Northern Ireland state.[59]

Sinn Féin have been challenged internally over their appropriation of the life and death of Bobby Sands in political speeches. In the 1980s, Sinn Féin used the deaths of ten republican hunger strikers to make political progress with both republican and nationalist communities.⁶⁰ These events proved to be a tipping point for provisional republicans, which eventually took them into mainstream politics. The continued references to Bobby Sands by Sinn Féin is seen by some republicans as an insult:

> Bobby is undoubtedly recognized as a great icon whose sacrifice had a profound effect on the political landscape of Ireland. However, to me it is heartbreaking that those who would idolize him as the epitome of the republican struggle, including those who were amongst his closest personal friends and comrades, would use his sacrifice to justify the current Sinn Féin strategy. It is a distortion of what he and the hunger strikers died for.⁶¹

This statement reveals an important challenge for Sinn Féin in the future. The decision to move away from armed struggle and adopt a constitutional route to Irish unity has taken Sinn Féin away from their radical politics and republican roots. Republicans are now faced with the practical reality that Sinn Féin could win an electoral mandate on both sides of the border and use the principle of consent to force a referendum on Irish unity. Constitutional politics have enabled republicans to change some aspects of the political system in Northern Ireland from within rather than fighting it. This has left provisional Sinn Féin with a complicated relationship both with their past and with their republican opponents.

Sinn Féin and their transformation

> I see no contradictions to Sinn Féin's outreach to unionists while simultaneously commemorating IRA volunteers, republicans are proud of our freedom fighters.⁶²

This response from the current Sinn Féin leader in Northern Ireland provides an insight into the philosophical dilemmas ahead for republicans. Their electoral successes both sides of the border indicate that they have growing political support for a united Ireland and proven success at working in governments in Belfast and Dublin. Radical republicanism poses a threat but none of the political groups have a democratic mandate and the scale of operations conducted by armed groups is small and localized compared to that of the Provisional IRA in the 1970s and 1990s.[63]

Sinn Féin, as a mainstream political party, is in a strong political position because their vision of a united Ireland through political means is becoming more tangible. Sinn Féin is also part also of a wider community of republicans across Ireland which shares a powerful legacy, and this differentiates them from their political rivals. Warrior talk has served an important purpose to unite republicans and sustain a strong sense of identity. In the period from 1969 to 1998, warrior talk allowed Sinn Féin to develop their political strategies but continue to demonstrate their solidarity with the republican armed struggle.

Their early colonized discourses were used subtly to introduce a changing perspective on the traditional republican relationship with the British. The Good Friday Agreement signalled a major shift in provisional republicanism towards a constitutional route to a united Ireland. Between 1999 and 2019, Sinn Féin's colonized discourses developed further and their political rhetoric now communicates that social reform and peace in Northern Ireland is their immediate priority.

Provisional republicans are now embedded in mainstream politics and their transformation from radical activists to constitutional politicians is complete. Warrior talk provides Sinn Féin with a familiar narrative to retain their republican identity, but it masks the reality that they have chosen to distance from traditional republican ideology and the republican principles of abstention and physical force.

Sinn Féin's use of warrior talk presents an issue for their credibility as leaders of transformational change and sustainable peace.

Chapter summary

In this chapter, the emergence of Sinn Féin's transformational discourses after the Good Friday Agreement was explored in order to understand more fully the role of warrior talk within their repertoire of political discourses. The entry of Sinn Féin politicians to the Northern Ireland Assembly was a pivotal moment in republican history because it represented a greater affiliation with mainstream politics and a significant shift from traditional republican ideology and principles. Transformational discourses appear to have multiple roles and reveal a balancing act for Sinn Féin leaders in their communications with both internal and external stakeholders. The visionary nature of transformational discourses was undoubtedly a strategy to win votes and secure political support from the grassroots across different communities in Northern Ireland. Sinn Féin political strategies became more inclusive and started to include unionists as potential voters. Sinn Féin recognized that the principle of consent could be used as a political opportunity if a democratic mandate could be achieved in both Northern Ireland and the Irish Republic.

Transformational discourses presented a positive future state, which included justice, freedom and equality for all citizens. Political visions are invariably light on operational detail but Sinn Féin had the advantage of serving in government in Northern Ireland and the Irish Republic. However, Sinn Féin transformational discourses have had limited success with radical internal opponents because they imply a transformation of Northern Ireland as a primary goal. For radical republicans, the continued existence of Northern Ireland is a manifestation of the power of unionists and the British government to block the unification of Ireland. In addition, evidence from the discourses of radical republicans reveals a deeply suspicious response to Sinn Féin's attempt to influence them.

An outline of models of war, conflict and has been provided to further explore the Northern Ireland peace process and the importance of distinguishing the causes of the conflict and the level of violence involved. The emergence of conflict resolution and conflict transformation, as approaches to war and conflict, were mapped to gain a deeper appreciation of the future challenges facing Sinn Féin. This has reinforced the view that warrior talk represents a disconnect between Sinn Féin's transformational discourses and their current position on radical republicans.

A pressing problem for Sinn Féin is their relationship with radical republicanism and its diverse groups, activities and members. In this chapter, 'dissident' discourses have been examined to understand the political implications for Sinn Féin's transformational agenda in Northern Ireland. Literature on 'spoilers' in a peace process has been used to assess the reputational risk to Sinn Féin of marginalizing other republicans. There is a strong argument that 'spoiler groups' are an important 'check and balance' to a sustainable peace process. If political groupings that are opposed to the status quo, as determined by politicians, are then demeaned and humiliated, the conditions for conflict transformation are undermined. In this context the probability of violence, whether direct or indirect, increases. It appears that warrior talk has a role in creating and sustaining the conditions for further conflict.

Suggested reading (chapter specific)

The focus of this chapter has been transformation discourses and their role in facilitating political and social change. The suggested readings in this chapter are a sample of key material on conflict resolution and conflict transformation. Further material can be found in the bibliography. Additional material on 'spoilers' and 'identity' can be found in Chapter Six.

If your interest is conflict within organizations then you will find material on transitional and transformational approaches in Chapter Six.
Tools for Transformation: A Personal Study (1990).[64] This is an excellent introduction to theory and practice in mediation as an approach to a conflict settlement. Adam Curle was an early researcher, practitioner and advocate in the field of conflict resolution that has expanded rapidly to include organizational conflicts.
Guns, Germs and Steel (1997).[65] This is an interesting book that will enhance your understanding of human identity and the common origin of our different histories. The notion of a global culture rather than conflicting national identities is good introduction to the importance of conflict transformation.
Identity: Contemporary Identity Politics and the Struggle for Recognition (2019).[66]

This book was recommended in Chapter Six and is relevant for this chapter on transformational discourses and warrior talk, in particular the material on human dignity in the transformation of conflict. The responses of a humiliated group carry significant emotional weight and a source of grievance that has the potential to keep escalating conflict conditions into violence and war. In Northern Ireland, the decommissioning of the provisional IRA was perceived to be a humiliation by some republicans and the reaction was to regroup and form new armed groups. The conflict transformation did not factor in the power of identity.

Global Politics in the Human Interest (1991).[67] This author proposed new perspectives on international interdependence and the possibility of peace across the world. This view calls for a transformation of attitudes and fundamental change in national and international structures. The context for this book is important when radical systems change was taking place across the world, such as the reunification of Germany and the ending of apartheid in South Africa.

Beyond Confrontation: Transforming the New World Order (1996).[68] This book has been cited in previous chapters and it essential to an understanding of global conflict and peace. The author was an early advocate of a global strategy for transforming ideas on peace and introduced the importance of interdependence between nation states.

Contemporary Conflict Resolution: The Prevention, Management and Transformation of Deadly Conflicts (1999).[69] This is an excellent resource, which gives a comprehensive view of theory and practice.

Handbook of Conflict Resolution: The Analytical Problem-Solving Approach (1996).[70]

This is a practical book that gives a good insight into how the problem-solving approach works in a conflict situation. This approach continues to be popular, but it is important to study later work on conflict transformation in order to appreciate how this field is evolving.

Practical study tasks

In this section there is an option to work through Task 1, which is designed for students and their tutors, or Task 2, which is a review of *Are we at war with Covid?*. From Chapter One. Task 1 is more structured towards an academic essay or assignment. Task 2 is a personal development task to help you apply your learning from this book to your own life.

Task 1: Assignment writing (students and their tutors)

This is an opportunity to research and write about a topic or issue that is relevant to your current situation or personal interest. The major themes of this book are:

- *Researching political discourses*
- *Transformational change*
- *Northern Ireland peace process*
- *Irish republicanism*
- *Conflict resolution*
- *Warrior talk*

If you are engaged in a programme of study that is accredited, then you may be expected to write essays or assignments. Educational programmes use different forms of assessment but, generally, essays can be quite flexible and you may have a choice on your essay topic, while assignments generally have a specific question and an outline structure for you to follow. Before you start, check the specific requirements with your lecturer or supervisor.

Here are a few typical assignment questions:

- *Discuss the relative importance of positive versus negative peace. Which is easier to define and why? Which is easier to achieve in practice and why?*
- *There is a striking contrast between a desire for peace and the recurring reality of violence. Discuss this paradox using a specific conflict that you are familiar with.*

- *What are the differences between conflict resolution and conflict transformation? Illustrate with a short case study from an international conflict. Which approach to conflict is more likely to deliver positive peace?*
- *Investigate the concept of 'peace spoilers' and illustrate with reference to a specific conflict. Notice how opponents of a peace treaty or peace talks were managed and state the outcomes.*
- *Choose a political speech from a politician and conduct an analysis of the discourses embedded in the speech. Prepare by checking the context in which the speech was made and the speaker's audience. Then explore how transformational discourses are being used to influence the audience.*

Task 2: My experience of warrior talk

In Chapter One, the exercise *Are we at war with Covid?* was designed to help you to become more aware of the role of warrior talk in your everyday life.

Review your notes from Chapter One and read the conceptual material, in this chapter, on peace and conflict. Consider the impact of warrior talk on your current thinking and personal experiences.

- *Where is warrior talk having a positive influence in your life?*
- *What are the benefits of warrior talk in a crisis?*
- *How have you used warrior talk in the past?*
- *What are your feelings about warrior talk now?*
- *Where does your warrior talk come from?*

In the next and final chapter, conclusions will be presented on the relevance of Sinn Féin's warrior talk to their political aspirations and the future of the republican project in Northern Ireland. The learning from the case study of the Northern Ireland peace process will be applied to the relationship between warrior talk, conflict and peace in other settings.

Notes

1. McGuinness, M. (2012). Easter Speech, *Irish Republican News*, 13 April 2012. The term 'New Republic' was a recurring feature of Sinn Féin transformational discourses especially after 2005 but notice the powerful link with the past.
2. See Chapter Two 'Decoding political discourse' for an explanation of how the terms 'core' and 'colonized' discourses are used throughout the book.
3. The principle of abstentionism and the principle of physical force are fundamental to the Irish republican cause. See Chapters Three and Four for a more detailed explanation.
4. Fianna Fáil, initially a republican party, split from Sinn Féin in 1926. The name means 'Warriors' or 'Soldiers of Destiny' and they are currently in a coalition government in the Irish Republic. Fianna Fáil was registered and recognized in Northern Ireland in 2007 and has a similar nationalist stance to the SDLP.
5. Adams, G. (2020). 'Partition Sucks. It Doesn't Merit Celebration', *Irish Republican News*, 4 September 2020.
6. Adams, (2012). Easter speech, *Irish Republican News*, 13 April 2012.
7. Wolfe Tone's proclamation, 1798. Wolfe Tone advocated a non-sectarian society that welcomed religious, social and political diversity. His influence on Irish republicanism is commemorated annually and his ideas resurfaced in Sinn Féin's transformational discourses post 2005.
8. Adams, G. (2002). Keynote speech to party conference, reported in *Irish Republican News*, 23 March 2002.
9. Adams, G. (2005). *The New Ireland: A Vision for the Future*, Dublin: Brandon Books.
10. The term 'agreement' refers to the Good Friday Agreement, 1998.
11. The terms of the Good Friday Agreement included permanent ceasefires and decommissioning by all parties to the agreement. Negotiations over decommissioning were protracted (1999–2005) with significant pressure on republicans to decommission first.
12. Adams, G. (2013). Speech to the Ard Fheis, *Irish Republican News*, 14 April 2013.
13. Adams, G. (2009). Extra-ordinary meeting of the republican Ard Chomhairle, Dublin, reported in *Irish News* 25 November 2009.
14. Adams, G. (2005). Speech to mark the 100th anniversary of Sinn Fein, Mansion House, Dublin, 5 May 2005.
15. Gerry Adams, Ard Fheis speech, reported in the *Irish Republican News*, 6 March 2010.
16. *Ibid*.
17. Adams, G. (2002). Elected representatives' conference, Monaghan, reported in *Irish Republican News*, 26 October 2002.
18. Adams, G. (2005). Address to a 100-year celebration, Dublin, Irish *Republican News*, 24 September 2005.

19. Gerry Adams, Easter speech, Bandon, County Cork, *Irish Republican News*, 13 April 2012.
20. Galtung, J. (1996). *Peace by Peaceful Means: Peace and Conflict, Development and Civilization*, London: Sage.
21. Schmookler, A. B. (1988). *Out of Weakness: Healing the Wounds that Drive Us to War*, Toronto: Bantam Books.
22. The IRA Green Book is a military manual using for training with regulations on the conduct of volunteers.
23. Galtung, J. (1996). *Peace and Peaceful Means: Peace and Conflict, Development and Civilizations*, London: Sage.
24. This nickname 'Chuckle brothers' was used to describe the working relationship of Ian Paisley and Martin McGuinness as First and Second Minister in the Northern Ireland government.
25. Galtung, J. (1996). *Peace and Peaceful Means: Peace and Conflict, Development and Civilizations*, London: Sage.
26. Jabri, V. (1996). *Discourses on Violence: Conflict Analysis Reconsidered*, Manchester: Manchester University Press.
27. The practical application of 'identity politics' in the context of provisional republicanism is explored in Bean, K. (2008). *The New Politics of Sinn Féin*, Liverpool: Liverpool University Press, pp. 138–173.
28. An example is the 'Black Lives Matter' movement, which started on social media in 2013, engaged in demonstrations in Missouri, 2014, and by 2016 had thirty local chapters across the USA. The death of George Floyd in 2020 brought international attention and political protests in major cities across the world. In the USA, activists became involved in violent clashes with right wing groups and state police. The escalation from legitimate protest to direct violence in 2020 was rapid.
29. Lewin, K., and Lewin, G. W. (eds) (1948). *Resolving Social Conflicts: Selected Papers on Group Dynamics (1935–1946)*, New York: Harper and Brothers.
30. Fisher, R., and Ury, W. (1981). *Getting to Yes: Negotiating Agreement without Giving In*, New York: Penguin.
31. Burton, J. (1990). *Conflict: Human Needs Theory*, London: Macmillan.
32. A team approach (however small) helps to avoid a conscious or unconscious bias and can reassure the participants that their third party is following instructions from one group.
33. Fisher, R. J., and Keashly, L. (1991). 'The Potential Complementarity of Mediation and Consultation within a Contingency Model of Third Party Intervention', *The Journal of Peace Research*, 28, no. 1.
34. Fisher, R. J., and Ury, W. (1981). *Getting to Yes: Negotiating Agreement without Giving In*, New York: Penguin.
35. Mitchell, G. (1999). *Making Peace*, London: Random House. This is worth reading for an insider's view of the early talks and tactics used by unionist politicians to stop

Sinn Féin from joining the peace process. The Mitchell Principles requested all paramilitary violence to end before talks. Republicans argued that loyalist (Protestant) paramilitaries continued to engage in sectarian attacks in Catholic communities. Unionist politicians distanced themselves from loyalist activity.
36. Lederach, J. P. (1997). *Building Peace: Sustainable Reconciliation in Divided Societies*, Washington DC: United States Institute of Peace Press.
37. This represented an important change in conflict theory, which had been largely paternal and conducted between political/military elites. Transformational change requires a shift of thinking towards grassroots and their role in conflict resolution and post conflict peace building.
38. In Chapter Four, there is more information of the failure of the Police Service of Northern Ireland to meet the recruitment requirements recommended by the Patten Report and which included 50 per cent Protestants and 50 per cent Catholics. This is an example of a structural change that was not supported by measures to change attitudes to policing in Northern Ireland. The previous police organization (Royal Ulster Constabulary) was viewed as an armed wing of unionism.
39. Tony Blair's New Labour discourses were dominated by terms such as 'transformational change' and 'transformational leadership'. In organizations, 'transactional' equated to management systems and procedures whereas 'transformational' became a new way to describe a visionary leadership style.
40. See Chapter Five for a description of collaborative discussions between Sinn Féin and SDLP, in the 1980s and 1990s which laid the ground for the Downing Street Declaration of 1993 and the Northern Ireland peace process.
41. Checkland, P. (1981). *Systems Thinking, Systems Practice*, London: Wiley. This is an early work by the author on Soft Systems methodology and is worth reading.
42. Jabri, V. (1996). *Discourses on Violence: Conflict Analysis Reconsidered*, Manchester: Manchester University Press.
43. McGlinchey, M. (2019). *Unfinished Business: The Politics of 'Dissident' Irish Republicanism*, Manchester: Manchester University Press, p. 37.
44. Michelle O'Neil succeeded Martin McGuinness in 2017.
45. Examples from 2019 include pipe bombs in Derry and Belfast, letter bombs in London, Glasgow, Heathrow and City airports, mortar bombs found in County Down, and attacks on vehicles owned by police officers in County Fermanagh and County Armagh. New IRA claimed responsibility for some of the attacks through a code sent to the *Irish News*.
46. The British government still has the power to impose Direct Rule from Westminster and have done so five times since the Good Friday Agreement.
47. Gerry Adams, *Irish Republican News*, 9 March 2017. The term 'progressives' refers to other political parties considered warm to the idea of Irish unity. This links back to the pan national work of Gerry Adams and John Hume of the SDLP in the 1980s,

when republicans realized that they could not achieve their goals without political support.
48. This is a statement made by Sinn Fein MP, Elisha McCallion, 13 August 1969, to commemorate the Battle of the Bogside.
49. Donnelly, G. (2012). Easter statement from the 32 County Sovereignty Movement, *Irish Republican News*, 13 April 2012.
50. McGlinchey, M. (2019). *Unfinished Business: The Politics of Irish Republicanism*, Manchester: Manchester University Press, p. 2.
51. See Chapter Six: these terms were used to label individual republicans with no affiliation to radical political groups or new-armed groups.
52. Stedman, S. J. (1997). 'Spoiler Problems in Peace Processes', *International* Security, 22, no. 2, pp. 5–53.
53. *Ibid.*
54. *Irish Republican News*, 21 August 2020.
55. McGuinness, M. (2016). *Irish Republican News*, 26 March 2016.
56. Jonathan Powell, a negotiator for the British government in 1997, and Tony Blair, the Prime Minister at the time, were complimentary about the calibre of leadership and courage demonstrated by the two Sinn Féin leaders. See Powell, J. (2014). *Talking to Terrorists: How to End Armed Conflicts*, London: Vintage, pp. 179–180.
57. The term 'resources' includes finance, access to power and media coverage.
58. The Sinn Féin leader in Northern Ireland, Michelle O'Neil, expressed 'regret' at a press conference on 10 September 2020 for attending a republican funeral during COVID restrictions. The funeral was for Bobby Storey and senior members of Sinn Féin, including Gerry Adams, walked in the funeral procession. This is a traditional republican expression of respect and part of Irish republican culture. There was significant backlash in the media and Michelle O'Neil expressed regret but did not apologize.
59. McGlinchey, M. (2019). *Unfinished Business: The Politics of 'Dissident Irish Republicanism*, Manchester: Manchester University Press, p. 3. This remark was made by Bobby Sands' sister, Bernadette Sands-McKevitt, a founder member of the 32 County Sovereignty Movement.
60. There are more detailed accounts of republican hunger strikes in Chapters Three, Four and Five.
61. O Fiach, S. (2017). *Irish Republican News*, 30 September 2017.
62. McAleese, D. (2017). *Irish News*, 1 May 2017. Report of an interview with Michelle O'Neill, current leader of Sinn Féin.
63. 'Bloody Friday', 21 July 1972, was an IRA operation when 19 bombs went off in Belfast. Currently, it is unlikely that current republican armed groups have the capacity for this scale of violence however localized violence and community-policing activities, from armed radical republican groups is on the rise.

64. Curle, A. (1990). *Tools for International Conflict: A Personal Study*, London: Hawthorne Press.
65. Diamond, J. (1997). *Guns, Germs and Steel: A Short History of Everybody for the Last 13,000 Years*, London: Jonathan Cape.
66. Fukuyama, F. (2019). *Identity: Contemporary Identity Politics and the Struggle for Recognition*, London: Profile Books.
67. Gurtov, M. (1991). *Global Politics in the Human Interest*, Boulder: Lynne Rienner.
68. Hauss, C. (1996). *Beyond Confrontation: Transforming the New World Order*, Santa Barbara: Praeger Publishing.
69. Miall, H., Ramsbottom, O., and Woodhouse, T. (1999). *Contemporary Conflict Resolution: The Prevention, Management and Transformation of Deadly Conflicts*, Cambridge: Polity Press.
70. Mitchell, C., and Banks, M. (1996). *Handbook of Conflict Resolution: The Analytical Problem-Solving Approach*, London: Pinter.

Chapter 8

Warrior talk and peace

Introduction

> Language is both a site and a stake in the class struggle – those who exercise power through language must be constantly involved in a struggle with others to defend it.¹

The purpose of this book has been to raise awareness of the potency of warrior talk and the forms it takes in political discourses. Warrior talk is not necessarily a product of war: the insights from the study of political discourses demonstrate that combative language is used as a communication tool in a broad spectrum of conflict situations from international and national conflicts to power struggles in organizations and groups. Conflict in any form requires a psychological investment in shaping each party's assumptions of the other, and the manifestation of this process can be observed in the language used to account for the dynamics of the situation.

Warrior talk appears to have a role in reducing a conflict situation to extreme positions and facilitating a transition to direct violence, or indeed to indirect violence and coercion.² The discourse findings from each chapter revealed a number of forms of warrior talk embedded in Sinn Féin's political discourses and which emerged in response to changing circumstances. Over the time period covered in the research study, 1969–2019, warrior talk evolved to serve multiple purposes which largely included the political strategies of Sinn Féin, their relationship with external stakeholders and the republican movement.

The Northern Ireland peace process was selected as a background to this study of warrior talk because of the abundance of discourse material to work with and the potential for an extended timeframe of fifty years. The research approach was an analysis of republican discourses spanning the 'Troubles' in Northern Ireland, the peace process and significant political change within the republican movement. A comparative study of discourses from other stakeholders in the Northern Ireland peace process was considered but realistically was not feasible for this book: other authors are welcome to follow up those intriguing possibilities. The selected case study also provided a practical context for an exploration of warrior talk in relation to conflict resolution and peace building.

An additional outcome from the research was a realization of the scale of appropriation of warrior talk in other settings: this provided an insight into how deeply embedded warrior talk is in our everyday lives. This chapter will close with a commentary on this 'taken for granted' phenomenon. In Chapter 1, the practical study task 'Are we at war with Covid?' illustrated the use of warrior talk in the context of a global pandemic and drew attention to the language of war used in a crisis. Governments frequently declare war on a spectrum of human conditions such as viruses, cancer, drugs and poverty. In a global or national crisis, warrior talk can become a predictable tactic to inspire the 'best' and, if necessary, police the 'worst' of human behaviour. The language of combat when used out of the context of war and direct violence reduces complex social, economic and political issues to binary choices. It may be appropriate to inspire people to have a 'fighting spirit' but what is the psychological cost of losing a 'battle' with a disease? The exercise on Covid-19 introduced the role of warrior talk outside a traditional conception of war and this kind of usage will be examined further, later in this chapter.

In Chapter 2, a detailed explanation of the research methodology was outlined and a conceptual model of discourse analysis introduced. This was followed, in Chapter 3, with an outline of the history and roots of Irish republicanism and the impact on republican warrior talk. The legacy of Irish republicanism provided a backstory for the detailed study of Sinn Féin's core and colonized discourses in later chapters. Chapter 4 charted the journey of Sinn Féin from radical activists to mainstream politics and the emergence of colonized discourses. Chapter 5 mapped Sinn Féin peace discourses and the subsequent republican involvement in the peace process in Northern Ireland. Chapters 6 and 7 introduced Sinn Féin's transitional and transformational discourses and significant evidence of their political trajectory towards constitutional politics in Northern Ireland. It was concluded that colonized discourses allowed Sinn Féin to navigate a complex range of expectations from internal and external stakeholders. Although they continued to communicate with core republican discourses, the development of colonized discourses signalled changes in political strategies that would, over time, impact the traditional republican relationship with the British state.

Chapter purpose

The primary purpose of this concluding chapter is to summarize the outcomes of the case study and to comment on the relevance of Sinn Féin's warrior talk to their political aspirations and the future of the republican project. A secondary purpose is reflecting on the practical implications of warrior talk for conflict resolution and peace building in other settings, which involve organizations, groups or individuals.

This chapter has a number of interrelated objectives:

- To consolidate the findings from all chapters and critically reflect on challenges facing Sinn Féin in Northern Ireland
- To comment on Sinn Féin's relationship with warrior talk and the political implications of its presence in their political discourses
- To compare the different forms of warrior talk employed by Sinn Féin and specifically their use of 'dissident discourses'
- To analyse the role of warrior talk in the context of conflict resolution and conflict transformation
- To reflect on the forms of warrior talk and their relevance to modern societies and the social and political interactions of their members

Chapter structure

Research approach and questions
  Summary of research findings
  Warrior talk and core discourses

Warrior talk and peace discourses
Warrior talk and transitional discourses
Warrior talk and transformational discourses

Reflections on the case study
Warrior talk and other forms of conflict

Warrior talk and polarization
Warrior talk and sacred values
Warrior talk and identity politics

Final reflections

Research approach and questions

The research study took a chronological approach to Sinn Féin core and colonized discourses from 1969 to 2019. Each chapter followed this timeline to allow for a comparison of the different forms of discourse production during key events in the 1970s, 1980s and 1990s. The Good Friday Agreement (1998) was as used as critical period in the republican movement.

The findings from each chapter resulted in a number of further questions which were used as an additional form of scrutiny of the discourse findings and forms of warrior talk. These questions were addressed, and the outcomes will be summarized in this chapter:

- What were the roots of Irish republicanism and how did their warrior talk sustain and legitimize the republican legacy?
- How did the provisional movement of the 1970s develop into a constitutional political power and what were the consequences for the republican movement?
- How did Sinn Féin become political champions of the Northern Ireland peace process and what was the role of warrior talk in their journey from war to peace?

- What was the impact on the republican movement of Sinn Féin's peace strategy in Northern Ireland and how were colonized discourses used to manage republican through the ideological change that the peace process brought?
- What was the role of Sinn Féin's transitional and transformational discourses and what part do they play in republican political aspirations for Irish unity?
- What is the current relevance for Sinn Féin's warrior talk and their ambition to bring transformational change to Northern Ireland?

Summary of research findings

The model of core and colonized discourses, introduced in Chapter Two, facilitated a comparative study between early republican core discourses and the later proliferation of Sinn Féin colonized discourses. Core discourses, focused on the republican identity, were used to maintain consistency and continuity for the Irish republican goal of a united Ireland. These discourses evoked the republican legacy and were used to justify radical action in the quest for Irish independence. Republicans were able to argue that their cause was as legitimate as any other country attempting to remove the British colonial system. During the 'Troubles' in Northern Ireland, core discourses were used to justify their armed struggle as a radical strategy and aligned to the republican principle of physical force. Warrior talk had a role as a linguistic tool, which communicated heroic stories and rallying calls to republican supporters and volunteers.

Colonized discourses included ideas and language from sources outside Irish republicanism. These forms of discourse emerged at different times in response to changing political opportunities and threats. For example, in the 1980s colonized discourses included themes such as transition and change and indicated a shift towards the Sinn Féin peace strategy. The research revealed that new colonized discourses were frequently used to test out proposals for strategic change that were likely to impact republican ideology. Sinn Féin proposals were debated across the local republican groups (Cumann) and at length during the republican annual conference (Ard Fheis). A clear pattern emerged from the discourse findings where colonized discourses started as a 'testing the water' exercise before evolving into political strategies. In their relationship with the republican movement, the Sinn Féin leadership was careful to deliver their message through core discourses and warrior talk.

The research illustrated that Sinn Féin continued to use core republican discourses during the peace process and in spite of their entry into mainstream politics in Northern Ireland. It could be argued that their use of warrior talk was a tactic designed to sustain their relevance to the republican movement. Certainly, the co-existence of war and peace discourses appeared to be more prevalent at times when the Sinn Féin political strategies were being robustly challenged internally. An example of this is the long saga of external talks and internal debates prior to the decision on IRA decommissioning taken in 2005.

The ability of the Sinn Féin leadership to flex between core and colonized discourses emerged in the 1970s, a period when they communicated through republican justification discourses. Justification for the republican cause allowed Sinn Féin to align themselves with those engaged in the armed struggle but at the same time present themselves as a purely political party. Since the 1970s Sinn Féin leaders have mastered the art of moving between different forms of discourse to influence both internal and external stakeholders. What could be regarded as a well-honed political skillset is seen by some as duplicitous.[3]

Radical republican discourses following the Good Friday Agreement (1998) revealed a significant level of frustration and anger at Sinn Féin's use of core republican discourses. The appropriation by Sinn Féin of republican hunger strikes in 1981 is seen, by some republicans, as politically and morally offensive. At the time of writing, Sinn Féin speeches at commemorations, special events and annual conferences follow a familiar pattern. Warrior talk and core discourses open and close their speeches with powerful references to the republican cause, while the main substance of each speech uses the forms of political and colonized discourses you would expect from mainstream politicians. This contrast between the language of their republican roots and the language of their current roles in government remains a paradox. The issue comes down to the motive and authenticity of their warrior talk.

Warrior talk and core discourses

In the period 1969–2019, the difference between core republican discourses and Sinn Féin's colonized discourses became more apparent and signalled the fundamental changes taking place in the republican movement. Core discourses represented an alignment of republican philosophy, ideology and principles and as such provided a consistent and continuous message from one generation to the next. The Irish republican legacy is communicated through their historical discourses and political justifications for radical protest and physical violence. The removal of the British state from Ireland has always been at the centre of traditional republican ideology. This clear goal continues to manifest in republican warrior talk and reflects a historic and combative relationship with the British government.

It appears that republican warrior talk acts as a form of shorthand which encompasses a long saga of war with the British state, a powerful demand for Irish independence and the tragedy of human sacrifice. The findings from republican core discourses confirm that Irish republicanism remains a political project with a shared vision and ideology amongst its members. The political message was, and remains, clear: to remove the British influence in Ireland and create a single Irish nation based on republican principles. The warrior talk used by both Sinn Féin and radical republicans present Irish republicanism as a noble cause. However, while Sinn Féin uses warrior talk to signal solidarity, some armed radical groups continue to see themselves as literal warriors and believe their struggle is not over. Warrior talk, for these groups, is an expression of the frustration that the republican goal has not been achieved and an acknowledgement that the conflict in Northern Ireland has not been resolved.

Against this background, the political development of Sinn Féin in Northern Ireland is an extraordinary story because it has been achieved largely through the adaption of discourses from outside the republican movement. As Sinn Féin developed their repertoire of political discourses, the emergence of colonized language in their speeches was a clear signal that they were moving away from the radical precision of republicanism. This shift was observed in Sinn Féin political discourses during the 1981 hunger strikes, which reflected their growing realization that the republican principle of abstention was blocking the political opportunities for republicans in Northern Ireland. At the time, Sinn Féin politicians elected to Stormont were unable take up their seats and fully serve the communities who elected them. It is interesting that the infamous statement 'Armalite and Ballot box' from Danny Morrison was, in retrospect, a discursive turning point for Sinn Féin.[4] Here was an early sign that Sinn Féin could influence a political change internally if it was communicated as warrior talk, creating an additional front in the republican armed struggle.

Warrior talk and peace discourses

The emergence of Sinn Féin's peace discourses represented a major shift in their political strategies. They became skilful at colonizing discourses from both conflict resolution theory and the best practice used with other international peace processes, for example in South Africa. Sinn Féin peace discourses presented a vision of a sustainable peace in Northern Ireland and recommended an integrated approach towards resolving the conflict. Sinn Féin proposed structural and systematic changes to address the root causes of conflict combined with the healing of the communities across Northern Ireland. This approach went further than a traditional problem-solving approach to conflict resolution and recognized the importance of forgiveness and reconciliation as a crucial human aspect of peace building.

Sinn Féin's peace discourses were remarkable in their colonization of language from other conflicts, which gave them a powerful moral high ground in the 1990s. Terms such as 'forgiveness and reconciliation' created an expectation that healing between unionists and nationalists in Northern Ireland was a crucial step in the peace process. Sinn Féin took a historic step closer towards political engagement with unionists by promoting reconciliation across all communities in Northern Ireland. After the Good Friday Agreement (1998) it became more obvious that Sinn Féin saw reconciliation across Northern Ireland as a politically acceptable precursor to Irish unity. The scale of peace discourses before and after the Good Friday Agreement indicate the effort that Sinn Féin made to build a credible explanation for this major shift from the traditional republican position.

The moral high ground of Sinn Féin peace discourses made it more difficult for republicans to challenge the leadership especially in the years following the Good Friday Agreement. The research findings uncovered an interesting development in Sinn Féin peace discourses where new forms of warrior talk were used to communicate issues both internally and externally. Terms such as 'armed for peace', 'killing the peace process' and 'peace is under siege' were used to blame unionists and the British and Irish governments for the lack of progress on the recommendations lodged in the Good Friday Agreement.

The emergence of warrior talk within established peace discourses was also directed at other republicans and specifically the armed republican groups who continued to operate in Northern Ireland. War-like language was directed at fellow republicans who challenged the Good Friday Agreement and the conditions that Sinn Féin had signed up to. New forms of Sinn Féin warrior talk were used to label and marginalize republicans as 'terrorists' and 'dissidents'. It is interesting that the political discourses generated by radical republicans since the Good Friday Agreement have not generally been focused on the merits of the peace process but on the terms of a peace agreement that has left the republican movement well short of their traditional goal.

Warrior talk and transitional discourses

The emergence of transitional discourses represented another shift in Sinn Féin's political strategies away from traditional republican principles. The development of transitional discourses emerged from the need to influence the republican movement to accept ideological change and were the product of Sinn Féin's pragmatic approach to constitutional politics. Discourse findings from the 1980s indicated that the Sinn Féin leadership had realized Irish unity was a long-term political project and unlikely to be achieved by armed struggle. This was an interesting moment in time, when an ideological gap appeared between Sinn Féin strategies and the traditional republican principles of abstention and physical force. It was, however, a discreet gap and internally managed using transitional discourses.

By the 1990s transitional discourses had developed further and now openly communicated that republicans could achieve their historic goal by working within the political system in Northern Ireland. Transitional discourses presented the future as a long road, which was now in a political phase and as such a respite from armed struggle. Terms such as 'phased demilitarization' and 'release of political prisoners' acknowledged the sacrifices of the past and prepared the ground for the controversial challenges of the Good Friday Agreement and later decommissioning. In the 1970s and 1980s, warrior talk had dominated the early forms of transitional discourses and reflected the dynamics between Sinn Féin and the IRA. By the 1990s transitional discourses had changed to reflect the ascendancy of Sinn Féin as the leadership of the republican movement. Now the language from change management theory and the appearance of metaphors such as 'engine of change' and 'agents of change' reflected a new paradigm of republican political discourses.

The situation changed after the Good Friday Agreement. With Sinn Féin politicians in government, transitional discourses started to lose the power to keep the republican movement united. The attraction of transitional discourses was that they had allowed Sinn Féin to present armed struggle as a legitimate step towards political change. Yet for some republicans this positive momentum was negated by the acceptance of the consent principle, stipulated by the Good Friday Agreement: it was arguably a betrayal of the republican cause and the architects of this flawed political strategy were identified as the leaders of Sinn Féin.

However, the research findings indicate that the notion of transition was a skilful way to adapt and refresh republican core discourses. Sinn Féin transitional discourses presented a subtle use of history which allowed them to reframe the republican cause as an evolving process of liberation. Republican engagement with constitutional politics was presented as the final phase in the struggle for Irish independence. It was clear that warrior talk was used to deflect attention from the continued existence of the political construct known as 'Northern Ireland' and the ongoing influence of the British government.

Warrior talk and transformational discourses

Sinn Féin transformational discourses developed considerably after IRA decommissioning (2005) and represented a distinctive linguistic shift from a phased approach to change (transitional) to a complete paradigm shift (transformational). The notion of transforming Irish society into a free independent nation was at the core of the republican philosophical lineage and political ideals. Sinn Féin's adoption of the term 'transformation' provided them with a multipurpose form of discourse that was at once visionary and flexible but still rooted in the republican dream.

The research findings revealed that Sinn Féin transformational discourses were ambiguous and used to communicate both the transformation of Northern Ireland and the transformation of Irish society. Beneath the surface of their transformational rhetoric, it is clear that Sinn Féin's long-term ambition was to govern a united Ireland. However, there was a practical realization that it would take a democratic mandate both sides of the border to achieve the political traction for re-unification. Sinn Féin transformational discourses were a powerful indicator of their complete shift towards constitutional politics: not only had they joined the Northern Ireland Assembly but they now sounded like any other political party canvassing for votes.

Transformational discourses convey a message of a paradigm shift in the system and attitudinal shift for the participants in that system. The distinction between transitional and transformational discourses is subtle but important to this study of warrior talk. Transition implies a series of planned stages to reach a destination and, therefore, previous history, especially paramilitary activity, can be explained as a means to an end. Transformation promises a new destination and requires powerful, evocative and inclusive rhetoric which can be directed at a diverse and wide range of voters on both sides of the border.

A pressing problem for Sinn Féin continues to be the presence of radical republican groups who follow the traditional republican principles of abstention and physical force to a greater or lesser degree. Transformational discourses are anathema to radical republicans who consider the republican message to be already distinctive and with principles that are sacrosanct. The idea of a changing Irish republicanism into another constitutional national party is regarded as unnecessary and a betrayal of Irish republicanism.

Transformational discourses tend to make Sinn Féin sound like mainstream politicians: this was clearly observable in the research study and forms a marked contrast to the clarity of republican core discourses. This disparity was an important clue to understanding Sinn Féin's ongoing use of warrior talk. At this time of writing, Sinn Féin continue to include traditional republican warrior talk in speeches, funerals, conferences and commemorations. Each of the radical republican groups have their own rituals and gatherings and use similar forms of republican warrior talk.

Reflections on the case study

> Your job is to pick out what is our warrior talk and what is relevant.[5]

This quote was instrumental to why this book was written. Twenty years later, the contrast between republican warrior talk and Sinn Féin's political aspirations remains a fascinating case study that has lessons for conflict resolution and peace building in other settings.

The recurring nature of warrior talk signposts a political dilemma for Sinn Féin politicians, both in Northern Ireland and the Irish Republic. Warrior talk could be perceived as a respectful gesture to the past but it also codifies a major challenge for Sinn Féin and their political aspirations. The romanticism, through poems, stories and myths, of republican sacrifice also acts as a reminder of a violent period. In the act of republican remembrance, Sinn Féin clearly respect their roots but risk damage to their political credibility and ability to influence a wider body of voters to accept the reunification of Ireland.

After the Good Friday Agreement, Sinn Féin could no longer claim to be radical republican activists because they had moved into a different political space and become a mainstream political party. The political space for a traditional republican position is now occupied by radical republican groups engaged in both political activism and paramilitary operations in Northern Ireland. The political discourse across these groups is both consistent and coherent: the removal of the British State from Northern Ireland and the reunification of Ireland. In short, the political position of radical groups is uncompromisingly republican and idealistic, and this is evident from the traditional warrior talk in their publications, speeches and actions.

Sinn Féin shares the same philosophical legacy and historical roots as other republican groups and individuals and this is an important issue for the future. Their continued use of warrior talk is potentially damaging because it positions them in the past when their political ambitions lie in the future.

The Sinn Féin leadership chose to distance themselves from their radical republican opponents by turning to war-like language to marginalize and demonize them. This is a very interesting tactical choice given Sinn Féin's engagement with the peace process in Northern Ireland. Radical republican groups, whether armed or unarmed, represent dissenting voices in the republican movement and display some of the characteristics of peace spoilers.[6] It is also interesting that several options were available to Sinn Féin in defining their relationship with radical republicans, such as to ignore, engage, marginalize or escalate and use violence. The pattern emerging within the discourses after 2005 indicated that Sinn Féin have opted to use a form of warrior talk which marginalizes and demonizes other republicans.[7] This form of polarization could be a flawed strategy because it fixes radical republicans as an enemy and sows the seeds for potential destabilization and future conflict.

Clearly, any transparent display of violence towards other republicans would be deeply damaging to Sinn Féin's role as custodians of peace.[8] The relationship between provisional and radical republicans has become a complex dynamic, which is unlikely to be resolved by further splits. Historically, internal republican splits have been ideological and centred around the 'means' to achieve a united Ireland. Sinn Féin are now embarked on a constitutional route and committed to a peaceful means to complete the reunification process. It could be argued that there is no room for warrior talk whether as a tactic to promote the solidarity of the republican movement or a mechanism of control against republican opponents.

Since the 1970s Sinn Féin's warrior talk has been used to communicate a strong sense of republican identity despite changes to their political strategies. This allegiance to the republican identity is clearly an important communication tool and is used both internally and externally. The research findings from 1969 to 1998 confirmed that warrior talk allowed Sinn Féin to develop their political strategies but also continue to demonstrate their solidarity with the republican armed struggle. The situation became more complex as Sinn Féin developed their colonized discourses and used them to propel the republican movement towards peace. The Good Friday Agreement changed the nature of the relationship between provisional republicans and the British government. The war was over, volunteers stood down and weapons decommissioned, and Sinn Féin transitional and transformational discourses reflect that.

At the time of writing, provisional republicans are embedded in mainstream politics in Northern Ireland and their transformation from radical activists to constitutional politicians is virtually complete. Warrior talk provides them with a familiar narrative and the means to reinforce their republican identity and masks the reality that they have also chosen to distance themselves from their traditional roots. The emergence and development of Sinn Féin colonized discourses has facilitated much of their political success, but their continued use of warrior talk now impacts their credibility as leaders of transformational change and sustainable peace.

Warrior talk and other forms of conflict

> We are always writing the history of war, even when we are writing the history of peace.[9]

The case study of the Northern Ireland peace process and analysis of Sinn Féin discourses has produced insights that are relevant to other forms of conflict whether in a national, organizational or personal context. A conflict situation may be small scale and non-violent, but language is an important contributor to whether the situation deteriorates or the parties opt to resolve their differences.

Warrior talk appears to have a significant effect on the capability of conflicting parties to adapt and deliver a sustainable peaceful outcome. The historical roots and causes of both latent and direct conflict create a potent legacy and the potential for violence is frequently transmitted through language – including before violence occurs. In Chapter Seven it was concluded that the transformation of a conflict situation required both structural changes to address the root causes and the reconciliation of the parties engaged in the conflict. A peace treaty may legislate for structural changes to address the causes, but the process of forgiveness and healing is highly emotive and for some an impossible requirement. A new legacy is created from the emotional and psychological scars to keep people focused on the past despite all the best intentions of the peacemakers. An outreach approach to engage communities in the peace process can work but it is clear from the case study that language has an important part to play is achieving a lasting peace.

The language of war exists across a wide spectrum of human interactions from violent conflict on a global/national level to the sports field or the thrill of imaginary heroes in a Hollywood film. Warrior talk exists in many forms, including within everyday communications between groups and individuals. In reality, an international sports team does not run onto the pitch with a mission to lose the game. A healthy display of warrior talk is an inevitable part of the sporting experience whether as a player, spectator or team coach. It is clear that warrior talk has positive attributes and a role to play in human motivation; the challenge is to understand how it used in different settings. It is also important to remember that the language we use to interpret our experiences and communicate with each other is frequently a product of the past, whether the time lapse is minutes or years.

A key issue is that warrior talk emphasizes difference and has a role in polarizing a situation and the responses of the participants involved. The use of warrior talk may not result in conflict, but the polarizing effect of its language contributes to the level of intransigence in the different positions that emerge. The dynamics of a small-scale confrontation has the potential to escalate, draw in other parties and develop into a conflict.

Warrior talk and polarization

The language of war instantly polarizes a complex political scenario or social setting into opposing positions and attracts the labels or 'right' and 'wrong'. Terms such as 'enemy' and 'battle' heighten emotional reactions irrespective of the form of the conflict. A competitive game may appear benign but the polarizing process that encourages requires participants to take sides can then become a tipping point for a conflict situation. In a competition both players and spectators engage in adrenaline-fuelled behaviours and the outcomes can be exhilarating and entertaining. However, the use of war-like language can swiftly take the emotional highs into negative reactions between different parties and spiral a competitive scenario into latent conflict. Warrior talk is deeply embedded in everyday language and interaction, frequently manifesting as aggressive behaviours and bullying in organizations, irrespective of their size and sector. An interesting rationale for aggressive behaviours, for example in schools and offices, can be observed in the terms such as 'healthy competition', 'just a bit of fun' and 'letting off steam'.

In Chapter Seven, the psychological basis of human conflict was explored using a concept known as 'splitting' which triggers an emotional response and reduces complex histories, political dynamics and human experiences to a duality of 'self' and 'other'. The gap between 'self' and 'other' can exist at macro and micro levels and is observable between individuals, groups, organizations and nations. The splitting process is open to further distortion when warrior talk is applied; the label of 'other' is replaced by another label: 'enemy'. If the term 'enemy' is used in a non-violent context, the language can evoke an image of threat and introduce the possibility of violence. The threat of violence impacts how people respond in the situation and is a factor in whether the situation becomes violent; for instance, war-like language in an interchange between two drivers can escalate a latent conflict into a form of direct violence, something which is euphemistically categorized as 'road rage'.

The role of warrior talk when applied to groups appears to make a direct contribution to the mobilization of opposing factions and a polarization into 'us' and 'them'. Political elections are a good source of material on warrior talk and speeches made by contenders for high office illustrates how their political rhetoric and personal insults reduce complex social, political and economic issues into a furious battleground. Warrior talk is used as a metaphorical weapon and the result is both a sad spectacle and a rallying call for political supporters; in some situations, a proportion of these supporters may well be armed for physical violence.

Warrior talk therefore polarizes and escalates tensions in what may be a benign social interaction or an established confrontational situation. A violent dispute between neighbours over land could mean critical access to water or it could be about a minor issue over parking. The escalation to direct physical violence is not always predictable and rarely proportionate to the situation.

Warrior talk and sacred values[10]

The findings from the case study illustrated the power of warrior talk as a transmitter of what may be termed 'sacred values'. Sacred values are powerful human attachments and used to communicate and sustain a group identity or a tradition that transcends short-term self-interest. Warrior talk is used to mobilize people to follow a specific cause and protect their rights as a group to hold values whether they are orientated towards religion, family, community, nation or the global environment. The existence of a noble cause inspires people to act now for the greater good of a distant future, and this is a powerful platform for radical action and the possibility of violence. A current example is the global cause of climate change where sacred values drive both peaceful and violent protests. The political rhetoric of a 'cause' mobilizes groups against a common enemy and promotes collaboration between supporters. The polarization between the 'supporters' of a cause and its 'enemies' is another example of the splitting process and the role of warrior talk in preserving the sacred cause and sustaining the group's identity.

The combination of warrior talk and a sacred cause is a combustible mixture and manifests both as peaceful protests and violent demonstrations. The tipping point into violence during a protest march for human rights or environmental issues can be observed in the chants, slogans and combative messages between protesters and their opponents. The image portrayed in the media is one of an army advancing on the enemy's castle whereas the experience for the marchers is frequently one of solidarity, comradeship and identity with a cause. Warrior talk can transform the situation rapidly as the 'enemies' of the cause whether perceived or real respond with their warrior talk.

Warrior talk and identity politics

The rise of identity politics is a modern social phenomenon which is fuelled through language and the impact of social media. Group identity is used as a primary driver to address inequality and reconfigure the power relations between different identities. Social media enables a rapid transmission of views and information, and this clearly accelerates the creation and maintenance of identities. The polarizing effect of strong identities is particularly noticeable in echo chambers where communications are conducted within a closed system of people who share similar views.[11] The politicization of identity is also influenced by the warrior talk generated by opposing groups and this can be observed in the disturbing trend of abusive and malicious communication on social media platforms.[12]

Social and political identities function as another form of 'self' and 'other' and although this may be a valid expression of discontent, the language of protest can deteriorate into the language of threat and violence. The emotional volume of human communication increases when a disadvantaged or disempowered group starts to protest, and another identity responds. Rational discussion about the structural conditions experienced by a disadvantaged group is frequently overtaken by a human propensity for conflict and violence as competing identities defend their positions. When a group's dignity has been disparaged or disregarded, warrior talk is a powerful tool to mobilize supporters and remind them of historic injustice.

Identity politics has a purpose in raising awareness of injustice and inequality. A humiliated group seeking restitution can became a powerful moral force for change. A vision of empowerment is frequently created using forms of warrior talk to communicate both the need to acknowledge the identity of a particular group and the necessity of restoring the dignity of its members, for example the Women's Liberation movement in the 1960s and the more recent emphasis on inequalities in civil rights, particularly in the USA, associated with the Black Lives Matter movement.

The question is whether societal change is simply a shift of power dynamics or a complete transformation to a new paradigm where power is shared. The problem is that the polarization between different competing identities does not solve the issue of inequality and merely signals a temporary reconfiguration of power dynamics. Warrior talk, in this context, sustains the conflict between different identities rather than promoting the possibility of a peaceful co-existence of new and multiple identities.

Escalation from legitimate protest into violent confrontation is a damaging process with lasting effects for all parties. If opposing groups feel justified in striking back, the resulting coercion and violence discourages communication and limits the opportunity to address the issues. Even a lack of retaliation can be perceived as a weakness and so the convoluted process of conflict continues, often spanning several generations. Acts of retaliation and violence fuelled by warrior talk can become a temporary substitute for the original grievances.

Final reflections

> The human self is created by the use of vocabulary.[13]

This chapter has summarized the findings from the case study of the Northern Ireland peace process and reflected on Sinn Féin's current relationship with warrior talk. Discourse analysis of a substantive volume of speeches and statements have illuminated the many facets of warrior talk in our social interactions and political exchanges. It is clear that warrior talk has some merits as a way of inspiring and motivating people to deal with change or indeed crises. However, warrior talk also has a polarizing effect on individuals and groups, and directly contributes to negative effects of a human attachment to causes and the identity politics, which inevitably flow from that cause.

At a macro level, warrior talk can tip a latent conflict into direct violence and war. Peace is not the direct opposite of war. An armed conflict may result in a ceasefire and negotiations between the conflict's parties, but a sustainable peace is not an assured outcome. A peace treaty may have conditions which change structures, redress grievances and reconfigure the power dynamics but this does not mean that peace is sustainable. The evidence from this book points to the importance of language in the transformation of conflict and peace building. If language which represents the past is constantly evoked and communicated between opponents then the opportunity to transform the situation is inevitably damaged.

The memories of past grievances, abuses and atrocities become the sacred cause for other generations to follow. This brings a complex dynamic between remembrance as a gesture of respect and a collection of memories that trap people in destructive cycles. Warrior talk is part of our human existence. On a global level, in localized wars and extended conflicts, the exchanges between opponents are frequently fuelled by combative language and threats. In theory, peace processes are possible through the transformation of societies and the healing of past grievances. In reality, the process of reconciliation and forgiveness is very challenging and for some an impossible act.

At a micro level, warrior talk can take many forms and is a 'taken for granted' aspect of human existence. From competitive sport and reality television to disputes between co-workers, warrior talk has an impact on attitudes and behaviours. Even the current fashion of 'declaring war' on a virus, cancer or poverty reduces complex societal issues to a polarized interpretation of a health or social crisis. The choice is delineated by warrior talk: fight an amorphous enemy or give in to it.

The term 'fighting spirit' illustrates an appropriation of language shaped by two global wars, 1914–1918 and 1939–1945, and the socio-political aftermath. Paradoxically, this language continues to shape our responses to health and social care. Currently there are a number of 'alternative wars' being waged in society from cancer and diabetes to mental health. On the surface, a 'fighting spirit' might be an asset but on closer inspection a failure to win these wars is framed as losing a competition. If an individual dies, they are perceived to have lost their battle. Warrior talk is a powerful linguistic device that requires a conscious appreciation of its potency and a thoughtful application to the situation.

The language used in any setting will shape behaviours and responses. Warrior talk can be fun and stimulating but it can also be hugely destructive. The challenge is to recognize the impact that language has on our social interactions and our perception of group identity. The differences between our intentions, our language choices and their impact on others are crucial to understanding how conflict manifests in our lives.

Notes

1. Fairclough, N. (1999). *Language and Power*, London: Penguin, p. 35.
2. See Chapter Seven for a more detailed explanation of forms of conflict and violence.
3. This remark includes external stakeholders and internal stakeholders with a healthy scepticism for political rhetoric and political opponents.
4. Danny Morrison made statement at the 1981 Ard Fheis which encouraged republicans to consider an '*Armalite and Ballot box*' approach to constitutional politics. It was a remark that opened up a middle ground between the republican physical force tradition and an electoral strategy. The 'Armalite' was a generic name for rifles used by PIRA in the 1970s and 1980s.
5. A remark made by Eoin Ó Broin to the author, 1999, which helped to shape a PhD, and inspired a twenty-year interest in how language helps or hinders peace. Eoin Ó Broin is now a Sinn Féin MP for Dublin West.
6. Stedman, S. J. (1997). 'Spoiler Problems in Peace Processes', *International Security*, 22, pp. 5–53.
7. Bowman-Grieve, L. (2010). 'Irish Republicanism and the Internet: Support for New Wave Dissidents', *Perspectives on Terrorism*, 4, no. 2, pp. 1–7. Accessible at <www.terrorismanalysis.com/pt/index.php/pot/article/view/97/html>.

    This is very interesting article which explores how different radical republican groups use the internet and brings another perspective to the study of republican warrior talk.
8. Some radical republicans have reported open intimidation from provisional republicans.
9. Foucault, M. (2003). *Society Must Be Defended*, London: Penguin.

10. In this context 'sacred' does not mean wholly religious but it is used as a term to describe a cause that is deeply meaningful to its members. In the context of the Irish republican cause, there is a strong religious (Roman Catholic) contribution to notion of freedom from oppression.
11. An echo chamber is an environment (for example, social media) where a person encounters opinions that reflect and reinforce their own. Echo chambers contribute to the polarization of groups and their social, political, ethic, religious and gender identities.
12. Aro, J. (June 2016). 'The Cyberspace War: Propaganda and Trolling as Warfare Tools', 15, no. 1, pp. 121–132, <https://doi.org/10.1007/s12290-016-0395-5> , accessed July 2020.
13. Rorty, R. (1999). *Contingency, Irony and Solidarity*, Cambridge: Cambridge University Press, p. 6.

Internet sources

32 CSM, <www.32csm.net/>.
Conflict Archive in Northern Ireland (CAIN), <www.cain.ulst.ac.uk/>.
éirígí, <www. eirigi.org/>.
Irish Republican News, irlnet.com.
Irish Republican Socialist Part (IRSP), <www.irsp.ie/>.
Office of First and Deputy First Minister (OFMDFM), <wwe.ofmdmni.gov.uk/.
Police Service of Northern Ireland (PSNI) for statistics on the security situation, <www.psni.police.uk/security_situation_statistics_user_guide.pdf>.
Republican Network for Unity (RNU), <www.republicannetwork.ie/>.
Republican News, republican –news.org.
Republican Sinn Féin, <www.rsf.ie/>.
Saoradh, <www.saoradh.ie>.
Sinn Féin, <www.sinnféin.ie/>.
Terrorist Research Initiative, <www.terrorismanalysis.com>.
The Blanket, <www.indiamond6.ulib.iupui.edu:81/>.

Newspapers

An Phoblacht
An Phoblacht/Republican News
Anderson Town News
Belfast Telegraph
Derry Journal
Irish Independent
Irish News
Irish Republican News
Irish Times
Republican Bulletin
Republican News
Saoirse
The Blanket
The Guardian
The New York Times
The Times

Journals

Academy of Management Review
Capitalism and Class
European Journal of Political Research
European Journal of Work and Organizational Psychology
Human Relations
International Affairs
Irish Political Studies
Journal of Conflict Resolution
Journal of International Affairs
Journal of Peace Research
Political Geography
Political Quarterly
Politics Review
Studies in Conflict and Terrorism
Terrorism and Political Violence

Bibliography

Adams, G. (2003) *Hope and History: Making Peace in Northern Ireland*, Kerry: Brandon.
Adams, G. (1995) *Towards a Lasting Peace*, Dingle: Brandon.
Adams, G. (1989) *A Scenario for Peace*, Dingle: Brandon.
Bell, C. (2001) *Peace Agreements and Human Rights*, Oxford: Oxford University Press.
Bew, P., Patterson, H., and Teague, P. (1997) *Northern Ireland between War and Peace: The Political Future of Northern Ireland*, Lawrence and Wishart: London.
Bew, P., and Gillespie, G. (1996) *The Northern Ireland Peace Process, 1993–1996*, London: Serif.
Bloomfield. (1996) *Peacemaking Strategies in Northern Ireland: Building Complementarity in Conflict Management Theory*, London: Macmillan.
Bourdieu, P. (1990) *The Logic of Practice*, Stanford: Stanford University Press.
Bourke, R. (2003) *Peace in Ireland: The War of Ideas*, London: Pimlico.
Bowyer-Bell, J. (2003) *The Secret Army: The IRA*, Oxford: Transaction Publishers.
Boyce, D. G. (1995) *Nationalism in Ireland*, London: Routledge, Third Edition.
Boyle, K., and Hadden, T. (1994) *Northern Ireland: The Choice*, London: Penguin.
Bregman, R. (2020) *Human Kind: A Hopeful History*, London: Bloomsbury.
Brown, A. D. (ed.) (2020) *The Oxford Handbook of Identities in Organizations*, Oxford: Oxford University Press.
Burton, W. (1990) *Conflict Resolution and Prevention*, London: Macmillan.
Butler, M. J. (2009) *International Conflict Management*, London: Routledge.
Chilton, P. A. (2004) *Analysing Political Discourse: Theory and Practice*, London: Routledge.
Chouliaraki, L., and Fairclough, N. (1999) *Discourse in Late Modernity: Rethinking Critical Discourse Analysis*, Edinburgh: Edinburgh University Press.
Coogan, T. P. (2003) *Ireland in the Twentieth Century*, London: Arrow Books.
Coogan, T. P. (1980) *On the Blanket: The H-Block Story*, Dublin: River Press.
Cox, M., Guelke, A., and Stephen, F. (2000) *A Farewell to Arms? From 'Long War' to 'Long Peace' in Northern Ireland*, Manchester: Manchester University Press.
Cunnningham, M. J. (1991) *British Government Policy in Northern Ireland, 1969–1989: Its Nature and Execution*, Manchester: Manchester University Press.
Curle, A. (1971) *Making Peace*, London: Tavistock Publications.
Darby, J. (2001) *The Effect of Violence on Peace Processes*, Washington DC: United States Institute of Peace Press.
Darby, J., and McGinty, R. (eds) (2000) *The Management of Peace Processes*, London: Macmillan.
Dixon, P. (2007) *Northern Ireland: The Politics of War and Peace*, second edition, Basingstoke: Palgrave.

Dooley, B. (1998) *Black and Green: The Fight for Civil Rights in Northern Ireland and Black America*, London: Pluto Press.
Edwards, D. (1997) *Discourse and Cognition*, London: Sage.
Ellison, G., and Smyth, J. (2000) *The Crowned Harp: Policing in Northern Ireland*, London: Pluto Press.
English, A. (2003) *Armed Struggle: The History of the IRA*, Basingstoke: Macmillan.
Fairclough, N. (1995) *Media Discourse*, London: Hodder.
Feeney, B. (2002) *Sinn Féin, A Hundred Turbulent Years*, Dublin: O'Brien.
Fisher, R. J. (1990) *The Social Psychology of Intergroup and International Conflict Resolution*, New York: Springer Verlag.
Frampton, M. (2009) *The Long March: Political Strategy of Sinn Fein, 1981–2007*, Basingstoke: Palgrave Macmillan.
Fraser, T. G. (2000) *Ireland in Conflict, 1922–1998*, London: Routledge.
Gabriel, Y. (2000) *Storytelling in the Organization: Facts, Fictions and Fantasies*, Oxford: Oxford University Press.
Garfinkel, H. (1984) *Studies in Ethnomethodology*, Cambridge: Polity Press.
Giddens, A. (1990) *The Consequences of Modernity*, Cambridge: Polity Press.
Gillespie, G. (2008) *Years of Darkness: The Troubles Remembered*, Dublin: Gill & Macmillan.
Haywood, K., and O'Donnell, C. (eds) (2011) *Political Discourse and Conflict Resolution*, Abingdon, Oxford: Routledge.
Hennessey, T. (2014) *Hunger Strike: Margaret Thatcher's Battle with the IRA*, Dublin: Irish Academic Press.
Hennessey, T. (1997) *A History of Northern Ireland, 1920–1996*, London: Palgrave.
Howarth, D. (2000) *Discourse*, Buckingham: Open University Press.
Huntington, S. (1996) *The Clash of Civilizations and the Remaking of the World Order*, New York: Simon & Schuster.
Knox, C., and Quirk, P. (2000) *Peace – Building in Northern Ireland, South Africa and Israel*, London: Macmillan.
Lederarch, J. P. (1997) *Building Peace: Sustainable Reconciliation in Divided Societies*, Washington DC: United States Institute of Peace Press.
MacGinty, R. (2006) *No War, No Peace*, Basingstoke: Palgrave.
Maill, H. (1991) *The Peacemakers*, London: Macmillan.
Mc Cann, E. (1992) *Bloody Sunday in Derry: What Really Happened*, Dingle, Co Derry: Brandon Books.
Mc Garry, J., and O'Leary, B. (1995) *Explaining Northern Ireland*, Oxford: Blackwell.
Mc Grattan, C. (2013) *Memory, Politics and Identity: Haunted by History*, Basingstoke: Palgrave, Macmillan.
McIntyre, A. (1995) 'Modern Irish Republicanism': 'The Product of British State Strategies', *Irish Political Studies*, 10 (1), pp. 97–122.

McKay, S. (2008) *Bear in Mind these Dead*, London: Faber and Faber Ltd.
Mckearney, T. (2011) *The Provisional IRA: From Insurrection to Parliament*, London: Pluto.
McKittrick, D. (2000) *Making Sense of the Troubles*, Belfast: Blackstaff Press.
McKittrick, D. (1996) *The Nervous Peace*, Belfast: Blackstaff Press.
McLoughlin, P. (2010) *John Hume and the Revision of Irish Nationalism*, Manchester: Manchester University Press.
Miall, H. (1992) *The Peacemakers*, London: Macmillan.
Miller, D. (1994) *Don't Mention the War: Northern Ireland, Propaganda and the Media*, London: Pluto Press.
Moloney, E. (2002) *The Secret History of the IRA*, London; Penguin Books.
Mowlam, M. (2002) *Momentum*, London: Hodder& Stoughton.
Ó Brádaigh, R. (1996) The Evil Fruit Has Ripened Once More, *Irish Reporter*, 21, pp. 19–29.
O'Malley, P. (1990) *The Irish Hunger Strikes and the Politics of Despair*, Belfast: Blackstaff.
O'Rawe, R. (2005) *Blanketmen: An Untold Story of the H- Block Hunger Strike*, Dublin: New Island.
Patterson, H. (2013) *Ireland's Violent Frontier: The Border and Anglo- Irish Relations during the Troubles*, Basingstoke: Palgrave Macmillan.
Powell, J. (2008) *Great Hatred, Little Room: Making Peace in Northern Ireland*, London: Bodley Head.
Rapoport, D. C. (ed.) (2000) *Inside Terrorist Organisations*, London: Frank Cass.
Rorty, R. (1999) *Contingency, Irony and Solidarity*, Cambridge: Cambridge University Press.
Rorty, R., Ruane, J., and Todd, J. (1996) *The Dynamics of Conflict in Northern Ireland*, Cambridge: Cambridge University Press.
Rupersinghe, K. (ed.) (1995) *Conflict Transformation*, London: Macmillan.
Saunders, A. (2011) *Inside the IRA: Dissident Republicans and the War for Legitimacy*, Edinburgh: Edinburgh Press.
Shanahan, T. (2009) *The Provisional IRA and the Morality of Terrorism*, Edinburgh: Edinburgh University Press.
Sharrock, D., and Devenport, M. (1998) *Man of War, Man of Peace: The Unauthorised Biography of Gerry Adams*, London: Pan Books.
Shirlow, P., and McGovern, M. (1998) Language, Discourse and Dialogue: Sinn Féin and the Irish Peace Process, *Political Geography*, 17 (2), pp. 171–186.
Silverman, D. (1993) *Interpreting Qualitative Data: Methods of Analysing Talk, Text and Interaction*: London: Sage.
Tonge, J. (2005) *The New Northern Ireland Politics*, New York: Palgrave Macmillan.
Toolis, K. (2000) *Rebel Hearts: Journeys within the IRA's Soul*, London: Picador.

Wallenstein, P. (2007) *Understanding Conflict Resolution: War, Peace and the Global System*, second edition, London: Sage.

Weick, K. (2001) *Making Sense of the Organization*, Oxford: Blackwell.

Widgery, J. P. (2001) *Bloody Sunday, 1972: Lord Widgery's Report of Events in Londonderry, Northern Ireland on 30 January 1972*, CAIN, at <www.cain.ulst.ac.uk/>.

Wilson, R. (2010) *The Northern Ireland Experience of Conflict and Agreement: A Model for Export?* Manchester: Manchester University Press.

Whyte, J. (1990) *Interpreting Northern Ireland*, Oxford: Clarendon.

Index

Adams, Gerry
   abstentionism 78
   acknowledgement of 'Long War' 108
   'Brownie' writings of Gerry Adams 76
   International credibility 82–83, 119–120, 196
   Language of inclusion 110
   management approach 142–143
   'New Ireland' 178
   Northern Ireland Policing Board 85
   rhetoric of 'phases' 140
   'the war is over' 115–116
   Wolfe Tone language and republican political discourses 108
Abstentionism
   impact on Sinn Féin politics 76
   colonization of peace discourses 120
   discursive use of term 'strategy' 83–84
   universal republican principle 54–56

Backchannel and the British Government 113
Bloody Sunday and republican historical discourses 44–45, 50

Conflict
   approaches 185–186
   resolution 187–188

transformation 189
Colonized discourses
   definition 29
   study task 96
Consent principle and radical republicanism 87
Core discourses
   definition 26
   study task 96

Decommissioning
   impact on republicans 145
   preconditions for peace talks 115
Discourse analysis
   conceptual model 25–26
   definition 23–24
Discursive shifts
   forgiveness 111–112
   inclusive politics 144
Dissident discourses 193–194, 197, 202
Downing St Declaration and expectation of IRA decommissioning 113

Easter Rising and legacy for republicanism 47–49
Éire Nua
   blueprint for a united Ireland 138
   power to the people 74
Electoral mandate
   impact of 1980s hunger strikes 219
   paradox with warrior talk 192–193
   republican strategy 84

Enniskillen
    catalyst for peace 71
    reputational damage 110

Foucault, Michel
    archaeological accounts 24, 59
    genealogical accounts 24, 59

Galtung, Johan
    forms of violence 184–185
    positive peace 184
Good Friday Agreement
    challenges to Sinn Fein leadership 146
    changes to Sinn Fein transitional discourses 147–148
    emergence of transformational discourses 177
    impact on Provisional Sinn Fein 89, 120
    radical opposition 80
    relationships with unionists 115
    shift in provisional republicanism 200–201
Goulding, Cathal
    frustration with provisionals 139
'Greyhound trained to race' 134–135, 165

Hartley, Tom language of invitation 111
Historical discourses
    definition 27
    republican legacy 75–76
Hunger strikes
    importance 51–52
    massive political victory 77–78

IRA (Irish Republican Army)
    cessations 144–145

Justification discourses
    definition 28
    republican consistency and coherence 173

Loyalist ceasefire 113–114

Mc Cartney, Robert
    impact on Sinn Féin peace discourses 117
    murder 117
McGuinness, Martin
    'chuckle brothers' and Ian Paisley 184
    frustration with armed republicans 194
    historic handshake 121
    relationship with radical republicans 160–161

New IRA
    unfinished revolution 149
    'vows to continue struggle' 166
New Republic and Sinn Féin rhetoric 91, 180
Northern Rock Bank raid and damage to Sinn Féin political aspirations 117

O'Neill, Michelle
    contradictions within republicanism 197
    impact of republican political legacy 190–191

Patten, Chris and policing reform 85
Peace Discourses

alternative route to Irish unity 102
colonization of terms 'forgiveness' and 'reconciliation' 112
critical shift in 1980s 107–108
metaphor of journey 121–122
pacification process 102
peace under siege 117
presence of warrior talk 93–94
PSNI (Police Service of Northern Ireland and RUC (Royal Ulster Constabulary) 85
Provisional movement and emergence in the 1970s 49–50
Provisional Sinn Féin
- appropriation of republican heroes 199
- building a nation 118–119
- current leadership dilemmas 191, 200
- economic discourses 89
- inclusive politics 89
- management approach 80
- 'New Republic' discourse 91–92
- outreach to unionists 111, 159
- peace makers 115
- political transformation 200
- relationship with radical republicanism 148–149
- republicans as change agents 147

Radical republicanism
- definition 87
- political views 150–157
Republicanism
- importance of abstentionism 54–55
- internal unity 56–57
- relationship with physical force 44–46
- roots 42–43

Scenario for Peace 109
Stages Theory 138–139

Towards Lasting Peace 109
Transformational Discourses
- constitutional politics 196–197
- contrast with transitional discourses 181–182
- emergence 174
- strong inclusive message 179
Transitional Discourses
- consensual language 142
- early forms 138–141
- emphasis on conflict resolution 162
- post decommissioning 147–148
- reconciliation and transition 159

War
- Are we at war with Covid? 12
- definition 183
- escalation of conflict 185
Warrior elite 183–184
Warrior talk
- commemorative role 199–200
- disconnect with transformational discourses 199, 202
- form of grieving 88
- identity politics 185, 201, 220, 230
- inhibitor of peace 93
- linguistic tool 215
- polarizing role 183, 194–195, 226
- relationship with peace discourses 220–221
- relationship with transformational discourses 223
- relationship with transitional discourses 221–222
- sacred values 229
- signifier of physical force 46
- spoiler discourse 193–195

"This volume offers readers not only an introduction to key issues in the orality movement, but also fresh contributions by leading practitioners and researchers. A welcome addition to the growing literature on orality."

—**Craig Ott**, Professor of Mission and Intercultural Studies, Trinity Evangelical Divinity School

"Unique and impressive tour d'horizon of the state of orality in missional ecclesiology. With extraordinary depth, thoughtful critique, and meaningful recovery of systems, the authors provide groundbreaking research and innovation that sets the course for the new decade. Steffen and Armstrong have created a brain trust. With delight, may I commend this book to you."

—**Samuel E. Chiang**, Orality Catalyst, Lausanne Movement

"I felt an unusual sense of elation as I went through *New and Old Horizons in the Orality Movement*. Nothing is as thrilling as seeing a living intersection between orality and theology. . . . I recommend this book to everyone interested in the Great Commission, but especially students, faculties, and libraries of all theological institutions across Africa and the world."

—**Ezekiel A. Ajibade**, Partnership Coordinator, The Nigerian Baptist Theological Seminary

"*New and Old Horizons in the Orality Movement* is a remarkable gift to cross-cultural workers and educators at a crucial time in missiological history. Steffen and Armstrong have pulled together a riveting compendium of the latest research and praxis for oral strategies. I was gripped by this book from beginning to end. . . . I highly recommend this book—it's a must-read for expanding your horizons in mission."

—**Robin Harris**, President, Evangelical Missiological Society

"This is a groundbreaking volume on orality. . . . Steffen and Armstrong have skillfully and successfully attempted to convince the church as well as the academy to take orality seriously as a strategic teaching-learning tool for disciple making. *New and Old Horizons in the Orality Movement* is an invaluable resource for missiologists, theological students, and educators, and of course, orality researchers. I highly recommend it."

—**Shivraj K. Mahendra**, Dean of Online Studies and Assistant Professor of World Christianity, New Theological College

"Listen up! This work is essential for anyone committed to twenty-first century mission with emerging generations and broken people among the *oral majority*. These seasoned practitioners examine the roots of modern Bible storytelling, wrestle with the limitations of highly literate theological education, and expand the application of 'orality' to *any* kingdom communication strategy. Their work applies to any context, from city streets to mountain pathways. Find out why and share it with others."

—**Charles B. Madinger**, International Director, International Orality Network

"What a breath of fresh air for missiology in general and orality in particular! . . . This book describes both the complexity of understanding/applying orality as well as the practicality for topics such as theological education and spiritual formation. . . . The reader will also be delighted to explore more recent implications to orality, such as oral hermeneutics applying character theology, various oral teaching applications in seminaries, and trauma healing, to name a few."

—**W. Jay Moon**, Professor of Church Planting and Evangelism, Asbury Theological Seminary

"This fine book delivers what the title promises. Its dozen contributors reflect insightfully on the development of the orality movement and highlight its core ideas and practices. . . . The authors think big and go deep, but they never lose sight of the practical challenges of carrying out Christian missions where orality and its associated phenomena are prevalent. . . . I commend this book highly."

—**Grant Lovejoy**, Director of Orality Strategies, International Mission Board

"Steffen and Armstrong compile a diverse and impressive collection of experienced contributors, delivering an extensive resource for missiology and the church. . . . In these pages, you will find a strong case for the value of listening, learning, and applying oral strategies to the farthest field, the classroom, and the church. . . . I heartily recommend this valuable book and encourage every serious learner to read it and expand their horizons in a whole new way."

—**Mark M. Overstreet**, Associate Director, Global Leadership Team, International Orality Network